ICE JOURNEY

A story of adventure, escape and salvation

ICE JOURNEY

A story of adventure, escape and salvation

BIG SKY PUBLISHING

Dave Morgan

First published in 2010

Big Sky Publishing Pty Ltd
PO Box 303
Newport, NSW, 2106
Australia
Phone: (61 2) 9918 2168
Fax: (61 2) 9918 2396
Email: info@bigskypublishing.com.au
Web: www.bigskypublishing.com.au

National Library of Australia Cataloguing-in-Publication entry
Author: Morgan, Dave.
Title: Ice journey : a story of adventure, escape and salvation /
Dave Morgan.
ISBN: 9780980658248 (pbk.)
Subjects: Morgan, Dave.
Vietnam War, 1961-1975--Veterans--Australia--Biography.
Veterans--Australia--Biography.
Meteorologists--Antarctica--Biography.
Post-traumatic stress disorder--Australia.
Antarctica--Biography.
Dewey Number: 305.906970994

Senior Editors Sharon Evans, Alistair Mival
Edit by Cathy Bay
Proofreading by Virginia Laugesen
Cover and layout design by Think Productions
Typesetting by Think Productions
Printed in Australia by Ligare Pty Ltd

Cover photo has been merged: Dave Morgan on the ice at Davis. Iceberg in distance as the *Aurora Australis* chews through the ice.

In memory of my mother, Sybil Ornsby (Cookson) Morgan.

To my wife Debra, daughter Michelle and son David.

To all the expeditioners I have served with and other expeditioners who have served Australia in South Polar Regions.

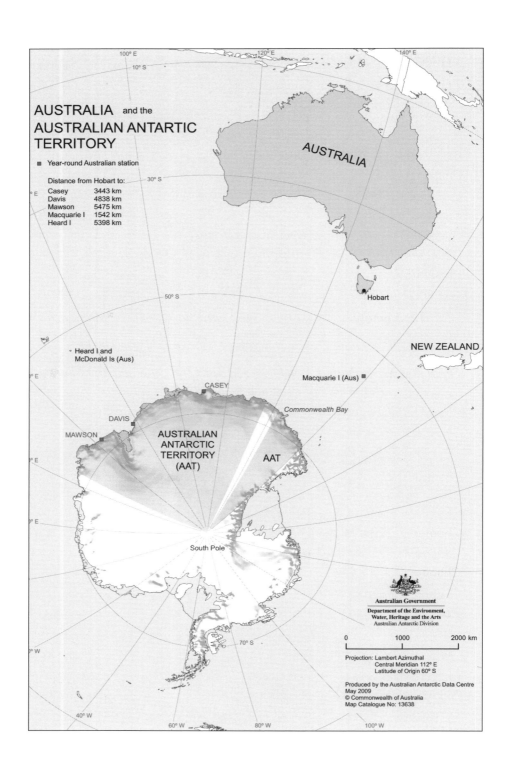

AUSTRALIA and the
AUSTRALIAN ANTARTIC
TERRITORY

■ Year-round Australian station

Distance from Hobart to:
Casey   3443 km
Davis   4838 km
Mawson   5475 km
Macquarie I 1542 km
Heard I   5398 km

AUSTRALIA

100° E
120° E
140° E
10° S
30° S
50° S

Hobart

NEW ZEALAND

Heard I and
McDonald Is (Aus)

CASEY

Macquarie I (Aus) ■

Commonwealth Bay

DAVIS

MAWSON

AUSTRALIAN
ANTARCTIC
TERRITORY
(AAT)

AAT

South Pole

70° S
60° W
80° W
100° W
40° W

Australian Government

Department of the Environment,
Water, Heritage and the Arts
Australian Antarctic Division

0   1000   2000 km

Projection: Lambert Azimuthal
          Central Meridian 112° E
          Latitude of Origin 60° S

Produced by the Australian Antarctic Data Centre
May 2009
© Commonwealth of Australia
Map Catalogue No: 13638

CONTENTS

ACKNOWLEDGEMENTS

I want to thank a few special people.

Nick Quigley OAM, a mate I served with in Vietnam. He was always at me to write a book about my adventures down south and was my initial inspiration to put pen to paper. Nick put me onto Nev Tickner, a Rockhampton writer, and also a Vietnam veteran. Nev helped me get started and encouraged me to write my story.

This led me to Paul Ham, the author of *Kokoda*. I received an email from Paul (through a Vietnam veterans' group) stating he wanted to talk to any Vietnam veterans about their experiences as he was writing a book on the war in Vietnam. As I had already written my story using my Vietnam diaries, I thought he might be interested, so I contacted him. Paul gave me encouragement to move forward with my Antarctica story.

Cathy Bay, who edited my book, is originally from Vancouver, Canada, but now lives in Queensland. From that first conversation I realised Cathy was the editor for me. I was enthused with Cathy because of her knowledge on freezing climates - she had lived in Canada - and her adventures on the sea and on ground, push-biking around Australia.

Before moving forward we decided it was best to meet. We hit it off straight away. Our writing sessions would happen once a month, sorting through my diaries and viewing the videos that I filmed down south.

Without Cathy, this book would not have been completed. She has three gifts - she is a good listener, very dedicated and a hard worker. I cannot express my gratitude to her enough.

Also important to this process, David Murphy and his wife Lizzy for editing the story – their help was invaluable. I would also like to thank Sharon Evans for her assistance in writing this book, and my publisher Big Sky Publishing, for giving me the opportunity to tell my story.

And of course, my family, who supported me every bit of the way on my trips to Antarctica. In total I was away from home just on two years. Some families probably would not tolerate it. Deb, Michelle, and David were very understanding and sacrificed a husband and a father so that I could satisfy my cravings for Antarctica.

I remember at my going away party, just before I headed off to Davis, my second posting, a lady said to me, "If you were my husband, I know what I would do. I'd either leave you or kick you out. I wouldn't stand for it. You must have the most understanding family in the world."

That sums it up pretty well.

I think all Vietnam veterans thrive on isolation. Looking back I enjoyed every bit of the peace and quiet at the Antarctic bases and at Giles in the Gibson Desert. All of which I couldn't have accessed without the goodwill of my family. Thank you.

Finally, all the expeditioners I served with down south - all characters and gifted people from all walks of life. To me there is not enough recognition for the men and women who serve at our Antarctica bases of Macquarie Island, Casey, Davis and Mawson.

Special thanks to Mark Maxwell, Gil Barton, Malcom Foster and Di Beamish for their stories and Dr Flanagan for his article on Post Traumatic Stress Disorder (PTSD) and Nanette Madan for her Antarctic painting.

From tradies, to science boffins, Met fairies, doctors, chefs, comms, Station Leaders, to all who serve - this represents your story.

Dave Morgan

PROLOGUE

Moments in life can often be categorised as "before" or "after" a defining event. Calendars revolve around Christ, families talk about divorces or deaths. My defining event occurred on a night that started like so many others but ended with me as a different person. I was young, idealistic and serving my country in a misunderstood war far from home in an "exotic" location.

It was mid-January 1969 and I was working at a forward fire support base called Julia in Vietnam. My unit, the 104 Signal Squadron, was part of the 1st Australian Task Force's Operation Goodwood.

The days were long. I worked in the signal centre (an Armoured Command Vehicle) from 0800-1700 hours before gun pit duty from 2200-2400 hours and again from 0400-0600 hours, or a similar variation. Sleep was no longer that well-deserved rest at the end of the day but an elusive state grabbed in small snatches a few hours at a time.

Every night we came under Viet Cong (VC) attack. I would slide into my pit hole, knuckles white as I gripped my SLR rifle, and watch as our armoured tanks and gun pit personnel fired into the jungle where they thought the VC were hiding. Night would become day as flares ignited around the base and incoming tracer bullets whizzed overhead. Nothing, not even the best training, prepares you for the awful sounds of war; the cracking of flares, the booming of guns, the sound of human confusion. Attacks continued through the night and by the time dawn arrived we were completely drained of physical and mental energy.

The night of my defining moment I was in a deep sleep in my pit hole. The Viet Cong hit our base at 0200 hours with small arms fire and mortar shells, one of which landed nearby and caused the left side of my hole to collapse.

I can't breathe ... oh my God, the whole world is falling on top ... I'm suffocating.

Pushing through the edge of consciousness, I realised the heavy dirt, sandbags and iron sheeting had collapsed and buried me. My head was throbbing with the pressure my ears had taken and the ringing drowned out my gasps as I struggled to breathe. The pure blackness fed my claustrophobic panic and I started thrashing my body. My feet were free; this discovery fed my adrenalin and I started kicking madly.

How long have I been here ... hell, what else is going to fall on me?

Time was confused, but I managed to thrust and heave to the right side of the pit hole and roll over sideways. Most of the debris had landed to the left and I scrambled past it to freedom, inhaling sweet fresh air.

I can't stand it.

Instinct led me to my SLR and I scrambled to the surface, thoughts of being buried alive in the tiny space driving me in a desperate dash to the nearby gun pit hole 8-10 metres away as tracer bullets flew low overhead.

I jumped in and the two diggers on duty were shocked when I suddenly landed beside them.

A startled Signaller, Brian O'Neill, yelled out, "Morgan, you crazy bastard, what're you trying to do, get your bloody head shot off? Shit man, you crazy bastard."

Shaken, I yelled back, "I didn't want to die alone under a pile of dirt."

I sat shaking and dry retching among the others, cuts to my head and scratched face throbbing for the few hours until daylight. I went to the first aid tent but was back on duty within a short time.

Though I didn't know it at the time, that night changed my life. It continues to haunt me during my sleep, sometimes seven, sometimes 10 times a week, in the form of a violent nightmare. They say war is hell and I think that's quite an apt description. It suggests an ongoing trauma, something just bearable, a situation which traps you in a constant state of "just coping".

Hell suggests a perpetual struggle - continuing discomfort, distress and pain. The nature of this personal hell requires that element of ongoing struggle. This fits the experience of many a Vietnam veteran, I believe. Conditions were just bad enough, often enough, or constant enough (as the case may have been) to be endured at the time. Just like a hungry predator, it picked off the vulnerable and the sick first.

Anyone with any stress from home, with injury or any particular sensibility which might leave them particularly open to depression or boredom or fragility, were the ones from among our ranks affected first. And the trauma moved inwards from there, encircling most, if not all, of us.

It caught up with many of us after being granted freedom from the army and returned to our homes and tried to live a "normal" life. It wasn't so much a matter of if, but when, you cracked. The pressure was immense and eventually something had to give.

Vietnam was tough. A lot of us were young. We were over there fighting for a way of life that we'd barely experienced ourselves. I came home to a place which hadn't changed, only to find how much I had.

It took a long time to come to grips with the notion that I'd just worked my guts out, facing night after night of gut-wrenching fear, living in a hovel, for nothing. For less than nothing. All because the "policy" had lost favour, because the media had spun things one way and public opinion had shifted accordingly.

Like many Vietnam vets, I struggled with psychological problems but tried to present a "normal" face to the world, raising our children with my wife, going into the office every day. I initially adopted this mask of normality as a way of coping. But over the years it became such a part of me I started to forget I was wearing it.

As I aged, my struggles with Post Traumatic Stress Disorder became harder. As the pressure built, escape became my obsession.

The dream of romantic isolation drove me to work my way through the channels of the Bureau of Meteorology until I earned a posting in Antarctica. When man fights nature, it's easier to forget that man is fighting himself. It was easier to appear normal while fighting my demons down there. Everyone who seeks the challenge of Antarctica has their own reasons for doing so.

Surrounded by intoxicating beauty and the challenge of various co-expeditioners, I believed I was in control. My mask was strong. Problems could be ignored. In this new world I could cope.

Casey taught me otherwise.

PART ONE
ANTARCTIC DREAMINGS

"In this life we only get those things for which we hunt, for which we strive, and for which we are willing to sacrifice."

George Matthew Adams

ICE JOURNEY

CHAPTER 1
THE CURSE OF CASEY

How to explain what drives a man?

It was April 2000, and I was sitting opposite an Australian Antarctic Division-approved psychiatrist at my old Enoggera Army Base in Brisbane answering questions while he studied my every move, searching for weaknesses.

I was a 52-year-old man, married with two teenage children, trying to get down to Antarctica. "Everyone has an Antarctica", Thomas Pynchon once wrote. As a young bloke standing on the edge of a windy, wintery Melbourne beach, I didn't understand the spirit that drove the early explorers and those during the heroic age to leave family behind as they battled towards "The Unknown South Land". I just knew, staring towards the cold vastness of the Southern Ocean, that one day I'd go beyond the horizon.

But you need someone's dollar to get there. Travelling as a tourist wasn't the challenge that I was looking for, and to be part of the Australian National Antarctic Research Expeditions (ANARE) group, you need a skill. I'd been working with the Australian Bureau of Meteorology (BoM) since 1972, and had just finished a six-month stint as officer-in-charge at Giles, perched on the edge of the Gibson Desert, the only staffed weather station in an area of about 2.5 million square kilometres. It ranks in BoM folklore with tiny Willis Island in the Coral Sea as one of the most isolated weather observation points in the country.

When I'd applied a few years later with ANARE for a position on one of Australia's four main bases, I'd proved I could handle remoteness. The BoM had flown me from my home in Rockhampton, Queensland to Melbourne, Victoria for a two-hour grilling from a three-person panel. I'd passed the first test – now all that remained was to pass the physical and psychological examinations.

The psychiatrist wasn't interested in boyhood fantasies of rip-roaring adventure, the human thirst for challenge and exploration. He wanted to know much more than that. In the early years, ANARE expeditioners weren't psychologically screened, but the Mawson winter of 1959 changed that. One of the two diesel mechanics, a German national named Henry Brandt, had a nervous breakdown in April. He'd been showing some problems in the months before, but in early April he entered the mess with a knife in his hand and the other expeditioners had to wrestle him down. He became violent and ended up being restrained in a hastily-made cell. The station doctor tried to control his illness with medication until the winter ended. The nearby Russians flew 600 kilometres to try and help. He improved after nine months of treatment and confinement at Wilkes and was flown back to Melbourne for further treatment. That was a big lesson to ANARE, and today's screening aims to ensure the mental health of any person facing that kind of isolation.

"Tell me about Vietnam".

That was the question I'd been anxious about. The Vietnam vet label had followed me around for years, changing in focus as society learnt more about the scars that so many were left with.

"Yeah, fine. A few nightmares, but nothing much." That was the most I was willing to say, knowing it would be hard to hide those once I started sharing space with other expeditioners.

In reality, I'd been diagnosed with Post Traumatic Stress Disorder (PTSD) just a short time before. My wife Deb had been after me for years to get help as my nightmares were getting more severe. After returning from Giles, I finally went to the doctor. He told me I had grounds to get out of the workforce as my symptoms were so brutal. I said that was the easy way out. I knew I'd never get down to Antarctica if it got out, so I ignored his recommendation.

I prided myself on the fact that I had a good job and a good family. I didn't drink much, didn't smoke or do drugs. As far as I was concerned, I was fine, unlike my mate Don who I'd worked with in the BoM and who'd also signed up for the army and served in Vietnam. He found his peace in Thailand, going over once or twice a year until he blew his brains out one day.

Somewhere in the back of my mind I knew that my anxiety attacks and nightmares weren't normal, but I figured that was my lot, and just to get on with it. I'd gone to Giles to see how I'd cope with nightmares as much as how I'd cope with remoteness. I was confident that while PTSD was an issue for me, it wouldn't be an issue for anyone else.

And I wanted a challenge. All my life I'd wanted to push myself. I learned to fly in my late teens, joined the Citizens' Military Force (CMF) in my sub-senior year. I must have convinced the psychiatrist as a few days later I got the call to pack my bags and be in Hobart at the end of August to join the 2000-2001 expedition to Casey.

It wasn't quite as simple as that. There were bulky manila folders full of forms to be filled out in triplicate, a checklist of sizes for cold-weather gear to be issued, and advice on how to prepare my family. In the meantime, I continued my shifts as meteorological officer at the Rockhampton (Rocky) Bureau where I found it hard to focus as everyone else kept shuffling along with their duties. I wanted to scream out, "I'm going. I'm really going".

Time was dragging, but for my wife Deb and my kids David and Michelle it was speeding up. Deb and I had to sort through the necessary financial and legal documents dealing with "what if" scenarios. Before I'd applied, we had sat down as a family to discuss what it would mean to us if I pursued my dream. It would mean more than a year away in a period when David and Michelle would want me around for advice and support. And it would mean leaving Deb to cope with everything by herself. I knew she was battling a sense of being left behind, an unfortunate reality for the families of expeditioners. However, it would also bring financial benefits, especially with private school fees owing and university fees looming. Most importantly, it would mean an end to working at Rocky with its long commute and shiftwork, especially the hated 2.30am starts.

It was only with their approval that I'd moved ahead, but as we prepared for my departure a sense of urgency weighed on everything we did. One morning as I was laying turf in the backyard, the pain in my groin that I'd been feeling on and off for weeks turned severe and left me doubled over.

The news wasn't good: "It's a hernia. We'll have to operate, but it's a straightforward operation and shouldn't put you out of commission for too long."

I couldn't afford to be sick right then, and tried to make the doctor understand. He wasn't swayed. "It'll have to be fixed, Dave. Look, the op itself should only last an hour at the most and we'll talk recovery time after that."

I went in at 1pm. When I managed to finally force my eyes open around the grogginess, saw it was after 4pm. *That's bloody strange, what's going on?*

Two hours later, Dr Renton-Power came to my bedside and told me I was a lucky boy. Apparently the hernia had strangulated a portion of my bowel. Left any longer, it could have burst with fatal results.

Two weeks later, I was back in Dr Renton-Power's rooms in Rocky for a follow-up examination.

"How do you feel, Dave?"

"Yeah, good."

He studied me for a moment, and then asked, "Anything unusual?"

"Well, I'm still bleeding from my bowel." I knew my news wasn't good, but certainly didn't expect his reaction.

"What?"

An undignified exam later, he said what, deep down, I already knew: "You've got problems".

The doc sent me urgently to the Mater Private Hospital in Brisbane to meet Dr Steadman, who performed a colonoscopy. It revealed 13 polyps in my bowel, the largest the size of a golf ball, which he burnt off. Not a man to mince words, he told me the large one looked nasty and I was more than likely looking at cancer.

Sent back to Yeppoon in Queensland to wait for the results, I was finding it hard to remain optimistic. August was drawing near, the beginning of intensive ANARE training, and I couldn't move or bend. And I was waiting to hear if I had cancer.

Luckily I didn't. Both Dr Steadman and Dr Renton-Power assured me I would be fit in time for the August departure, and I concentrated on getting fit and getting organised.

One day I received a phone call. The professional voice at the other end introduced himself as Dr Peter Gormly, head of ANARE's medical division. After some small talk, he asked about my health.

Hoping it was a stock-standard question for all expeditioners, I answered in my usual manner: "Yeah, good."

He paused. "I believe you've been having some medical problems."

I knew neither of my doctors would've said anything and figured it must've been someone at the Rockhampton Meteorology office who'd told him. If that were the case, I assumed he wouldn't know too many details. "Where'd you hear that? No, doc, I'm fine."

The doc's tone changed and he asked me again, this time telling me there was a Commonwealth Act which meant if I didn't tell the truth when questioned, there could be severe penalties.

Well, when you put it that way. "I did have a hernia op in May and they found a golf ball-sized polyp."

"In that case, you're not going to Casey."

The last two months of worrying had finally come to this, and I wasn't going to back down. I argued with him, saying that both my doctors said I'd be medically fit by August. Dr Gormly said I would need medical certificates from both doctors before I went to Hobart in Tasmania, and we left it at that. I spent the last few weeks training up my replacement at work, spending time with my family and friends, and enjoying a farewell bash at the Yeppoon Sailing Club.

Saying goodbye to Deb, Michelle and David was hard. After a final hug, I didn't want to linger. On the trip down to Hobart I was hollow, questioning the fairness of what I was doing, especially as the kids were at an age when they should have their dad nearby.

At the Antarctica Division's building in Kingston, I met the other 20 expeditioners who were also to head down to Casey. One introduced himself as the station's doctor and said he wanted to talk. What he actually wanted to do was examine me. Afterwards he said: "I'm not happy to take you, Dave. I just don't want the risk".

I froze. Surely I wasn't going to be turned away now, not after all it took to get there. I argued I was fit and asked if he'd received my certificates from Dr Steadman and Dr Renton-Power. He said he did and that we'd have to refer the decision to Dr Gormly. After his examination, the two doctors conferred.

Dr Gormly delivered the news. "Dave, I agree with the station doctor. You've got problems."

I tried to explain I was fit, that my problems were fixed.

"Sorry. You can go any other year, just not this year." And with that I was dismissed.

I was devastated. And angry. That night I stayed at a friend's place and rang Deb with the news. I couldn't understand why Dr Gormly let me say goodbye to family, leave work and come down if my acceptance was always going to be conditional. I felt he should've been clear there was a chance I wouldn't be going. Instead, I'd organised the medical certificates they'd wanted and they'd dismissed me.

I returned to Yeppoon and tried to pick up as if I'd never gone away, but it wasn't working. Having to face all the people who had been celebrating with us a few weeks before was hard, but going back to work was claustrophobic. The Rockhampton Bureau of Meteorology is based at the airport. It's a major regional airport with substantial aircraft operations, including choppers landing about 100 metres away. The flat shuddering sound of these is a noise anyone who went to Vietnam recognises, and the relentless slapping noise made my stomach tighten, especially when the Singapore military used the airport for their annual exercises.

Besides the choppers, the politics and the in-fighting amongst the staff became intolerable. I'd escaped once before by going to Giles, but when I'd come back I found the stress built and I couldn't cope with the pressure, finding even taking phone calls from the public hard. The period at Giles had been heaven. Even with the added responsibility of being officer in charge, I'd found peace there. The disappointment of the aborted Casey expedition rested heavy as I forced myself to go back to work and answer questions from well-meaning people.

***

Where to from here? It seemed that all the choices I'd made in my life, and the twists and turns life had thrown, had brought me to this point.

"We might be poor," my mum Sybella often said to us kids, "but as long as we're always good honest citizens, people in town will respect us for that."

Mum was the backbone of our family, single-handedly raising us after my dad died. One minute she was with my dad Gerald (Gus) running a café in Alice Springs in the Northern Territory, 'The Sybella', raising my brother Gerald and sister Sybil (known as Patsy) and newly pregnant with my twin brother and me. The next she was widowed. Perhaps Dad's death shouldn't have been that unexpected as he'd been a heavy smoker most of his life, smoking up to 60 cigarettes a day. Mum not only lost her husband that day, but the inheritance she'd invested in the family business vanished with him. With no money and no income, she took Gerald and Patsy to Melbourne to be near her family. In March 1948 my brother Don was born. I followed seven minutes later.

Those early years were marked by hard work and bad health, moving and adventures. When I was four we moved to Somers, a small Victorian seaside town on the Mornington Peninsula. Shortly after, Patsy accidentally knocked the kerosene lamp off the cupboard which shattered on the floor, bursting into flames and trapping Don in the kitchen. Mum rushed through the blaze to carry him out to safety before heading back in to fight the fire. She inhaled a considerable amount of smoke and was sick for weeks which, on top of her chronic cough, badly affected her health. On doctors' advice, she decided we would move north to Mildura on the banks of the Murray River. After a teary farewell, we headed to Melbourne to catch an overnight "Red Rattler" to our new lives.

The move and our father's death affected our family deeply. Being much older, Gerald and Patsy missed Dad and their loss caught up with them. Gerald found a job and moved to Melbourne. Patsy ran away from home and refused to return, living instead in a government house in Adelaide. Mum decided to move back to Alice Springs, reasoning she had friends there and it would help her deal with Dad's death if she could visit his grave.

Once again our worldly belongings were packed into a couple of suitcases and we were off on The Ghan for a three-day journey to The Alice. With no accommodation available, Don and I stayed in the Church of England Hostel for a week, until Mum found a job and a place for us all to live. While she worked as a housekeeper at a holiday farm, a whole new world opened for Don and me at the Alice Springs Caravan Park, sitting around campfires with travellers or Aborigines who lived nearby. Gerry and Patsy came to join us and once again we were one big happy family.

After a year Mum decided it was time to head south again but became ill shortly after we'd arrived back in Melbourne and required hospitalisation.. The doctors diagnosed tuberculosis (TB), telling Mum to expect the worst. Dad had been an officer in the Merchant Navy so Mum's doctor, who was a good bloke, arranged for Legacy (the Australian organisation established in 1923 by ex-servicemen dedicated to caring for widows and dependants of deceased soldiers) to keep an eye on us. Patsy, who was 17, could only look after us at night so the doctor arranged for Don and me to be put into a Legacy holiday camp program. We went to Blamey House to join 50-odd other boys in one of the best periods of my young life. To our complete amazement, we were even given two shillings a day as pocket money. I'd never felt so rich.

Once out of hospital, Mum eventually found a job looking after a farmer and his two sons on a sheep and wheat property up near Balaklava, South Australia, and Don and I, nine years old by then, were assigned jobs around the farm before and after school to pay for our keep.

A failed move to Tasmania followed, with our return to Melbourne and onto Echuca on the Murray River. In Grade 5, I had my first job working for a small greengrocer on Saturday mornings, earning one bob for each five-hour shift. I did that for 12 months and near the end of that year, Mum was again admitted to hospital with TB. For several months Don and I lived with her friends from church.

When I was in high school, Mum's health deteriorated to the point where Legacy found us a rental house in Caloundra, Queensland, for the warmer climate. Here I got a job working a milk run Friday and Saturday mornings from midnight to 8am, and school holidays Monday to Saturday. They were hard hours to balance with studies, but I managed to put some money aside for the two years I kept the job.

Just after Don and I sat our junior exam, the headmaster called us into his office to tell us Mum was in hospital in Brisbane. She had fallen and broken her hip at the site of some council works. For six weeks we fended for ourselves while Mum was in Brisbane. We got holiday jobs as postmen, working from 5am until 3pm, though as Christmas approached we'd work until 5pm.

After gaining our Junior Certificate, Don and I decided to keep going at school and began our sub-senior year (Grade 11). One of my teachers was an officer in the Citizens' Military Force and I decided to join. My commitment to the CMF included a weekly parade at the drill hall and one weekend a month. I loved every moment.

I was getting average marks in sub-senior so I decided it would be my last year at school. I was thinking of trying to pursue a career in the army or perhaps as a pilot so, as well as continuing in the CMF, I started taking flying lessons. I'd always wanted to fly since the day in my first year of primary school when a biplane came down in a paddock and all the kids went running out to see it. Three times a week I took a one-hour lesson, eventually flying solo. I would've kept going indefinitely but money, or rather the lack of it, had become a challenge. After a request to Legacy for help to continue with lessons was denied, I applied to join the regular army, hoping to get into the aviation program indirectly.

My army career started like everyone else's: the trial of training, the shaping of a soldier and the selection of postings. I got my first choice of the Royal Australian Signal Corp and was eventually posted to 139 Signal Squadron based at Enoggera in Brisbane, which served as a reinforcement unit for 104 Signal Squadron stationed in Vietnam.

Selected to attend a cipher course at Balcombe, I learned how to code and decipher messages on different machines and how to set them up. When we arrived back at Enoggera, we learned that our postings to Vietnam had been confirmed and we could expect to depart sometime in January. I'd be heading to Nui Dat in Phuoc Tuy Province, about 50 kilometres south-east of Saigon.

I completed my posting at 139 Signal Squadron in mid-December 1968 and started my leave. While at home, some of my ex-school friends approached me, criticising Australia's involvement in the war and I got into pretty heated arguments with them. A few weeks later, at 4.30pm on January 1, 1969, I took the train from Brisbane to Sydney for the flight to Vietnam. It was time to leave not only my home, my family and friends, but also my country.

Just over a year later, my tour of duty over, I returned to Australia disillusioned and struggled to settle into my old life. Nothing seemed to matter and after six months, I decided to take discharge from the army. That came as a shock to my unit as everyone thought I was a "lifer", but even talks of my bright future couldn't change my mind. It was time for Civvy Street.

I left the army July, 1969. I didn't waste any time in applying for different jobs, I started with the Department of Supply in Melbourne on August, 1970.

After 12 months in Melbourne, I had my first nightmare. One night, after heading out to watch the footy with a friend, I fell into bed exhausted. It wasn't long before I woke, gasping for breath and screaming out in horror. I couldn't remember the last time I'd had a nightmare but as I scrambled for the light switch, my body shaking all over and covered in sweat, I realised that's what had just happened. News that my mate Robert "Scotty" Wilson had been killed in Vietnam on his second tour of duty made me realise the futility of what I had been doing and set off what would be a pattern of nightmares and anxiety that would curse me for the rest of my life.

After Scotty's loss I seemed to get very angry within myself feeling guilty that I had left the army and let my mates down including Scotty. A lot of anti-Vietnam war demonstration marches were being held in Melbourne at the time. It made me angry and disgusted. All I wanted to do was to get out of Melbourne.

In the following weeks I applied for different jobs, and even considered rejoining the army. They offered me my rank, trade and subjects back and said I could have my old posting at 139 Signal Squadron in Enoggera, but I was also offered a job with the Bureau of Meteorology and a job with Foreign Affairs.

Antarctica kept haunting the back of my mind. After I left the army I met an ex-army bloke who had been to Antarctica as a radio operator and talked about his experiences and this became a dream of mine. I knew the Bureau of Meteorology had a strong history down on that continent.

I chose the Bureau. It was a chance for a new environment and I opted to be posted to Darwin as a communications operator, where I'd send out forecasts and synoptic weather observations via teleprinter to the main Communication centre in Melbourne and media outlets. Much as I loved Darwin, the humid climate was aggravating the chronic conjunctivitis I'd developed in Vietnam and I transferred to Brisbane.

The Brisbane staff were great and we made a good team, we proved this during the Brisbane floods caused by Cyclone Wanda in January 1974. Those of us who were working when the river flooded were trapped for the duration. In a 72-hour period I worked for 60 hours, followed by another 12-hour shift. Others worked even more.

While I liked my work and the people I worked with, I continued to struggle with nightmares and felt unsettled. I headed to America to visit my sister, who'd married her long-lost boyfriend and moved with him to Portland, Oregon. I also caught up with an American friend from Vietnam. When I returned, I started dating a beautiful young lady who worked in the Bureau's administration section, Debbie Leabeater, and we married six months later.

It was the beginning of many changes. I was selected for the Bureau's observers' course and started my training in Melbourne on October 24, 1977. After completing the course, I took a posting at the Amberley Air Force Base and over the next 20 years we moved around Queensland - Oakey Army Base, Longreach, Rockhampton and back to Brisbane where our daughter Michelle was born. From there we headed to Cairns, back to Brisbane and out west to Charleville, where David was born. After that came Gladstone and, finally, Rockhampton, with each posting bringing me further skills.

Through it all, I kept searching for something more. As my children grew older, I started seriously considering the possibility of trying to make the dream of Antarctica a reality. I knew my experience could lead me into a spot in the Australian National Antarctic Research Expeditions (ANARE) which have served Australia in south Polar Regions since 1947.

The Bureau of Meteorology is one of several Australian government agencies involved with Antarctic research, including the Antarctic Division (formed in 1948 to administer ANARE), the Australian Geological Survey Organisation, the Australian Surveying and Land Information Group and the Commonwealth Scientific and Industrial Research Organisation (CSIRO), as well as other non-government organisations such as universities.

I also knew that I'd have to prove that I could handle isolation before I'd be taken seriously, so I sat down with Deb and talked through the idea of applying for Giles. A weather station located at the edge of the Gibson Desert south of the Rawlinson Range, 750 kilometres west-southwest of Alice Springs and just over the West Australian border, it would be a good test to see how I'd handle isolation.

We'd always travelled together as a family but this time I'd have to leave them for six months. It was a big ask for them, but without this experience I'd have little weight behind my application to go south.

In March 1998, I was accepted and headed out to meet the other four guys I'd be living with for the next six months. I'd lived at Longreach and Charleville but Giles made those experiences feel like a joke. This place was seriously isolated. The only staffed weather station in an area of about 2.5 million square kilometres (Australia's second largest State, Queensland, measures 1.72 million square kilometres), it ranked in Bureau folklore with tiny Willis Island in the Coral Sea as one of the most isolated weather observation points in the country.

Established in 1956 by the Weapons Research Establishment (a division of the Department of Defence now known as the Defence Science and Technology Organisation), Giles was designed to provide weather data for the UK atomic weapons tests at Emu Plains and Maralinga and to support the rocket testing program based at Woomera. It transferred to the Bureau of Meteorology in 1972. Today its weather balloons go straight into the core of Australia's subtropical jet stream, making the station vital for forecasting over most of eastern and south-eastern Australia, particularly for rain.

I went in as officer-in-charge and learned very quickly to juggle the different demands that the role brought. Apart from the isolation, there was pressure to keep everything running on a tight budget and the need to be self-sufficient. When something broke, you couldn't just order in equipment or ring up a repairman. We became quite handy with the good old Aussie tradition of jerry-rigging, learning quickly how to fix things ourselves.

Harder than that, though, were managing the human relationships. As the person in charge, I was always aware that the people who'd apply for a position at Giles would be independently-minded and would likely have been attracted to the remoteness to escape the normal bureaucracies and rules of everyday life. Being officer-in-charge, I was concerned about being able to balance the social side of the lifestyle with ensuring we stuck to our program, but soon learned to read the moods of the other blokes.

When my six-month stint was over, I went back to Yeppoon where I decided that if I could survive Giles, I could certainly survive anything Antarctica could throw at me. The next step was to apply for Willis Island, located almost 500 kilometres off the coast of Cooktown in Far North Queensland, where my job would be to provide cyclone information. It would mean another six months away from my family, but after talking it through with them, I decided to apply.

I was assigned the June-December 1999 stint, but the day before I left, David broke his arm. Faced with my son's injury, I had no choice. I just couldn't abandon them.

Instead, I stayed at home and in March 2000 applied for a position directly on Casey, one of Australia's four main bases in Antarctica. That had been the failed Casey position.

Now I was struggling with the disappointment. One night I sat down and talked to the family. We needed a change, so we packed our bags and headed to North America for a break, enjoying our first white Christmas in Helena, Montana, with my Vietnam friend Ron and his wife Sandy. I sat at the window, watching the snow fall outside and tried to pretend I was in Antarctica.

Staring at the snow, I realised that pretending wasn't working. It was pretty, yes, but it wasn't "on the Ice". When we returned to Australia, I would have to try again.

***

I was back at work in Rockhampton in March, preparing my application for the 2002 year, when I received a phone call from the head of the ANARE Meteorology program Ian Hickman.

"You interested in going to Macca?"

Apparently pulling me from Casey had caused a problem with station postings. The bloke who was due to head to Macquarie Island ("Macca") had filled my place at Casey and they had found someone from Launceston who would go to Macquarie Island, but only for the winter. Now they needed someone to fill the 2001 officer-in-charge summer season role.

"You'd head to Hobart for training in early September and leave later that month," Ian said.

"I'll be in like Flynn. Count on it." I wasn't going to knock back a chance to get my foot through the door and went through the physical and psychological examinations. By now I was fully recovered and couldn't believe my luck; if I went to Macca and did well, I'd have a good chance at one of the continental stations.

Once again, I had to prepare my family. Though they'd supported my decision and sympathised with what had happened in Hobart, I was back home with them again. Now we were preparing for a seven-month separation. On 2 September I left Rocky for Melbourne after another emotional goodbye at the airport. It wasn't any easier the second time around, and I felt wretched as I headed down the plane's walkway.

***

First up was training at the Bureau's Broadmeadows training school with Jim Easson, the chief physicist of the ozone section. The Bureau has an Ozone Monitoring Unit which maintains an extensive commitment to ozone measurements helping to piece together the big picture of global climate and ozone depletion. I needed training in the ozonesondes used at Macca - the only subantarctic site to launch them. This balloon-borne device profile ozone concentration from the ground up to an altitude of about 35 kilometres and measures the ozone concentration of the sampled air. A standard meteorological radiosonde is incorporated in the balloon payload, and provides additional data on pressure, temperature and humidity every 10 seconds during the flight. An on-board global positioning systems (GPS) receiver provides location information for wind speed and direction. All these readings are transmitted to a ground-receiving station providing ongoing information on exactly what was happening to the ozone layer.

Three 12-hour days with Jim were followed by training on the Dobson spectrophotometer which measures atmospheric ozone and electrolyser training, needed to make hydrogen gas for the weather balloons, before I flew out to Hobart and moved into Trinity House.

The next day I met Graeme Taylor, who was in charge of all BoM training. He brought me to the Australian Antarctic Division (AAD) headquarters in Kingston for the time-honoured kitting out of extreme cold weather clothing. A kindly, grey-haired man met us and answered my questions with the patience of a someone who'd been asked many times. He was former expeditioner Don Reid, known to all as "Uncle Don", and there wasn't anything about Antarctica he didn't know. As he sized me up and disappeared down the back to gather the brightly-coloured bits, I studied the walls plastered with photos from previous expeditioners. The amount of survival gear he piled up seemed immense, and I would have to separate it into three categories before leaving.

My red survival clothing kit bag contained mandatory survival clothing: freezer suit, AAD First Aid Manual, AAD Field Manual, sunglasses, balaclava, socks, woollen thermal top and leggings, polar fleece top, pants and gloves, and walking boots. I'd be required to take this as part of my carry-on luggage and keep it in my cabin in case of shipboard emergency musters and all aircraft flights.

Don recommended I take the windproof jacket, sun hat and neck gaiter in my cabin luggage, and pointed out the limit on this was 30 kilograms (excluding the survival kit). All my other expedition clothing and equipment, which had a limit of 15 kilograms, had to be packed and delivered to the AAD main warehouse before boarding the ship, and would go into the cargo and therefore unavailable for the duration of the voyage.

***

It was early morning, and my head was busy with the DigiCORA training, used to track the weather balloons, that Graeme had given me the day before. I flicked on the television and stared at the screen for a while before realising I was watching Armageddon. Planes slammed into buildings, people jumped from incomprehensible heights, white ghosts calmly walked out of the city in shock. September 11 in America was chaos as terrorists attacked New York's Twin Towers.

I rang my family, who were also watching, and we tried to make sense of what was happening. We couldn't, although we sensed its impact. It was raw and unprocessed, and it stunned us. That night I spent hours watching "America Under Attack". As I watched the Towers collapse over and over again on screen I recalled visiting them in 1975. My disbelief and terrible sadness for the families whose worlds had been shattered left me with an overwhelming need to be with my family. It didn't escape me that I was about to put even more distance between us. *If I got injured at Macca, or God forbid one of the kids got injured while I was there ...* It was a lonely night.

***

Further Meteorology (Met) training followed – DigiCORA, how to reset logs, rainfall, computer, how to put weather profiles into various programs to send to Hobart. Ian and Graeme briefed me about my duties as officer-in-charge, and I spent a half-hour on the phone with outgoing Macca Officer in Charge (OIC) Andrew McGifford discussing station life.

After three days of forklift training, it was time for the serious field training at the Bronte Park Highland Village, located midway between Hobart and Queenstown in the geographic centre of Tasmania. Expeditioners need a wide range of skills to work at the stations and it was mandatory to undergo the four-day pre-departure training. We were divided into two groups, one going to the heated village accommodation while our section headed off to set up camp for outdoor training.

Spring in Tasmania can bring some unpleasant weather, and this time it chose to give us cold and rain. I crawled into the small space in the polar pyramid tent and set up next to my tent mate.

Night-time had become my enemy, and I knew I'd have to warn him. Since Vietnam I'd relived being buried alive, but as I got older it became more vivid and more frequent. I'd also had the occasional shakes, but since Giles everything had become worse, including my anxiety attacks. My wife Deb had been pressuring me to see a doctor, but it wasn't until I started going to a drop-in centre for veterans at the Naval hall in Rockhampton that I had to admit I was affected. The other vets could see my shakes and told me I had Post Traumatic Stress Disorder – Vietnam's calling card. After talking to them about things I couldn't share with my family, I finally went to see a doctor who confirmed the PTSD.

"If you hear anything during the night, it's just me having a nightmare," I warned my tent-mate. "I'm not violent or anything, but it'll take me quite a while to come out of it."

He was okay with that, and while I luckily didn't have any that night, I still couldn't sleep. Unfortunately, he sounded like an engine about to seize. I curled up, desperate for sleep while he blissfully bounced his snores off the tent wall.

Next morning, over breakfast, everyone complained about the miserable night. Sympathy was not forthcoming from our trainers: "Consider it good training for Macca". We worked on navigation, radios and compass skills, and tested what we'd learnt with a search and rescue exercise. Another crappy night with wet clothes and my snoring tent-mate left me rather exhausted the next morning, but thankfully our field work was done.

After packing up the tents, we drove the five kilometres back to the village itself and swapped places with the other group. While they dealt with the cold, we had classroom sessions on environmental management, coping with separation from family and friends, occupational health and safety, harassment and issues in community living. We finally got to use the four-wheel-drive Honda quad bikes before ANARE put on a formal dinner and drinks session with all the executives.

The next day back in Hobart, my confidence was slammed at the TasFire training school in Cambridge. It was hard physical work, rolling and unrolling hoses and setting up the equipment. Although I was fit, I was in my fifties and for the first time I really struggled. It really knocked me around and convinced me that my stamina wasn't what it used to be.

**

Departure day, 28 September, was bittersweet. Excitement at finally heading out, apprehension at leaving family. I left Trinity House at 8am and dropped the rest of my personal gear off at the Bureau office at Macquarie Street before heading out to Kingston for a lecture from Dr Gormly. Quite a few people have lost their lives at Macca, something he wanted us to understand so we wouldn't repeat past mistakes. I knew he and I would have to talk at some point; it would've been too awkward not to.

"I see you made it."

I nodded.

"Where're you going?"

"Macquarie Island."

"Good spot, Macca. How do you feel?"

"Yeah, good." And that was it.

Surprisingly enough, I'd lost my anger. One reason was so much time had passed. Another was that finally I was heading out on an expedition.

As the head of the medical department, he had an enormous amount of responsibility and I could see his point. In the end, he was just doing his job.

The bright orange icebreaker, *Aurora Australis* (AA), affectionately known as the "Orange Roughy", was waiting at the waterfront for us. Named for the southern hemisphere's night phenomenon, she's Australia's Antarctic flagship, and was purpose built for the program by P&O Polar. The ship accommodates 116 passengers, and at 94 metres long and 3911 tonnes, can break ice up to 1.5 metres thick. Three helicopters can be housed in the hanger and operate from the deck at the rear of the ship.

We boarded and practiced safety drills for several hours. Antarctica doesn't offer many avenues of escape if something goes wrong, and the AA had experienced that first hand. In July 1998, fire broke out in the engine room when the ship was in sea ice about 1300 nautical miles (2500 kilometres) from Hobart, and 100 nautical miles (185 kilometres) off the Antarctic coast. The engine was stopped and a quick response from passengers and crew contained the fire. It took about two days to get the engine going before they could head to the mainland and on to Newcastle for repairs.

After the drills, I headed back to the Met office for lunch and a few beers with friends. I had time for one last phone call to the family. I hadn't wanted them to fly down to see me off; I couldn't handle the intensity of trying to keep them in sight as we pulled further and further away. As I walked through the groups of wives smiling bravely and kids getting last hugs, I knew that decision was right. It was gut-wrenching enough watching the others. Going up the walkway, I could see that the others walking towards the ship felt the same.

Finally at 6.30pm, the ship's horn blasted and we pulled away. Thin paper streamers connecting expeditioners with their "other" life snapped one by one until finally we were on our own.

PART TWO
MACQUARIE ISLAND
FINE ONE MINUTE, LOUSY THE NEXT

"Never regard study as a duty, but as the enviable opportunity to learn to know the liberating influence of beauty in the realm of the spirit for your own personal joy and to the profit of the community to which your later work belongs."

Albert Einstein (1879-1955)

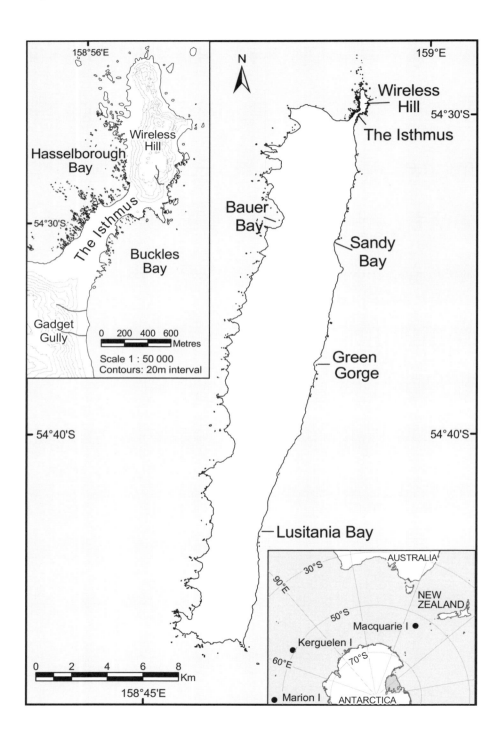

Cold, wet and windy, Macquarie Island ("Macca") rises from the Southern Ocean about 1500 kilometres south south-east of Tasmania, halfway between Australia and Antarctica. After a long history of sealing, it became a nature reserve under the control of the Tasmanian government and is now a breeding refuge for southern elephant seals, fur seals and penguins. Approximately 34 kilometres long and 5.5 kilometres at its widest point, it became a World Heritage area in 1997.

CHAPTER 2

GOOD GOD!

October 2001 weather details:
Extreme max 10.3 °C, min -4.6 °C
Mean daily sunshine (hours) 2.8
Days of precipitation 25, average monthly rainfall 71.6 millimetres
Days of strong winds 24, days of gales 9
(Based on averages to 1989)

The island was beautiful. Rugged. It poked up through the mist just after 11.30am three days after we'd left Hobart. We gathered on the deck to stare at the desolate cragginess which would be home for the next six months.

The Southern Ocean had served her reputation well. I was desperate to get off. I'd spent the better part of the journey with my head in a toilet bowl as the "Orange Roughy" rolled. The shape that gave the vessel the ability to ride up over the ice and break it with her weight also meant an uncomfortable trip. I'd lost the battle against seasickness fairly soon after reaching open water.

"Sorry, too rough to land." The captain dashed my hopes, announcing that the 20-25 knot winds and white-capped water meant we'd have keep moving and wait for better conditions. We sailed past the ANARE station, clusters of buildings on either end of a narrow isthmus, and continued down the east side of the island, 34 kilometres to the southern Hurd Point.

Massive clusters of penguin colonies were just white dots against green, and seemingly comatose elephant seals dotted the grey-black pebbled beaches. The first of these pups had started appearing in September as mothers, pregnant from the previous year's mating, returned. The breeding season was in full swing, and though keen to see the alpha seals fight for their territory, we were too far away. Behind the beaches the land rose sharply to the plateau uplands. Although I knew Macca was going to be green thanks to all the rainfall it receives, I wasn't prepared for the wild beauty. Parts of the land were scarred, stripped bare by landslips following heavy rainfall or seismic activity.

A few hours later the ship returned to Buckles Bay near the station. Winds had dropped to 10-15 knots making it safe to start the transfer. I donned my survival dry suit and gathered my kit bag. As I waited I studied a bird seemingly stationary in the distance. Despite all efforts against the wind it appeared to be hovering in one spot. The Zodiac pulled up and I climbed down the rope ladder, sat and grabbed the slippery red tube for purchase. Though I nodded hello to a young woman with long hair, I didn't recognise her as Cathie Saunders, my BoM tech from Giles, who I'd seen a few months before in Hobart on the aborted Casey expedition. She'd been down there preparing for Macca, and would be one of the team during for my stay. I was too mesmerised by my surroundings to notice anything but the old buildings growing larger as we covered the few kilometres to shore. At the southern end of the station is the fuel tank farm which holds 300,000 litres of diesel oil and small quantities of petrol and kerosene. As we approached I could read the large white letters on the tanks which spelled out the station's name.

As the Zodiac hit the sand, a figure wearing a flimsy dress, bad makeup and long red hair was racing up and down the beach. *Who the heck is this ugly sheila?*

I was distracted from this sight by the station leader, Robb Clifton, who shook my hand and officially welcomed me, and by finally meeting outgoing BoM officer-in-charge Andrew McGifford. It was nice to put a face to the voice. I followed him up to the Met office after handing my dry suit to the beach master.

Most changeovers last about four or five days, and normally the outgoing officer-in-charge would have fully prepared me to take over the station. However, Andrew only had time to point out the essentials: "This is my diary, this is the office, here are the keys, I'm off, need to get on the ship". The state of the weather meant the crew of *Aurora Australis* wanted to leave immediately and 15 minutes were all I was going to get. I shook hands again with Andrew and watched him head off, his figure receding into the distance. I slumped into "my" chair in the office, the excitement of finally arriving wiped out by anxiety at coming in like "Blind Freddy".

I knew I'd figure it out, that all my training would kick in but at that moment the responsibility, my unpreparedness and the unknown was claustrophobic. A face popped around the corner. It was Ailsa Brady, the other Met member. Both Ailsa and Cathie had wintered and were staying on, and I was going to have to depend on them to show me the ropes. Ailsa's light manner helped ease my tension as we spent the rest of the afternoon going over basic duties.

Late that afternoon the *Aurora Australis* sounded her horn and disappeared, and we headed up the wooden walkways into the mess, the Hasselborough Club, for the official welcome. Robb went over the rules and safety issues of the island, and as I listened I studied the strangers I'd be living with. Isolation does funny things to people, and those that had spent the winter together would be finding the arrival of 34 strangers disruptive, though they didn't show it.

I rang Deb and the kids. They were full of questions but I was still trying to take everything in, and only had time to say I'd arrived safely, that everything was okay and I'd ring again in a few days. Two things I was certain of – that night my bed wasn't going to roll, and I would sleep.

And I did. Until the nightmare pulled me back to the claustrophobia of my flashback. The stress of being in an unfamiliar place and the tightness in my stomach at being unprepared for my new role teased my subconscious back to being a 19-year-old sitting in the bottom of a dark, cold hole again.

I can't stand it.

Screaming, I raced from my bed in a fear-driven frenzy until my conscious caught up with me again. Gasping for breath, I sat back down on the edge of the bed. The room was basic – bed, desk and chair, wardrobe with a mirror on the door and drawers – but it was unfamiliar, and I crashed into it as I tried to find a way out.

I can't stand it.

Resting my elbows on my knees, my body shook uncontrollably for the better part of an hour. Luckily I was next to the main toilet and shower/laundry room on one side, and only had one person in a room next to me. I'd met Col Rendall, the carpenter earlier and hoped he hadn't heard me cry out. Eventually my gasps stopped and my breathing became more regular, and once the shakes stopped I drank some water and climbed back into bed. I knew I'd be tired the next day.

The next few days I worked at the Met office with Cathie and Ailsa. The stress at being underprepared threatened to explode through the calm exterior I struggled to maintain as I learned my new role. Sensing this, Cathie asked me how I felt.

I'd first met Cathie back in 1998 at Giles when she'd flown in from Darwin to service our Met equipment. A pretty woman in her mid-30s, she was intelligent, a hard worker, a brilliant technician, and there wasn't any equipment she couldn't fix. She was also a compassionate woman.

"Too much going through my brain." And wasn't that the truth. I spent days frantically writing down any bit of information that might be relevant and learning what had to be done each shift. Those first few days I was just looking at shiftwork, not even looking at my officer-in-charge duties, while also meeting with the station leader and other expeditioners for a tour of the station.

The Met office ran two shifts: 8am-4pm and 4pm-12.30am. Each shift had specific duties, including releasing a weather balloon, undertaking synopses (weather situations), working the Dobson ozone spectrophotometer to get data, and ozone preparation for packages (there were three stages for each package). On the fourth day, Cathie and I released an ozone package, my first. Luckily it was successful, and I started to relax. By the fifth day, I was confident enough to tackle the morning solo, and managed to release my first weather balloon.

One of the daily duties was heading to the clean air lab on the west side of the island to check on experiments. Often getting there could be a challenge and I'd struggle against strong blustery winds. Experiments ran unmanned around the clock, but daily we would have to check everything was working, change filters and occasionally pump air through cylinders. The lab had emergency back-up in case of power failure. It was here air was taken and tested, and data sent to the CSIRO and various universities, including Princeton in America. I'd change the filters and was amazed at how much pollution there was - not a lot, but it still shouldn't have been getting down to Macca.

***

That night, a violent earth tremor jolted me out of a deep sleep. Macca had emerged from the sea between 90,000-300,000 years ago as a result of an uplift created through interaction of the Indo-Australian and Pacific tectonic plates, a process that continues today all along the Macquarie Ridge. Macca is its exposed crest. This was partly why the United Nations Educational, Scientific and Cultural Organisation listed it on the World Heritage List in 1997. Earthquakes are a fairly regular occurrence along the ridge with, on average, a tremor of 6.2 or greater on the Richter Scale once a year, and one registering 7.2 or greater once a decade. What can be rationally understood by day comes as a bloody shock in the pitch black of night. Slowly I realised the terror wasn't a nightmare and jumped out of bed for the doorway, trying to remember if Robb had mentioned anything about emergency plans for quakes. Nope. Next morning, all the winterers said, "That's normal. We've had worse." *Couldn't wait.*

Routine has a marvellous calming effect. As I started becoming comfortable with the job, time off was a priceless opportunity to explore my surrounds. The isthmus is a narrow patch of sand, no more than one and a half football ovals wide. In all the years people have worked at Macca, only rarely had the storm surge gone completely across, though a few years earlier one wave nearly took a female expeditioner heading back home after work. Today the seas were relatively calm, though the winds weren't. They never were.

Not having gone through field training, I was restricted to the station boundaries but could still explore the protected historic domed corrugated buildings, part of the original base before the construction project of the 1980s. These old buildings now serve many purposes: one was the stores, nicknamed "Woolies"; another was the official Macquarie Island Post Office. One of the expeditioners, Mick Eccles, had been trained as the official Australia Postmaster, and he was the only one allowed to open the sealed bags delivered during the summer shipping season.

I took a chance to approach the elephant seals basking in the sun. These massive animals were everywhere around base, and the sight, sound and smell wherever they gathered was unforgettable. Their acidic stench burned my nose. A female noticed me and looked up, very disinterested, before putting her head back down and going to sleep. Her baby beside her, no more than a week old, rolled over onto his back, wriggling and clapping his flippers. He looked at me and patted his tummy. I was amazed at his attitude towards the strange two-legged thing watching him. In the distance, two males lifted their great heads and bellowed warnings at each other. I knew one male would have this colony of females, but sometimes a younger one would try to take over. It made for impressive viewing, but I felt sorry for the old boy having to look over his shoulder at the younger pups literally biting at his heels, and empathised with the younger ones just wanting a shot at their turn.

As they took time out from their testosterone rituals, I suddenly realised it wasn't the seals that were on display. It was me. The tables were turned. The seal must've thought: "What is this tall thing in a funny fur? Why is it watching me? Would it taste good?" It was a strange feeling. It must be what it's like to be an animal in a zoo. For that moment, it made me realise that I really was outside my element here, standing among animals that had managed to survive and thrive for hundreds, if not thousands of years, while I was just a simple man standing here because of a structured program to allow me to survive in this wild land, just grateful to be allowed a glimpse.

***

Remote living means that of course there are no outside services available – no hairdressers, no ringing 000 for fire or medical needs, and most importantly no domestic help. We were the domestic help, a first for many of us. All the bases in Antarctica have a well-established roster service for domestic chores. Every day one person does morning cleaning duty, which is called "Baywatch". "Slushies" (kitchen assistants) take turns at scrubbing pots, peeling potatoes, scrubbing floors and wiping down tables and restocking serviettes and other essentials for several days at a time. Everyone on base had Saturday duties, aimed at keeping everything running smoothly and giving everyone a chance to socialise and see other areas. For us Met staff, whoever was on shift would clean the Met office otherwise we got assigned duties.

Hasselborough ("Hass") House (the sleeping quarters) was to be my responsibility that first week. I had spent my married life in the privileged position of having my Deb take care of the running of the house. Now I found myself scrubbing the toilets, cleaning the bathrooms and vacuuming the quarters, passageway and rooms if expeditioners wanted (doors kept open was the signal to go in and clean).

Woolies was next. The green historic building held all the supplies needed for the year and was brimming after the summer restock. Wandering around the shelves gave me an idea of just what was needed to keep the place ticking. As I tossed in items required to top up supplies, I thought it was the best shopping I'd ever done. And I didn't have to stand in a massive queue at the end.

Saturdays was more than work though. It was the major social night of the week, usually with a huge feast and possibly a themed night, an excuse to dress up and let loose. We made our own entertainment, and depending on the night, had a chance to dress up in costume or dress up in formal clothes. Either way, it brought a sense of togetherness that bonded the group closer. The scientists and tradies always had the night off to enjoy, but us Met workers had to enjoy these nights in roster. Our staff had to keep to our shifts so every Saturday night one of us would miss out on the social night. On the first week it would be mine, and I stole a few minutes to join the others in the mess for a quick meal.

The cook, Gerbil, without a doubt, was the most important person on base. His talents could make or break the season. After a while, as the excitement of being at Macca wore off and the isolation set in, food became a huge part of people's morale. Meal times were a highlight in the emotional centre of the station – the canteen.

When I'd first met Gerbil, his innocent face emphasised by round glasses and cheeky grin spoke of an easy-going man in his mid-thirties. The rest of the expeditioners had already spent months watching his larrikin ways and improving their spirits with his jokes and easy manner. A brilliant chef, he liked everyone to be in a good mood because of good food.

Gerbil told me later he'd tried at least five times to get into the ANARE program and succeeded on what was going to be his last attempt. Most people would have given up after two tries. A seasoned professional, he was a major part of keeping morale high and was recognised for his work with an Australian Antarctic Medal in 2005, which recognises contributions above and beyond day-to-day Antarctic service. He ended up spending nine summers and four winters feeding expeditioners at Casey, Davis, Mawson and Macca, and had served in a variety of roles including search and rescue leader, deputy fire chief, hospital theatre nurse and boat driver providing logistic support to field science. When the award was announced, it made mention of the fact he was best known for his culinary talents and for his contribution to station harmony and involvement and dedication to community duties. He deserved it.

***

By now we'd already had light snow, and the reaction of some of the expeditioners who'd never seen it made me laugh. I remembered feeling the same way my first time in North America. The weather was amazing - sunshine, small hail, snow and rain showers in the space of one hour. A Met bloke's dream.

I'd been talking regularly to my family but knew what I was trying to describe wasn't doing the island justice. I decided to grab my video camera and record the various highlights, accidentally disturbing some Gentoo penguins on my way to the clean air lab and having to side-step elephant seals on my way back home. I headed to the west side to tape an elephant seal chasing some King penguins down the path, the howling wind drowning out my words.

One of the Kings walking by stopped to peer at me. *National Geographic* made this breed famous with its cover of mother and baby. The brilliant yellow of their neck markings and narrow eyes make them easily recognisable. They spend much of their lives at sea feeding on squid and amphipods, but there are always some around, especially the chicks in their moulting cycles. Kings have been nesting on Macca for at least 5,000 years. By the late 19th century, as seal numbers dwindled after years of aggressive sealing, focus turned to penguin oil, an industry believed to have been unique to Macquarie Island. After the slaughter ended, penguin numbers quickly recovered and now numbers are over 200,000. Lucky for this bloke. When he was done peering at me, he started walking away like an old man with hip problems. One step, a second, and a rest. Then he'd start again.

My spirits lifted and I as I explored I felt more settled in my new home. I could rest my overloaded brain here, and that night after I finished my shift I recorded, simply, "Quite a pleasant day" in my diary.

I jumped as a loud intrusive noise took over Hass. Fire alarm. Robb had warned us on the first night that these were to be taken seriously, with everyone expected to meet immediately at the fire hut at the main gate. Fire is one of the greatest fears on any Antarctic station. Macca was better off than the other continental bases as ships could reach it year-round in the event of an emergency, but fire drills and awareness are still continually enforced.

In 1959, programs were wiped out when fire took over several laboratories on the shores of Hasselborough Bay at the top of Macca. Even though expeditioners tried to put out the fire, it destroyed the ionospheric and cosmic ray labs, and important equipment like the Dobson ozone spectrophotometer. That disaster further reinforced the need for everyone in every expedition to know fire safety rules, and for the station leader to know where everyone was at any time. Anyone leaving the perimeter of the station (the isthmus area extending from Gadgets Gully to the summit of Wireless Hill) had to get permission from the station leader, and turn his or her tag over in the fire hut.

A few days later, a phone call disturbed my newfound routine. "Morg, how'd you like a chance to stay at Macquarie Island for 12 months?"

Graeme Taylor was ringing from Hobart, giving me a chance that a year ago I would've jumped at. Twelve months ... a chance to winter ... but it wasn't on the Ice". I told Graeme I'd have to talk it over with my family.

"Yeah, great. Have a think, let me know. I'll need an answer in a month."

The night before I headed out to field training, I had to make a special call. Calling Australia was fairly straightforward – phones are in the workplaces and bedrooms in the main sleeping and medical quarters. There was also a "public" phone booth in a small room in the mess, and each expedition is given a four-digit code to enter when making a call, which is then summarised and debited against pay each month. Even with the AAD subsidy of 20 cents a minute, each call had a 15c flag fall and was 48c a minute, which limited long chats, though sometimes it was worth it just to hear their voices.

Michelle was turning 18, a big day for my little girl, and hearing her voice before her big party was bittersweet. Knowing I was missing it brought a powerful wave of homesickness, and I talked to her for as long as I could.

***

Finally it was my turn to head off for field training. The months of preparation in Kingston and Bronte Park continued upon arrival in Macca with a field session emphasising survival skills. Scientists and others needing to get out of the station perimeters were first priority for the training, and then Met and communication officers. I was looking forward to seeing the island outside of station confines, and of the challenge of the training itself.

Still tired the next morning, I got dressed and packed, ready for the field trip. I'd done a first aid refresher with the station doctor, Dr Cath, the day before, and after morning tea our group headed off under the guidance of field training officer Psycho (Christian Gallager). Ken Roberts, a carpenter, and Rob Gregor, communications, were low priorities for getting off base, like me, and Bec McIntosh, a zoologist on the fur seal program, wasn't starting her work for a few weeks. Psycho's enthusiasm for showing us the wonders of the island hadn't been diminished by the non-stop stream of people needing training and we started out energetically.

From Gadget Gully we climbed up to the plateau. I'd thought I was fit, but it didn't take long for my body to convince me otherwise. As I crawled up the rocks, my back was screaming at the weight - clothes, bivvy bag, heavy survival food and water - that kept shifting each move I made. On any day trip away from the station limits, regardless of the length of the journey, each person had to carry the ANARE Field and First Aid manuals, windproof parka, windproof overpants, woollen jersey, windproof mitts, woollen balaclava, goggles or sunglasses, sleeping and bivvy bags, camp mat, whistle, compass, a second pair of mitts and socks, high energy food such as chocolate, and a thermos, and each party had to carry a VHF radio and map. Everything we packed went first into plastic bags. Gear at Macca had to be waterproof (no surprise as it rained most of the time) and we had to be prepared to finish the day at least partially wet. So all together it weighed the odd kilo or two.

I glanced over at Ken, who was around my age, and felt better when I saw that he too was struggling. Even fit young Bec was feeling it. The only one happy was Psycho, who was a natural both physically and mentally.

A wiry man, slender with not much muscle, I wondered where Psycho got his energy from. With dull red scruffy hair and his fair skin, he looked to be in his late teens, though I knew he'd have to be in his late twenties or early thirties. I learned he'd wintered a couple of times as a carpenter (chippie) before he switched over to be a field training officer. Highly experienced in search and rescue, he'd worked on the August 1997 Thredbo landslide and the rescue of Stuart Diver.

So-called because of his love of doing adventurous or dangerous things, Psycho had once canoed from the tip of Australia to New Guinea, and climbed several mountains overseas. In October 2006, he was a member of a six-man team dropped at Cape Denison, Commonwealth Bay, for six weeks to restore Mawson's huts, serving as chippie and medic.

Now he was showing us the way. When we got to the top, the view down at the isthmus and across to The Nuggets momentarily silenced the voice inside my head telling me to blow this for a joke and to head back down. Then Psycho cheerily told us we had only five kilometres to go across the plateau and we could rest at the field hut at Bauer Bay. Great. Five kilometres of gut-wrenching, bloody hard work later, we could see the welcoming corrugated iron shed, complete with its little verandah, surrounded by tussock grass. Gas cylinders were piled up on one side, and fuel cans on the other.

By now my back was strained, and I struggled to put one foot in front of the other along the boardwalk path to the entrance. We still had more training to do. Among other things, we were practising navigation and search and rescue techniques. But, right now, I was looking forward to the bivvy training. Someone - caught out alone - unable to build an emergency shelter is in serious danger, especially as they may not be able to see the early signs of hypothermia. Enter the bivvy bag, designed to conserve energy and body heat. The theory is to get into a wind-free area, either behind a rock or even the slightest depression in the earth, lie on whatever insulation was handy, dig yourself in and leave an air vent open. Basically, bury yourself in a bag and wait it out.

At least I can rest my poor old body.

I wriggled in and fell into an exhausted sleep for a few short minutes before the nightmare hit. Screaming, I thrashed in the bag trying to find an opening and finally clawed a space large enough to get my head out. Realisation hit, and I stopped moving and looked at the other forms to see if I'd woken anyone. The wind was whistling and I think it must've swallowed my screams, as there was no movement from anyone in the other bivvy bags. Shaking and gasping, I pulled myself back inside but left my head poking out. I just couldn't handle going back to the suffocating darkness. After about 10 minutes the gasping stopped, and I slid the rest of the way in and shook until Psycho kicked me in the ribs to tell me to get into the hut.

Inside, we started to relax in the cosy heat and spent the night telling stories while Psycho gave us rubs. My body had finally calmed down and I forced myself to talk with the others. I was enjoying the company until nature called.

Going to the toilet at the base was straightforward. There were at least two toilets in each accommodation block, one toilet in the mess, plus a few other buildings. If I wanted to go to the toilet while at work, all I'd have to do is make a mad dash to the nearby science building.

I'm a bloke who likes to take my time on the toilet, not be rushed. At Macca, I found there were not many times when I could sit in comfort on the throne and meditate, or read a magazine or two. There was always someone straining or grunting in the next cubical to mine, or someone waiting impatiently for me to get off the seat. At other times when I wanted to go desperately, the toilets would be occupied.

With all the warm toilet comforts at the base, it was not so when expeditioners ventured to the huts on the island, as I learned that first night at Bauer Bay. That was my initiation into going down to the beach to do your business the way Mother Nature intended.

I'd grab a small shovel, a roll of toilet paper, a cleaning washer, and head down to the beach. It was recommended you do your business near the water's edge so you could shovel it into the water or small tidal waves. On getting down to the beach, I found it quite hard to make a decision about where to go. For starters there were hundreds of pairs of penguin and elephant seal eyes gazing at me. I soon discovered there were two options for going to the toilet Macca-style.

Option one: Go to the water's edge, dig a small hole in the soft sand, drop your daks, bend over, then squat down leaning forward with both hands on the sand for support, and then start grunting and straining. Pray that no skuas or no elephant seals take a liking to your flashing bum hole. Pray that no big freezing waves wet your daks and body. After completing the grunting stage, get up from the squat position, take the toilet roll from your pocket and then wipe while in the graceful bent-over position. Deposit the used toilet paper into the hole. Pull up your daks. Shovel the lot into the open sea of tidal waves. After completing this, get your washer from your coat pocket, dip it into the sea water, drop your daks again and give yourself a fresh wash. Repeat until comfortable and cleansed.

Option two: (definitely the preferred option.) Find a small waterhole in the rocks. When a suitable one to your liking is found, drop your daks, sit on the edge of a rock hanging onto other rocks for support, and then start grunting and straining. Once again pray that no skuas or elephant seals take an interest. Pray also, that you don't slip off the rocks, and no big waves come in. For this option, you have an automatic toilet hole with the tidal waves taking away your mess. After completing this stage, crawl carefully over the rocks and find another fresh pool of water to wash with. Note: this option does not work if there are big waves. Each option takes at least 10 to 15 minutes to complete.

As I struggled to learn this new valuable skill, the weather's little joys added another layer of complexity. We'd had snow, hail and ice pellets overnight and into the morning, and it continued after we woke and prepared for another day. Before we left, all perishables had to be rat and mouse-proofed from the populations of ship rats and mice brought to the island in the early years.

The navigation and medical training continued as we trudged along the four kilometres to the east. I wasn't sure if it was the sleep or Psycho's rubs, but the day wasn't so bad. We walked along the east side to Sandy Bay and down the wooden steps to the beach. This was one of the prized spots for tourists, and the steps helped with erosion and preservation. We continued with the navigational work on the way to the hut, an Antarctic "apple" at Brother's Point.

The red, apple-shaped huts, also known as igloo satellite cabins, are designed for lengthy stays in the field. Made of fibreglass, they're supposed to sleep three comfortably and are insulated using double-glazed polycarbonate windows and fire-retardant polyurethane spray foam. They can be extended into a "melon" using additional side and floor panels. This alien-looking shelter was a welcome sight, tight as it was with the five of us. I staggered up the front steps and chucked my pack down before grabbing my camera to capture the stunning view - the bright red apple nestled in the green valley close to the ocean.

Cautiously I scoped the area for seals, preparing for the trip I knew I would have to make later that night, and hoping they wouldn't be too amused by my clumsy skills. As I chatted with my companions into the night, exchanging stories of families, loves and how we ended up at Macca, I felt a sense of camaraderie that I hadn't experienced for a long time. In Vietnam, our group had grown close. Back then all of us were missing family, facing the unknown and depending on each other. Huddled in the tiny apple, talking with these people, I realised I'd missed that feeling.

The next morning started well, with Bec taking a right to our left, to head down to Green Gorge hut alone. She'd finished her training and was free to go her own way while the rest of us headed back up the island towards base, into the famous Macca wind. Gusts up to 90 kilometres per hour toyed with us, pushing us back one step for each two we took forward. The nearly nine kilometre trek took us a very wet six hours. The rain cut our visibility, and made heavy work of slogging through the sand. Each step made me think of trying to walk through "featherbed" fibrous layers of plant roots and other organic material floating on top of deep ponds of water which looks like a smoother green carpet, but which you can fall into. We'd been warned about it, that walkers with heavy packs could sink into it up to their armpits. This sand was solid, but still as difficult to get across.

At The Nuggets we slid over the rocks and pebbles before a treacherous climb in from the sea, up a rock cliff and along a narrow walkway. I hugged the cliff side, fighting the wind's attempts to pick me up and throw me over. Psycho calmly warned us if that happened we should try and land in the sea on our backs so the packs would cushion the fall. With all his experience, I trusted he knew what he was saying, but was reluctant to test out the theory.

There have been several periods in my life where I've faced fear and to this day I still live with the after-effects. That was fine. This, however, was self-inflicted, and as my heart thudded in my ears, I questioned why the hell I was doing it. In my view, survival training didn't mean putting yourself in a crappy situation; it meant running away from it as far as possible. As we struggled towards the base, Ken slipped and I glanced around to see he'd suffered a deep cut, and that Psycho was pulling out the first aid kit.

It felt like the movie Groundhog Day. I kept putting one foot in front of the other but nothing seemed to be moving or getting closer. Finally, the station in the distance, which had been teasing us, got close enough to be real. I can honestly say that walk was the hardest of my life, much harder than the endless days of walking through Vietnamese jungle. Easily. Back at base, I rewarded my aching body with a hot shower and clean clothes.

That night the Saturday social was an '80s Rock theme. Never had I felt less like bouncing around imitating the high-energy stars of that decade. The way my body was aching, all I'd be good for was an imitation of a comatose rocker. I was supposed to be on the afternoon shift but Cathie took one look at me and offered to take my shift. I devoured the meal and enjoyed everyone else's energy before collapsing into bed, feeling myself sink into a deep sleep within seconds.

When I finally opened my eyes on Sunday, I realised I had managed to sleep in, a rarity for me. As I swung my legs around and stood, pain shot up my leg. My calf had seized and was useless. Dr Cath said it was badly sprained, put on an ice pack and told me to rest.

The damage I'd done became more apparent during the next few days. The ice pack hadn't fixed it, and I had to start a massage regime. Of course, hobbling across the compound to get a massage seemed rather surreal with the weather we were getting. Heavy overnight snow was leaving several centimetres on the ground. I could only imagine the picture I must've presented as I shuffled gingerly across the white like an old man. Gerbil and Ailsa, both trained as nurses, took turns treating me.

I had to cross the isthmus at least six times on a working day. On each trip I was careful to watch my step and avoid Gentoo penguins and elephant seals. For obvious reasons it was worse at night. Limping back to my quarters after midnight one night, I stepped in a pile of faeces left behind by an elephant seal dreaded, stinking stuff.

As soon as my boot hit, I knew straight away what I was in for, and I hobbled back to Hass House, one boot heavier than the other. Usually we'd leave our boots on the cold porch area, but on these dreaded occasions I had no choice but leave mine on the outside steps of the building. Within seconds of removing the boot, I was surrounded by that unforgettable and indescribably foul smell. Clean-up was always left until the next morning. You had to put the boots back on, walk to the beach area of the isthmus and drag your feet through the shallow water. Trouble was the boot sole had ridges on it, so you'd have to find a sharp rock to pick the compacted mess out. The smell was so foul I'd often dry-retch in disgust. No matter what I tried, my boot always carried the smell for a few weeks.

Nearly a week after The Big Walk, my calf still wasn't healing and Dr Cath confined me to base. My injury was probably expected - things happen - but my reaction to it made me have a good think about my situation. I knew missing my family was part of it, but so was the fact I was struggling physically. I'd always thought of myself as a fit bloke able to handle any challenge thrown at me as part of the Antarctic program. Now, here I was, temporarily crippled by a little muscle, and not getting any younger. That was the part I kept coming back to. I didn't mention it to anyone else, but the site of my hernia operation was giving me problems too.

You're in your 50s, mate, and not getting any younger.

I wanted the Ice. If I stayed the full year at Macca, the delay in getting to Antarctica could mean I wouldn't have the stamina to do it. I finally picked up the phone and called Graeme. I knew he'd understand.

Graeme wasn't there, so instead I explained my decision to Phil Littlehales, who was temporarily filling Ian Hickmann's position. I knew Phil, and as we chatted, I knew I'd made the right decision.

***

After a weekend of rest, basking in the "heat" (the top maximum temperature one Sunday was 8.3°C), I went to see Gerbil for the first session of an ultrasound treatment program Dr Cath recommended. It was to be the beginning of an interesting series of meetings. Gerbil was in love. With my legs, that is. I lay on the table, and as he started rubbing cool gel over my legs, his hands hesitated before stroking the muscles. Never one to let slip a chance to lark about, he decided that I had the sexiest legs he'd ever seen. I peered down at them, then at him, before deciding he'd led a very sheltered life. He had a way of making sure everyone left his space a little heavier (stuffed with his cooking), or a bit lighter (after laughing their problems away).

People's characters had started to become clearer, and cracks had begun to show among some of the expeditioners' relationships. Isolation, both geographic and from friends and family, brought frustrations which began to spark clashes. As a "summerer", it took a while to catch on that there was an undercurrent among some of the "winterers". As the officer-in-charge of the Met program, I'd had to try and resolve problems between Ailsa and Cathy. They'd come in as friends, but differences in values and lifestyle choices had caused tension, which often broke out under the guise of work issues. Complaints like ozonesondes not being properly prepared and corners cut on shift duties would come in and, though I tried to mediate, often fights would break out. They weren't the only ones on station involved in skirmishes, but everyone coped in different ways. The return of ships with the summer season alleviated some of the pressure.

New faces, fresh food and mail arrived. I hoped I'd be able to keep the peace among my new group of friends.

***

Peter Sprunk's (Sprunky) end-of-month duties included checking the fuel supply, and I went along to give him a hand. At the southern end of the station, Macca has a fuel tank farm, which holds 300,000 litres of diesel oil and small quantities of petrol and kerosene. Sprunky measured each tank with a dipstick, and I recorded the readings.

"Getting fuel ashore that may sound easy enough and straightforward, but there is a lot more to it than meets the eye, particularly in today's world with increased emphasis on environmental protection," Sprunky told me later.

"Fuel is the life blood of an Antarctic station. Without it there would not be much science or stations as we know them. The fuel, called Special Antarctic Blend (highly refined diesel fuel), is used for the production of electricity, heat (for buildings) and, of course, for transport. Pumping the fuel ashore is fairly straightforward and yet quite demanding."

He told me how at Davis, for example, the fuel may have to be pumped nearly four kilometres from the ship to the station tanks, depending on how close the ship could break its way in through the sea ice. The fuel was then pumped over ice in a special lay-flat hose at a rate of more than 30,000 litres an hour.

"At the other Antarctic stations, the fuel is pumped over open water, through a floating fuel line. The added difficulty then is that the fuel line has to be deployed and constantly patrolled by inflatable boats. In some of the weather conditions, that is not an easy task," he said.

"Here at Macca, the refuelling is also over open water but there is the difficulty of the rough seas. The swell is always at least a couple metres and sometimes the waves really pound onto the shore. The difficulty then is to get the fuel line safely through, without it getting stuck in kelp beds, and do the pumping without spilling a drop into the environment."

We compared our experiences so far, and in the companionable routine, I thought how pleased I was to have met people like him. It'd been a good start to the journey.

CHAPTER 3
LURE OF THE WILDLIFE

November 2001 weather details:
Max temp 10.7 °C, min -3.3 °C
Mean daily sunshine (hours) 3.4
Days of precipitation 24, average monthly rainfall 68.2 millimetres
Days of strong winds 21, days of gales 4
(Based on averages to 1989)

Days were becoming slightly longer, and the temperature a touch warmer. The summer expeditioners had finally started to fit in with the winterers, and the atmosphere around the station was comfortable. The relatively uncomplicated life of the contained environment was satisfying; the predictable pattern of a good hearty meal and well-earned rest at the end of the day was relaxing.

Several events helped keep spirits up, such as Melbourne Cup Day. Any Aussie knows it's the race that stops a nation, and we didn't let the distance from Flemington Racecourse in Melbourne take away that pleasure. The 3,200 metre race for three-year-olds and over is generally regarded as the most prestigious "two-mile" handicap in the world. We took an hour off work to gather in Hasselborough House and I plunked my money down for the sweeps. I drew Rum – good name but it ran like a bloody donkey, finishing 15th.

Then we celebrated the 12-month anniversary for the wintering crew. They'd arrived on November 9, 2000, but with changes to shipping and the changeover, would have to stay for 16 months. Such is the life at stations. It's why we have old sayings like: "If you want to make God laugh, tell him your plans".

We had to watch our water supply which was dwindling and an ever-vigilant eye was kept on fire safety. One drinks night we gathered and toasted Ken, who'd had to put a slab of beer on the table as penance for accidentally setting off the fire alarm. The island's water supply comes from a small dam in Gadget Gully, about 1.5 kilometres from the station. Careful rationing didn't stop Gerbil maintaining his creations. I found myself elbow-deep in suds as Gerbil's slushy one Saturday, cursing him as I tried to keep up with the pots and pans he'd use up as quickly as I cleaned them. Once my fingers pruned, he switched me over to cutting up cheese and bread and whatever else he needed, then peeling garlic by the bucketful until my hands stank. The sheer volume of food we went through was incredible. I finally staggered into bed one midnight after working for Gerbil from 8am until my afternoon BoM shift.

A federal election was held on November 10. Though we were miles away from home, we still had the chance to vote. Unlike on the mainland, voting in Antarctica is not compulsory. Sometimes it isn't even possible for an expeditioner, depending on which State they're from. One winterer is trained to be an electoral officer, and he'd get the relevant electorate voting card for each expeditioner. In our case it was Col Rendall, a carpenter, and after I handed back my card, he sent my choice to the ANARE division in Tasmania. That night, along with the rest of the country, we heard that John Howard had been voted back in for his third term.

***

By mid-month, my calf was showing signs of improvement, allowing me to start venturing outside the station again. The lure of the wildlife was strong, and I helped Bec with her fur seal research program until her offsider, Alistair, arrived on a tourist ship later in the month.

There are three kinds of fur seals around Macca the *sub-Antarctic tropicalis*, which had a creamy coloured chest and face, the *Antarctic gazelle*, which was grey to dark brown, and the *New Zealand forsteri*, which was coarser and a darker brown. Unlike the other two species, the later didn't breed at Macca. Bec was looking for pups, which she would weigh, measure and bleach their fur for easier identification.

Unlike the dominant Elephant seals, these fur seals don't have layers of fat but instead rely on thick fur coats to stay warm. The killing of these animals for their furs has decreased, but marine debris such as nylon string and fishing nets is still a threat.

"These two calling out all the time ... they were born sometime today," Bec whispered as she pointed to two little wriggling pups. Covered in down, they weighed somewhere between three and seven kilograms. She trained her binoculars on some of the larger pups in the group, looking through the snow and rain to see if she'd already numbered them.

A warning grunt from the bull made me jump, but Bec just watched him carefully, measuring his agitation as he hopped forward several times, then back, trying to move us along with his bellows.

"I can't see," she said, studying the pups while the bull blustered and a female seal peered around a rock with her big soft eyes locked on us.

"I need a different angle," Bec said, and led me around in a wide berth to a different spot. She'd found an unmarked pup. Bec made soothing *"tsst, tsst"* noises to the agitated bull. At the right moment, she leapt out, swept the pup under her arm and raced away from the group to hide behind a rock where we'd previously laid out our gear.

As a team we worked to weigh the pup, me holding the weights, Bec putting the pup in a sling. Then sitting knee-to-knee in the sand, I'd hold his head while Bec took a biopsy from his backside. When it was all done, I cuddled number 14's wriggling body in my lap before we took him back to his family. It was interesting how, once we'd scooped the pups and taken them away, it as if their families immediately accepted they'd lost their baby and didn't follow.

One day we went to a bay on the west side of the island, and Bec repeated her dance with the bulls. She headed towards her chosen pup, taking quiet steady steps in a slight crouch. As the bulls became agitated, she took several steps forward, then back. Again and again, she played a game with the bull. All of a sudden, she swept in, grabbed the pup by the scruff of his neck and scooped him into her arms. Ignoring its pitiful wail, we raced him back to the gear and performed the well-rehearsed routine.

***

One Sunday, thankfully with no slushy duties, I grabbed my video and headed with Dave Gillies (Tubby) to North Point on North Head. Tubby, about my age, had become a good mate, someone to share a beer and story with around the bar at night. We headed up the very vertical climb a good test for my calf. My puffs were drowned out by the howling wind as we struggled up for about 15 minutes before finally reaching the summit.

Surrounded by beaches, we could see down past The Nuggets, across the rugged coastline towards Antarctica. The view was hypnotic, but the wind felt like it was searing away our throat lining, and we decided to head back. It was cold, no more than 5°C, but the wind chill factor of the 40-knot winds made it seem colder. Breathing through your nose in the extreme cold is best, as it warms the air as it passes through the nasal passages before hitting the lungs. Exertion, however, easily ruins this theory.

As we started our descent, a skua (the bird known as Antarctica's scavenger) glided overhead, its *"ah ... ah ... ah"* competing with my groaning against the cold. I stopped to watch Tubby through the camera's viewfinder, focusing on his yellow raincoat flapping in the wind as he followed the guided track down. The wind kept pushing him sideways, and I lost track of the number of near falls. He planted his feet wide, taking cautious steps, trying for a secure grip on the ground, while rocks I'd dislodged bounced down around him. I started laughing, and mentally tagged the trip Tubby's Run because of his humorous attempts to stay on his feet.

Tubby is one of those tough-but-kind characters, and the communications experience which put him in charge at Macca also took him to all the bases Mawson, Davis and Casey. He'd wintered at Macca, and would head to Casey afterwards before retiring.

He'd told me that he and the comms crew had been busy that month mending broken equipment on the station and in the field. He'd spent five days at Eitel Hut, Green Gorge and Windy Ridge repairing radios and the Mt Jeffries repeater site, and that he'd been keen to hike up the point with me for a "relax".

***

November was search and rescue training month, and after a few days of gale-force winds, snow and showers, we took advantage of a clear day to go to North Head. We spent the days climbing up by rope and abseiling down. Some people had to do a stretcher rescue from Wireless Hill, where they located a "patient", administered first aid, built an anchor and lowered the stretcher. They weren't as lucky, having to struggle through 50-knot gusts, snow, sleet and hail. Ailsa and Cath were happy to be patients immediately wrapped up while the rescuers battled on through the harsh conditions.

Wireless Hill served another purpose besides providing the terrain for exercises. Douglas Mawson of the Australasian Antarctic Expedition established the first scientific base on the island in 1911, and built a radio station at Wireless Hill, the first communication link between Australia and Antarctica.

The Tasmanian Parks and Wildlife Service (TASPAWS) rangers team of Chris Hall, Sandy King, Georgie Hedley and Phillipa Foster had been preparing for the influx of summer tourist ships, with the first due to arrive at the end of November. There are boardwalks at many of the places the tourists explore in an effort to minimise the impact on the environment, and the team had to get signs and tracks ready. Since the late 1980s, the increase in Antarctica tourism meant ANARE had to address its impact. Ship-based tourism brings large numbers of people ashore by boat to sensitive areas, including penguin rookeries. Everyone wants to experience the unique wildlife at close quarters, but getting too close to animals causes stress and lowers their chances of breeding successfully.

As Macca is a State nature reserve managed by the Tasmanian Department of Environment and Land Management, special attention is given to ensuring no unwanted foreign seeds or vegetable matter are unknowingly brought to the island by tourists. The boardwalks and lookout platforms near penguin and sea bird rookeries were built in 1989 by the Tasmanian government, and in 1995 it set a limit of 500 visitors to the island each year.

Whenever a ship was due, expeditioners were chosen to show tourists around the island to give them the maximum experience possible. We treated them just like anyone coming into your own home, by making them feel comfortable. I never led groups, but would talk to them when they visited the BoM buildings and explain our program. At the end of their chilly explorations, Gerbil would put on a good spread.

These ships were especially welcome for two reasons: fresh fruit and mail. After many weeks without either, waiting for the mail to be distributed was agonising. All mail for expeditioners was sent to the Antarctic Division in Hobart, whose staff then arranged for it to get to the various bases. It was official mail and we had to wait for Postmaster Mick to cut the ties off the mail bags and lay each person's bounty out on the pool table. I searched among the piles. Deb and the kids hadn't forgotten me; they sent me more film for my video, letters and newspapers.

It didn't matter that all the newspapers and magazines were out of date. For us, it was a touch of home, something to be savoured. Eight ships visited over the summer, and each time they left in their wake a good feeling a sense of being a little less isolated.

***

The first ship of the season, the *Kapitan Khlebnikov*, which had brought the bounty, was on anchor in Buckles Bay as Bec and I headed out to Secluded Beach for a day of catching pups. I knew Alistair, the other person on the fur seal program, had just arrived on the KK and would soon be helping Bec with her work, and I was anxious for at least one more day of interacting with these gorgeous creatures.

As we approached some weaners on the beach, we kept a careful eye on two males lining each other up, grunting warnings.

"What we might do here, because the boys are having a spat, is go up behind them, just in case they decide to ..." Bec didn't get to finish her sentence, as both of us decided to run to some rocks. The boys took their spat into the ocean, butting each other as waves broke over them.

Wisely, Bec headed off in another direction, to where a bull was staring at us, but wasn't overly aggressive.

"Funny how some days you can get really close and others you can't," Bec said as we weighed and marked two pups. They were the only two alone in the group as their mothers had returned to the ocean. Other groups still had pups and mothers, but they too would be heading out shortly to feed on fish and squid close to shore.

"The old fella's pretty quiet today," I said, pointing to the bull.

"Yeah, he's happy," Bec replied, obviously pleased he was.

"Must've had a big night."

Bec grinned and we went back to our business. As we worked, I picked her brains about how she ended up here. She'd studied zoology, and this was a "dream come true".

Good on you, mate. We were all here for different reasons, but all of us had the same dream. Although I was still having several nightmares a week, in this new world I'd found camaraderie, and an understanding that we were part of something bigger than just a collection of individuals. For the first time in many years, I could breathe easy, surrounded by people who had my back against the common opponent: Mother Nature. In this world, I was doing just fine.

CHAPTER 4
THE ULTIMATE CHRISTMAS

December 2001 weather details:
Max temp 12.5 °C, min -1.7 °C
Mean daily sunshine (hours) 3.4
Days of precipitation 24, average monthly rainfall 77.1 millimetres
Days of strong winds 19, days of gales 3
(Based on averages to 1989)

The festive month started with gale-force winds, registering 57 knots. I was getting complacent, comfortable in my surrounds. One morning I left my room and discovered I'd locked my keys in my room. After trying to break back in without success, I found Robb and asked for the spare key, but that was also missing in action. Eventually, carpenter Col was called and he managed to pry off the ventilation screen at the bottom and jimmy a stick through the opening to unlock the door.

Nature continued to throw glimpses of her talent, bringing killer whales to Garden Cove. I gazed out of the Met office window as four graceful forms broke the ocean surface, playing for a good 15 minutes. Whales were occasionally seen in the waters around the base, the most common being orcas. They often fed from the penguin colonies, but occasionally were seen taking elephant seals close to shore.

Tubby and I took a chance to leave base and head to Bauer Bay via the beach. On this trip, as opposed to the field training, we took our time, though the 40-knot winds kept slamming into us. Before we headed up to the plateau, I sat on a rock at Finch Creek near The Nuggets, surrounded by Royal penguins, nature and beautiful clear air. It was a virtual penguin highway a parade coming down to the sea and a second parade returning with food. I moved to a rock in the centre of the creek to take pictures and watch these amazing creatures. Their rhythm was fascinating, hopping on a rock, down into the water, onto another rock; the splat-splat of the masses of feet never stopped. It was just like driving in Australia they kept to the left and never crashed into each other. Actually, maybe it wasn't quite like Australia!

One stopped and stared at me, then pecked my boot before waddling off. He didn't even turn back when I laughed. Before moving on I watched a Rockhopper penguin, with its punk hairstyle, tackle a cliff – a fast movement to a point, then using his wings to balance, he stopped and studied his next move, just like a mountain climber, before taking off again.

We headed up the plateau via Gadgets, then to the hut for steak and good conversation. The cosiness of the environment allowed for some good bloke talk, though I had to prepare Tubby for the possibility of a noisy night. Darkness was a fickle lover: sometimes she'd wrap me up and keep me safe, other times she'd throw her full rage, trapping me as my mind relived the horror of being buried alive. Every night I'd have to share my space with someone, I'd have to tear open a part of me to warn them about the uncertainly of how the night would pan out. I couldn't say I was sick of it. At that point, it was just another facet of my life, just as the shakes and anxiety attacks which would come unannounced.

Having survived the night, we woke early to snow, strong winds and hail. Life out in the field huts has a unique and uncomplicated quality that for me remains the highlight of my time at Macca. Working out of the huts allowed us to be immersed in the environment; the animals, the moods of the weather and the ocean. Being able to work in with so few distractions was wonderful.

After packing, we headed through the weather and over the plateau to check out some of the lakes. Two figures in the distance gradually approached, and I recognised Brian and Al.

"I like coming up here," Brian said as he got nearer, balancing his poles as we looked out towards the ocean. "Quick and easy."

As Al passed us, he turned around so we could see Grover, and then turned so Grover could get the view too. A lot of people had brought mascots with them, and Grover, from Sesame Street, was a familiar sight around camp. Actually, he'd seen more of the island than anyone as he was continually pinched for new adventures. His photo album was better than most of ours.

***

The tourist ship *Akademik Shokalski* had arrived, bringing 35 tourists to the station's Met office to watch my morning release. The arrival of this ship meant the departure of Ailsa, who had decided to return to Australia, as well as Mel and Brian, summer scientists with the human impacts program.

Despite everyone's best efforts, the cracks in the friendship between Ailsa and Cathie had grown to a point where Ailsa had elected to leave the program. While on a personal level I wished her well, as I knew this was what she needed to do, her departure was going to have a big impact on the BoM program. Cathie and I would have to split Ailsa's job between us for the remainder of the season. I'd also have to take over the storeman's position, supplying any clothing needed.

The night before the trio left, we held a grand farewell at the Saturday night "Under the Sea" social. I went as a fisherman, wearing old dirty trousers, a chequered shirt, earring and my treasured Essendon Bombers beanie. It was a great night, with everyone determined to send the three off with a lasting memory. The mess was transformed with fishing nets, buoys and all things maritime. The costumes were very imaginative: we had turtles, hammerhead sharks, fish scales everywhere. Grover came as an octopus with eight papier mâché legs. Bec put on a huge papier mâché diver's helmet, but then couldn't get it off. Try as we all did, that helmet would not budge. As she staggered around, Gerbil took to one of the buoys (cleverly disguised exercise balls), his sponges (sewn to his body to represent scales) flying up and down with his movements. The fun went on late into the night, and I hoped the three departees wouldn't have to face the ocean swell with hangovers.

As the Zodiac faded into the distance towards the *Akademik Shokalski*, I felt sad that one of us felt a personality conflict took precedence over the beauty of the island. As OIC I had been unable to resolve the girls' differences, so I was anxious when, a few days before Christmas, I had to front deputy station leader Cal and station leader Robb for my ANARE Personal Performance Indicators review. A necessary part of the ANARE program, the review was a chance for feedback on an expeditioners overall performance, personal effectiveness, how they related to others in the community and addressed general requirements. Besides this review, I'd also have to face a full assessment before returning to Australia, as well as an end-of-expedition summary before reaching the mainland.

Having decided to opt out of staying at Macca for the full year in an attempt to get onto one of the Antarctic stations, I was nervous. I really needed this to go well. Cal and Rob said they were pleased with my progress, and I felt the knot in my stomach start to loosen.

***

One of my occasional duties was the restocking of various supply huts by Zodiac boat. Whenever we needed to head out on the ocean, the rule was a minimum of two boats with at least two people in each one. We had to carry radios, bivvy bags and other essential gear. As the BoM bloke, my job was to pick safe weather days, but if something went wrong we had to be prepared. The strong wind and heavy seas meant boats could only go out on the west side when the weather was good. Several crews had got stuck during the summer after the weather turned and were forced to stay in huts along the coast.

Getting out on the ocean was a chance to see the island, and my little world, from a different perspective. I was with Helen Achurch (elephant seal program) and Mick Eccles (comms). We headed off south along the coast, penguins swimming beside the boat like dolphins until we were surrounded by blurs of black and white and the constant sound of splashes. Along the way, we stopped so Helen could set up her antennae to scan for any transmissions. As part of the elephant seal project, time-depth recorder units are attached to the backs of females after they've moulted (around January) and retrieved when the animals returned for the breeding season (around September). These units record data on the breeding cows' foraging habits. Juveniles (aged from one to five) returned to the island to moult, and as many of these were also fitted with data-logging units on their backs. The team involved in the project Corey Bradshaw, Kathryn Wheatley, Helen and Matthew Webb had spent a good part of November combing the beaches for these young animals to remove the units before the moult did.

Helen scanned the area, but as she stood in the boat, balancing against the swell and sweeping the antennae back and forth, she only picked up static.

We dropped off supplies for the scientists at Bauer Hut before heading back to prepare for Christmas Eve activities. The others had been planning a barbecue in Market Square and we arrived to a happy crew.

Soon it was Christmas, for some the like those experienced in the Northern Hemisphere. All those carols started to make sense. As opposed to the great Aussie Christmas of prawns, beer, barbecues and heat, we gathered outside in the cold waiting for Santa.

He didn't disappoint. Standing on his sled, Santa (Mick Eccles) made his entrance, pulled by his two reindeer, Dancer (Cal) and Prancer (Al Baylis) on quad bikes, with two elves (Simone Ingham and Bec) keeping them company. The reindeer were dressed in white chemical suits with antlers made of blue dishwashing gloves blown up and tied off. Ringing bells, tooting horns and big cheers made a festive mood. Santa jumped off and pinched an Expeditioners bum. Then it was handshakes (for the blokes) and kisses (for the ladies) all round.

Inside, the mess had been transformed for the special dinner. Cathie and Kathryn used some tussock grass to make a tree, and Gerbil had made a gorgeous gingerbread house and gingerbread boys and girls (candies helped sort out which was which) to represent us expeditioners.

The champagne flowed and the festivities lifted everyone's mood as did the fact that we each had to have a drink before sitting on Santa's lap.

The first time I sat on Santa's lap, he got a friendly Christmas kiss on the cheek. He boomed to the crowd: "I've received about 53 letters from this young man. Always wants to see his friends and family." Santa had a kind word for everyone, and as we each took a turn, the rest laughed along in good humour.

Presents were exchanged only after a spin of the Wheel of Humiliation. And humiliating it was. I spun and got "Gerbil's Wish is Your Command". He commanded me to do a lap dance with Santa. I looked around, desperate for help, but the grins and laughs on the others' faces told me I wouldn't escape this one. Santa lay down; I straddled him and gave a few hops. The crowd was not impressed. So I wiggled my bum and waved my arms, knowing damn well I looked like a demented penguin. Finally, the crowd took pity on me and clapped.

The next time I sat on Santa's lap, I found it hard to look him in the eye and certainly wasn't game to give him a friendly kiss on the cheek! I patted him on the shoulder instead.

An exquisite Christmas feast was accompanied by eggnog and an unlimited selection of reds, whites, beer, cider, ports, champagne and spirits. I rang my family and listened to them describing the heat and their day. I missed them. Deb said later that it had been a hard day for them, too. Christmas is all about family, and we weren't together to share the joy._

***

Between Christmas and New Year, the *Kapitan Khlebnikov* returned with 70 tourists. The TASPAWS team showed them around, but their highlight of the month was the discovery of a nesting Cape Petrel on North Head, the first recorded on the island, and the discovery of the mandible of the long-extinct Macca Parrot. This bird hadn't been seen on the island for more than a century. The Tasmania Museum was just as excited.

As the year drew to an end, we gathered at Robb's patio for a spit-roasted lamb and barbecue. Fire chief Col had prepared a bonfire earlier in the day behind the Garden Cove donga, and after eating we gathered and toasted the journey so far.

Earlier that day, we'd mounted a rescue for an elephant seal who'd wanted to join the party. After deciding we weren't worth watching, she tried to return to the beach but found a fence in her way. No matter what we tried, she wouldn't flop over to the opening a few metres away. Instead, she became agitated as she tried in vain to force her way through. We could see the heat beginning to affect her as the steam rose from her body. We knew we had to do something quickly. One dismantled fence later, we farewelled one very happy seal.

We gathered around the bonfire, chatting as we waited for the count of midnight. With the limited hours of daylight, it seemed a long time, but when 2002 arrived, kisses and best wishes were shared. It was easily the most unusual place that I'd finished out a year. And overall it had been a good year.

CHAPTER 5
A CLOSE CALL

January 2002 weather details:
Max temp 14.4 °C, min -0.6 °C
Mean daily sunshine (hours) 3.4
Days of precipitation 25, average monthly rainfall 79.2 millimetres
Days of strong winds 19, days of gales 3
(Based on averages to 1989)

New Year's Day it may have been, but there are no public holidays on Macca. I woke refreshed and headed off to the office to deal with my end-of-month reports. As I hailed others with a cheery 'happy New Year', the cheer wasn't often returned. Apparently the last of the revellers had staggered off to bed only a few hours earlier.

A few days later, I had to lug out the lawnmower and tackle the grass on the back lawn of the Met office. Inside the enclosure were the surface observation instruments - the snow recorder, temperature reader in a Stephenson screen (wet and dry bulb), the automatic weather equipment, ground thermometers to record soil temperature, rain gauge and sunshine recorder. As I pushed the mower back and forth, I wondered how many other people that day would be mowing in sub-Antarctica.

Bec asked me to give her a hand, so we headed back to Secluded Cove to look for pups that weren't tagged. All I could hear were the waves and the weaners' grunts when they noticed us. By now most of the mothers had left and gone out to sea.

I heard a squeal and turned to see three fur seal pups in the tussock grass. I focused in on one with my camera and when he saw me, he rested his head against a tuft of the long thin grass and stared. They had such beautiful eyes and I was saddened by the knowledge most wouldn't survive once they went out to sea on their own. For killer whales, the pups are nothing but little sausages.

We watched as one found Mum, wriggling like a puppy, squealing and slapping himself with his little flippers before diving in for a feed. We pushed on and found two playing in rock pools, one in the water blowing bubbles. Bec pointed one out and mock-warned me: "Watch yourself. Number 28's going to have a go at you."

We caught a pup which was more placid. As I held him, Bec named him "130" and called him my new mate. I gave this little one a cuddle before putting him down. The breeding populations were being monitored, but I wondered if this one would escape the predators of the sea and make it back as an adult to start his own family.

We were on the downwards stretch of the summer and had to start planning for the resupply, including ordering all the equipment needed for the coming winter. It was a big job to figure out how many ozone and regular sondes we'd gone through during the year, allowing for some failures (as I did earlier that day when the string broke again and the ozone package landed on the main beach) and remembering all the little details like pens and pencils, paper pads etc. Regular duties still had to be fitted in. I'd been trained as a fire co-ordinator, and my job was to check the blokes' air time. If there was ever a fire, I would have to monitor each person's time, calculate how much air they had left, and tell them when to get out. Luckily, this duty remained theoretical, but maintenance chores still waited.

The tourist ship *Akademik Shokalski* was visiting and the tourists visited the office to watch while I explained the Met program while filling the weather balloon. I heard a hissing sound and raced out to release it. I'd had a few tricky releases, especially when the gales were south-west and they'd push the balloon back into the shed as I was bringing it out, but I hadn't encountered this before and quickly released the balloon before it exploded. I chatted to some of them afterwards, including a Russian ship's engineer and a tourist, who had worked for the English Meteorology Office during World War II. It always fascinated me to see the variety of people who found their way down south.

Tourism had become a norm in the ANARE program, with visitors from tourist ships and special Qantas flights which took passengers over the island. These 12-hour non-stop over-flights started in 1994, and take in Macca as well as other stations on Antarctica. Approved by all the Antarctic Treaty nations, they fly at 10,000 feet, an altitude which doesn't affect wildlife habitats. Robb Clifton had a live radio link to the plane while it circled overhead, giving the passengers and idea of what it was like down below. During the flight, a panel of onboard experts such as Antarctic scientists, glaciologists and explorers provided more information. Considering that prices at the time of writing ranged from $900 for a seat that doesn't rotate to a window to more than $5000 for a First Class seat, everyone did their bit to make the experience memorable.

***

A few days later, I sought out Robb for some advice. I'd been encountering hostility from a fellow expeditioner, who was once a friend. A bloke close to my age, we'd spent quite a bit of time chatting at the bar, laughing and enjoying a growing friendship.

One night, a group of us passed the time telling yarns and talking about our lives, our partners and great loves. When it came to his turn, he said, "This is all shit" and left. We stared at each other, puzzled. It was innocent talk, but it had obviously struck a chord. I knew he'd had some personal problems before coming down to the island, a bitter divorce scarring his view on relationships, but didn't expect that reaction.

Then one night, while sitting at the bar chatting with him, one of the female expeditioners asked me to join the others in a dance. It seemed to upset him. The next time I sat down next to him in the mess, he grunted, picked up his plate and left. He didn't speak to me again.

The tension of living in close quarters with this hostility was getting to me. I talked it over with Robb, and asked him to approach this bloke to find out what his gripe was. I didn't usually involve others in my problems, but trusted Robb.

An ex-SAS officer, he was a great leader and had all of our respect. Always very calm and collected, he knew how to handle all sorts of people and I never saw him lose it. He'd graduated from Duntroon and served in Rwanda, and I suspect he had issues with his service there, as well as the Black Hawk helicopter disaster in 1996 where 18 servicemen, mainly SAS soldiers from his unit, were killed. He had the sharp mind of a former military man and keen mountaineer and had made trips to the Himalayas, Peruvian Andes and New Zealand Alps. He had also climbed Mawson Peak, the highest peak of the Heard Island's "Big Ben", with three others.

Robb knew this bloke's history and said he'd have a word with him to see if we could resolve the problem. It was the first time in my life I'd encountered such a situation and didn't think it was smart to let it grow, especially as we all had to depend on each other.

That dependency became apparent on the 18th, when we had a serious accident. The day started well enough, with three teams heading out to resupply the huts at Brothers Point, Green Gorge, on the east coast of the island, and Hurd Point at the bottom. I was in one boat with Cal. Psycho and Paul Gleeson (Fiji) was in the second and Gerbil and Rob Gregor (Robbo) were in the third.

The trip was relatively calm and penguins kept us company along the way. At Green Gorge we picked up some rocks from a geologist, Steve Lewis, after dropping off his supplies, and headed further south. Then the weather started to turn, with the winds picking up to around 25 knots and the seas rising to three metres. The leader of the boating party decided to keep going, but by then it was hard to see the other boats over the waves. With the wind howling, I started to feel uneasy. I carefully wrapped my video camera in a waterproof bag and tucked it away as we approached Hurd Point.

Cal and I were the first boat to attempt to catch a wave in, watching for kelp as we timed our entrance. A huge wave caught us and we flipped into the dangerous rough waters. I'm not a strong swimmer, and as I gasped with the cold and the shock, trying to get my bearings, I could hear Gerbil behind yelling "Where's Dave?" My beanie had slipped over my face and I couldn't answer as I struggled through the mess and surfaced from under the boat, shoving my beanie up to see Cal still attached to the Zodiac. Gasping for breath, my lungs burning, I felt time slow as a second large wave picked us up and slammed us into rocks. Choking on water, I grabbed onto what I could, but a strong rip pulled us back out into deep, swirling water. My chest was burning, and I kept gasping for breath, desperate for sweet air among the claustrophobic water. My confused mind was trying, in slow motion, to focus on something. Helplessly, I watched as a powerful third wave approached and picked us up.

This is it. I knew that wave would slam us onto the rocks again and I was tiring. I felt my body rise, shattered by my struggle and the cutting cold, and watched the dark, angry rocks approach. The expected impact didn't happen. Instead, the wave spat us out on the beach, and Cal and I stumbled across the hard sand and pebbles and dragged what was left of the Zodiac onto the shore. We collapsed, drysuit pulling tight and deep cuts stinging from the salty water. Cal was bleeding from the head. Shock and exhaustion silenced us. Psycho and Fiji managed to ride in safely on a big wave, but Gerbil and Rob's boat flipped. Their wave was kinder, bringing them onto the beach straight past the rocks.

We'd lost all the supplies, tied down in plastic containers, from two of the boats as well as the rocks Steve had entrusted us to return to the station. Our boat was ruined. We sat and stared at the wreck, the waves and the chatter of thousands of penguins surrounding were the only sounds. The stench of the penguins was overpowering.

Finally someone spoke. "Well, what do we do now?"

It was decided we'd try to bring the ruined boat back with us, but whatever we tried, the logistics defeated us. We would have to pack three of us in each of the two remaining boats, plus what we could salvage from the beach. We decided to take the motor from the wrecked boat, and leave the shell behind.

Cal was by far the strongest swimmer and it was decided he would help launch the Zodiacs before swimming through the breaking waves to his boat. Studying the waves, we counted a 15-second gap between them and prepared to break through.

Psycho and Fiji went first, with all of us pushing their boat into the swirling water. They timed the waves and suddenly gunned the motor, pushing over a series of big waves on their first attempt.

Cal, Gerbil, Robbo and I returned to the shore and pushed the second Zodiac out. Cal pushed as we jumped in, and Gerbil tried frantically to start the engine. The tiny window of opportunity closed. Just as he got the engine started, we got picked up and flipped over into the angry water. Luckily, the wave pushed us straight past the rocks, but as I staggered out onto the beach again, I'd had it. In shock, and shaking with fear, I refused to try again.

"This is a bloody joke," I said to Gerbil, trembling with cold and panic. "I can't do this."

"Mate ..."

"I mean it. I'd rather walk the 34 kilometres back to base than try that again."

Gerbil stared at me, and then quietly promised if we survived this, he'd cook me a beautiful, tender steak. I stared at the waves, frustrated at feeling terrified. I was grateful for his strength, and hated that I was living a nightmare in the middle of the day. I could cope with the night-time demons, but not with this helpless feeling. And yet I knew I had no option.

"Yeah, okay."

Quiet, I joined the others and we started pushing the boat back out, fighting to keep it straight against the movement of the water. I was up to my shoulders in the icy water, and when I got the signal, struggled to lift my body through the heavy water and into the boat. Robbo heaved me in and I slumped on the floor. Gerbil was struggling with the motor again, and I tensed, expecting to feel the boat flip again. The sound of the motor roaring to life was beautiful. I felt the boat rise up and over the waves. Once past the danger of breaking waves, we pulled alongside the other boat and waited for Cal.

The waves were picking us up and dropping us down so far that Hurd Point would disappear entirely for the few seconds until we rose again. Cal swam under a wave, and we waited for him to reappear. And waited. As the waves threw us around, we started panicking as we could see a thick patch of kelp where he'd disappeared, and knew he was caught up beneath it.

Finally, he reappeared and made it to the boat. Anyone else would have drowned, but he was very fit, very athletic, and very lucky.

The return trip to the station was quiet and slow. We had to stop along the way to pick up Kathryn Wheatley, who'd flagged us down from one of the huts. After re-arranging the boats once again, we crept back to base overloaded with four people in one vessel, three and the remaining supplies in the other.

We finally returned to the station late that afternoon, four hours behind schedule and feeling sore, bruised and sunburnt. Robb met us and was relieved to see we had all survived. They'd known something was wrong when they couldn't contact us after the radio went in the drink. After cleaning up, I headed back to Hass House for a short, hot shower, desperate for heat to ease the aches in my tired body.

I'd gotten as far as the main building when I was fronted by the expeditioner I'd been having trouble with.

"I want to see you. I'm fuckin' sick of you. So when can I fuckin' see you?" he snarled, poking a finger in my face. Apparently Robb had talked to him earlier at my request, and he wasn't happy at the interference. I couldn't care. The adrenalin and fear of the past few hours had left me with an emotional hollowness, and I just couldn't be bothered to make the effort.

"You'll have to wait. I've had a pretty bad day, mate. I'm going to have a shower, then we can talk. I'll meet you in the Met office shortly," I said, walking past him. His answer wasn't polite.

Dressed in dry clothes and feeling better, I went back to the office and waited. It took a while to realise he wasn't going to show and the attempt at talking things over was probably for show. I left.

In the mess, surrounded by the warmth and friendship of the others, I sat down to a beautiful, tender steak, cooked to perfection by the unflappable Gerbil. It was one of the best steaks I'd ever eaten.

The next day we had a big debrief about the accident with Robb. A number of recommendations and instructions were instigated, including the requirement to turn back if the weather became uncertain, of having an observer at Hurd Point advising by radio of the weather conditions and of not beaching at Hurd Point unless there was someone at the hut.

Near misses are taken very seriously, and they should be. Each was a lesson to learn from to keep expeditioners safe from future incidents. More people (six) have died on Macca than on any other Australian base.

After the debrief, I tackled slushy duties but was very sore, sunburned, and still mourning the loss of my favourite Essendon beanie. Actually, one of my jobs that day was restocking everyone's beanies, all swallowed and lost forever in the sea.

***

Near the end of the month, while the *Sir Hubert Wilkins* came in with its load of tourists, I went out with the elephant seal team to record the capture of a female so a time-depth recorder unit could be attached.

The team of Kathryn Wheatley, Corey Bradshaw, and Matt Webb, with Dr Cath lending a hand, found their target seal and slowly approached her. She wasn't having a bar of it, and kept attacking the stick Matt was holding out, and then backing up. Quietly he walked forward and at the right moment, threw his stick away and covered her head with a bag while another member of the team straddled the cows behind and put the anaesthetic needle in her rear. Matt kept moving the cow's flippers and rubbed her head, helping her relax until the drugs took effect.

Once the cow was under, the team quickly organised the gear. One took a blood sample from the vein that runs down the cow's spine while the others prepared the stretcher, and they rolled her into the net. She was measured before the net got wrapped up, tied and a pulley set up on a tripod. After weighing, the cow was returned to the ground and measurements continued while and an area was shaved under and behind one flipper. One member of the team did a biopsy. Kathryn explained to me they were measuring the cow's back fat in six different places. The blubber biopsy provided fatty acid measurements which told the team what the cow had been eating. The amount of blubber she was carrying indicated the state of her condition.

To attach the unit, Kathryn applied a rectangle of glue, forcing it well into the shaved skin. Corey made an impression in the glue, and then removed the unit for Kathryn to fill the indentation with more glue before he attached it. More glue was applied around the top of the tracker.

The cow awoke less than 30 minutes after the capture. Everyone was cautious, as they can wake up grumpy and aggressive, but this one just looked at us with big sleepy eyes before heading off down the beach with a big blue bump on her back.

The 29th was a special day Gerbil's birthday. He always made a special effort for people's birthdays, and had an above average number to celebrate in November. We also celebrated two milestones in December. Col hit a half-century and Al D a quarter century. Now it was Gerbil's turn, with Cathie and Cal taking over the meals.

At the end of the month, Robb called in to talk about the bloke who'd been causing me the problems.

"Did you sort it out?" he asked.

I told him he'd fronted me but had refused to turn up to the office. Robb said he was really disappointed with him, but I told him to forget about it. With only six weeks to go, I could live with it.

CHAPTER 6
DISTURBING NEWS

February 2002 weather details:
Max temp 12.3 °C, min -0.6 °C
Mean daily sunshine (hours) 3.6
Days of precipitation 24, average monthly rainfall 83.2 millimetres
Days of strong winds 21, days of gales 4
(Based on averages to 1989)

Early in the month, the station leader broke some disturbing news to us all: there were only a few rolls of toilet paper left on the station, and we'd have to ease up on what was left. I heard a few murmurs of "oh shit" among the others, and we all knew we'd be facing painful moments in the month left. Our changeover date had been pushed back as the *Aurora Australis* had gone to the rescue of the *Polar Bird*, which was lodged in thick ice. Until the AA arrived, we'd get no more supplies.

I like to use a lot of toilet paper when I go but was now facing a ration of two small strips, which soon ran out. A mad rush to find newspapers began and they quickly became the most prized items on the station. I made sure to keep hidden in my room two *Melbourne Herald-Sun* papers I'd brought with me at the beginning of the summer. Several options were discussed. Someone observed that the pages of magazines were no good much too smooth for the job. Others considered using wet rags. Nothing was satisfactory.

After a few days of this dilemma, an expeditioner down at Hurd Point discovered a full box of toilet paper. As Robb broke the good news, one person yelled out above the cheers of relief: "Now my bloody bum can get back to normal". A couple of the younger, athletic blokes were given the important task of walking to Hurd Point and bringing back the valuable box.

***

My niggling injuries continued to bother me. At the beginning of the month, in spite of Gerbil's mock-ecstatic treatment of my leg, I had to go back to Dr Cath. I was also having problems with my neck after the boating accident. She tried to take an X-ray but couldn't get a good image. All I could do was take it easy and stay positive. The accident at Hurd Point had intensified my nightmare, and I was trying to keep a routine going to counter the lack of sleep.

I headed out with TASPAWS ranger Chris Hall to relocate some tracks. Certain areas are closed at the start of November due to nesting albatrosses and it was time to put the trail markers back to their original positions. The nests had failed, but we didn't know if this was due to feral animals or some other issue.

Chris was a top bloke, and a very busy man. Besides shepherding tourists around, he and the others on the team would survey different birds and lay out rat bait and Myxomatosis in a virus form.

Rabbits and wekas (flightless birds from New Zealand's Stewart Island) were introduced as a source of fresh food for sealers. There had been no plant eaters on the island before rabbits were introduced and they dramatically altered the vegetation. A strain of Myxomatosis virus was introduced in 1978. Since then rabbit numbers had dropped from 150,000 to 10,000 by 1993.

Native wildlife was also threatened by feral cats, which by 1972 had become such a problem a program was begun to eradicate them. As I helped Chris move markers around, he told me most cats had been killed but he still walked the area with a rifle in his pack just in case. One of the other TASPAWS members, Sandy, was in charge of dogs Tua and Kim, whose job was to help hunt for any remaining cats.

As rabbits became scarcer, the cats had turned to the wekas which had been wreaking havoc on burrowing petrels, eating the birds as well as their eggs. The wekas were eliminated by the end of 1988. With their food sources dwindling, cat numbers also decreased.

A few days later I had the chance to head back out to sea for another run down the coast. As I climbed in the Zodiac, I checked myself for any nerves and was surprised to find I was okay. We headed out to Green Gorge and unloaded supplies. While I waited to head back out, I watched an elephant seal lazing in the path of incoming waves. Each wave would wash into his face, and he'd snort in disgust. Every few seconds it would happen again. I wondered who would win, nature or beast. As we left and headed back up to Brothers Point, they were still locked in battle nature splashing, beast complaining. At Brothers Point we dropped Al and Nick off to continue their work with the penguins and headed out.

On the way back to the base, I knew we were passing by the sites of a number of shipwrecks; victims of shipping in the treacherous waters off the island. There are nine known shipwrecks: five between the isthmus and The Nuggets (*Campbell Macquarie* 1812, *Clyde* 1911, an unknown one, *Countess of Minto* 1851 and *Ben Clough* 1877), two between The Nuggets and Sandy Bay (*Gratitude* 1898 and *Jessie Nichols* 1910) and one on the south-west corner of the island (*Caroline* 1825). As well, the *Kakanui* (1891) and the *Endeavour* (1914) were lost without a trace after leaving the island.

And it wasn't only in the days of old. In 1988 the ANARE resupply vessel *Nella Dan* was also wrecked off Buckles Bay when she'd dragged anchor.

Though I never actually saw any of the wrecks, as we passed these watery graves I spared a thought for those early settlers who'd tried to forge a living on this island. During my stay I'd explored many of the relics which dotted the island. Remnants of the old sealers' huts, try-works, and steam digester plants lie abandoned along the coastline. They remain in situ, protected by a 1982 policy of leaving artefacts where they lie.

Macquarie Island is one of the few places in Australia where private enterprise, rather than the colonial government, initiated settlement. You had to feel for them. These men endured months of isolation and harsh conditions to scrape a living from the island's natural resources. In the early days they lived in mud and tussock huts, and killed fur seals for their pelts. As the seals died out the sealers turned to elephant seal blubber and penguins for oil. New Zealand entrepreneur Joseph Hatch brought great capital investment to the island from the 1880s to 1919. The remains of this period, especially the squat rusting penguin steam digesters, are easily spotted around the island. They stand among penguins that have never seen hunting in their lifetimes, at least not by man.

***

I had some spare time one day and asked Gerbil if he'd let me video him as he worked. It was 10°C and miserable outside. Inside his kitchen it was a cosy 20°C and I thought it'd be a good way to spend some time.

"Sure, Morg," he said before explaining how he made bread. He demonstrated each ingredient and step. He efficiently fashioned four loaves for toast and some rolls and left them to prove for about half an hour.

"Come back then, Morg, and I'll show you the next step."

When I returned, he talked me through the rest of the process. After he took the loaves from the oven, he turned to me with a deadpan expression.

"I really hope you enjoy this, Dave." Thinking he was talking about the bread, I kept the video on him as he abruptly turned to leave. Before I could yell out my thanks, I registered through the viewfinder something awfully white his bum! He'd taken off his pants and daks, and had been walking around, naked under his apron, waiting for the right moment. I sure as hell wasn't expecting that, and it was quite a few minutes before I could stop laughing long enough to give him some cheek.

***

That night we experienced another boomer of an earthquake. I hung onto the desk while the office shook, the noise an incredible roar, the ground a trembling mess. I'd just let go of the desk, having decided I'd have to make a run for it to the open space outside when it stopped. Tubby said later the quake was 5.3 on the Richter scale, with the epicentre 40 kilometres away and 10 kilometres deep.

A few days later I finished my application for the 2003 ANARE program with the Bureau of Meteorology. After turning down the chance to stay on for the full year, my focus was on getting to one of the other stations on Antarctica. As I faxed off the application, I crossed my fingers.

***

It was Sprunky's birthday. We gathered in the mess to await the feast. Before he'd left for the island, his lady friend had baked him a cake to save for the event, and he brought it out to share with us. The cake looked good, the icing perfect, until Sprunky tried to cut it. During the previous four months, the icing had set like cement. He tried everything to break into his cake. Finally someone brought him an axe. As we all rolled around laughing, he sheepishly broke through at last using a knife and hammer. Inside, it was amazingly good.

Macca was Sprunky's first summer expedition, but he had wintered seven times with ANARE (Davis in 1985, 1987, 1992 and 1994, Macca 1996 and Casey in 1998 and 2000). He was another expeditioner who'd been awarded an Australian Antarctic Medal in 2001 for outstanding effort and innovation in support of scientific fieldwork and station communities.

He told me once what had driven him there. "For me, that was in Rabaul, the main town on the island of New Britain in tropical Papua New Guinea; it was there that I heard stories about Mawson (the station) and became interested in icebergs.

"I have always liked nature," he said. "Deserts, tropical rainforests, the world underwater, extreme nature at its best. It didn't take long and I became fascinated by icebergs. I wanted to see them for myself ... touch them."

He first tried to work for the Germans but missed out. "My next try was to take part in the Dick Smith Explorer expedition to the Rauer Islands, near Davis, around 1982. The purpose of that voyage was to let a small sailing boat get beset in sea ice, over winter, and study how a small group of people copes with the isolation and challenges. In the end I didn't sign on because the operation was heavily subsidised by the National Geographic. That meant that not only would I have had to pay my own way, but I also would not have been able to publish anything until National Geographic did so. I know from other people that this could take two years and more.

"So, what to do? I then applied to work in Antarctica for the Australian Antarctic Division and at the same time see this magnificent place in all its glory. And at times, in a 100-knot blizzard, for example, when it's not so glorious.

"My first trip 'down south' was around November 1984 on the Nella Dan, the well-known ship that exists these days only in the memories of those who have been associated with her and in photos. As the saying goes, the first trip was an unforgettable experience. It was one of the first voyages of the season, a Fly-Off, and, basically, we had everything that could be experienced.

"The ship rolled, in rough seas with 15 metre waves, 48° to each side. We got stuck in the ice pack for two days or so, and we called in at all three Australian Antarctic stations. What an experience that trip was.

"My first winter was at Davis, in 1985, as a "dieso", short for diesel mechanic. In those days we were only two myself and the PI (plant inspector), Charlie Weir. That year we had an enormous science program and, of course, it kept us extremely busy. Part of the science was a major diving program that went on through the winter.

"In that year, we drilled and cut more than 300 dive holes through the ice. In the end, when the ice was averaging around 1.8 metres thick, that became quite an operation. We used to cut the ice into manageable blocks and the divers would push them under - one standing on the shoulder of the other. There was no easy way of doing it in those days.

"Our year (Davis 1985) was the first time Jiffy drills were used with ANARE.

"My second time down south was in 1987 and that was the year the first ANARE-SAT station was set up in Antarctica, at Davis. That too was an experience. For the first time, expeditioners could make direct-connect STD calls and even send and receive faxes. Gone were the days of the 'rad-phone' calls, telephone via high frequency (HF) radio, usually through Sydney Radio."

Antarctica was critical for Sprunky in a big decision – to naturalise or not. In 1987, his 20th anniversary of arriving in Australia, he lodged his application for Australian citizenship. He was naturalised at Davis on January 1, 1988. While he was not the first person to receive their Australian Citizenship in Antarctica, he was the first to go through the whole process, application and all, from down there.

CHAPTER 7
HOME, BUT NOT FORGOTTEN

March 2002 weather details:
Max temp 12.6 °C, min -2.3 °C
Mean daily sunshine (hours) 2.6
Days of precipitation 26, average monthly rainfall 91.6 millimetres
Days of strong winds 25
Days of gales 7
(Based on averages to 1989)

It was the beginning of the end. The station was preparing for the end of the summer season. Voyage 8 would be arriving in a few weeks to drop off the winter crew and bring us all back to Australia. The *Aurora Australis* would be doing Voyage 8 (V8), so I'd be leaving on the same ship I'd arrived on, finishing the circle. We were briefed on what to expect during the arrival and changeover period, and what our duties would be to support the new arrivals. It would be a big changeover as they wouldn't have the luxury of visiting tourist ships. V8 would be the main restock for the winter and following summer period.

The delayed changeover meant a lot of smokers were now caught out with no cigarettes left. For a while there was a round-robin of bumming, but eventually they all ran out. One bright young spark had a brain wave and collected all the old butts from the ashtrays and bins. Then they figured out a way to turn all the tobacco left in the butts into normal ciggies. Every late afternoon and evening on the mess verandah, at least half a dozen desperate smokers worked in a production line to produce a new brand to satisfy their cravings.

It was during this period I went into my room one night and found Ming Lee, dressed in black silk lingerie pyjamas, lounging on my bed. It was my birthday, and Gerbil had decided I shouldn't have to climb into a cold lonely bed. Ming Lee was his blow-up doll, who got around Macca quite a bit. Her favourite pastimes were late-night rave parties, meeting new men and going with the lonely ones to different huts around the island.

It was the first time Ming Lee had come to see me, though. I'm a bloke who likes faithful ladies, so she ended up sleeping on the floor for the night. While that sounds cruel and cold, I never heard a word of complaint from her.

***

Before we left, I had to front Robb and Cal again for my APPI full assessment and end-of-expedition summary and was rated "very good", which I knew would help support my application for the next tour of duty. To celebrate, Tubby and I went for a walk after lunch to Handspike Point to view the nesting of the King shags, or King cormorants around the mud pool. These beautiful birds breed in 19 colonies around the island, and because of the steeply shelving sea bottom, their feeding grounds are close to shore and quite restricted in area.

That night was the big end-of-summer-expedition party, and the mood was bittersweet. Reality had intruded into our tight group, and we were conscious that in a few days we'd be in different directions, living different lives. I wasn't ready, having fallen in love with this simple life and companionship with these like-minded people. Bec and Al pulled out guitars and serenaded us with a specially written song highlighting our Macca experience while I concentrated on making sure this moment was imprinted in my memory.

When we woke the next morning, the *Aurora Australis* was anchored in Buckles Bay, shimmering in the morning light. She'd arrived at 5.30am and already Zodiacs were zooming out to bring the massive fuel lines out. Sprunky's tanks started to fill for the next year. The "chump-chump" of heavy helicopters started to bring in supplies, beginning five or six days of sun-up to sunset restocking and removal of all the empty containers and rubbish from the finishing expedition. Incoming supplies were sorted and stored, and outgoing crates marked 'RTA' (Return to Australia). Besides the main base, the choppers would also deal with the gas bottles and rubbish from all the huts used by scientists.

During the organised chaos, I caught up with Mick Eccles in the communications room. The comms blokes were always busy, but during this period they were in their element. Usually there would be morning and evening schedules (skeds), or timed radio schedules, from all huts to the main hut with Tubby, Robbo or Mick taking these in turn. There was also a radio in the mess, so in effect there was a 24-hour service. Besides this, they would also be servicing radios, batteries, and Tubby or Robbo would fix any computer or internet problems. During handover, they had to coordinate everything, linking the ship to the helicopters and the station leader.

My replacement, Christine Spry, was waiting at the beach. I'd met her in Hobart, and knew she was an experienced ANARE technical officer (observer) with several seasons on the Ice. She was being joined for the winter by Adam Grimes, taking over as the technician from Cathie, and Rod Leewin.

As our team was short-staffed since Ailsa's departure, I had to also show Rod his duties as Cathie was busy with Adam. The problems with the equipment that Cathie had struggled with and nursed along meant that Jim Easson, the senior physicist for the ozone program, and engineer Roger Meagher had come to assess the viability of changing the electrolyser.

During the next few days, I briefed Christine on the administrative side of things, and talked to Roger Meagher about hydrogen safety, my version after six months' experience. The AA lurked in the background, teasing me with how close I was to going home. Now that the new crew was here, there was a subtle shift in camp and, for me, the magic of being at Macca was broken. I couldn't wait for the duties and handover to be finished and to start the voyage home.

On Saturday night, we gathered in the mess for a big party to both farewell and welcome. It was a heavy night, and very crowded. The mess was cramped with 60-odd people and after a few hours I went to the solitude of my room. I knew it was irrational, but I felt invaded. Just six months ago I would have been the one making others feel the same. It was common to every expeditioner, but knowing this didn't make it any easier to deal with. My shakes were visible as my body tried to cope with the anxiety of the crowds.

It's a small world. I discovered there was another bloke from Yeppoon, John Hoelscher. Unbelievable. I'd read about him and had envied him in the past. Now he was with the incoming crew to replace us, and I found it ironic that two blokes from a small place, thousands of miles away, would meet up in this exotic setting.

Finally, on the 19th, we were ready. I rang Deb and the kids and told them I'd be leaving shortly and that I'd call in two or three days when we arrived in Hobart. As I talked to the new Met crew on the beach, waiting for my turn, I covered my nervousness with jokes. Having the choppers flying back and forth over my head for days had been bad enough, but now I was going to have to climb into one.

"You been on the slops all night?" one bloke asked me.

Puzzled, I stared at him and shook my head. I thought it was a strange question. Later, someone told me there was a rumour going around that I was a drunk. The new arrivals had seen me shake, and assumed I was an alcoholic going through withdrawals, or waiting for my next drink. People who knew me had been quick to fill them in that I was a vet and suffered anxiety.

Now I stared at the chopper which had landed and was waiting for me. I knew I had to get in, and I thought I was ready, but now that it was a reality, I didn't think I could. Psycho knew what I was going through. Dimly I registered him talking, fear spreading up my spine to the base of my head, each pump of my heart increasing the pressure until I couldn't think clearly. He got me in, and nodded at Rick, the pilot, who knew my background, and he worked at getting us up quickly. The flashbacks of Vietnam kept coming, and I kept spinning out until we started moving.

Once we were up, the spinning slowed. It was getting in that was the hardest, the part that 30 years later I still couldn't deal with. Being up in the air, looking down at the craggy beauty of the island's coastline and the buildings dotted along the edge of the isthmus was so very different from what I always remembered seeing from a chopper. I grabbed my camera and focused on recording that beauty to show my family.

The trip over to the AA was short, probably two minutes at the most, and the helicopter settled gracefully onto the helipad deck. All we had to wait for was the last containers to be loaded. The day was miserable, with heavy snow showers and hail, but that didn't stop us from crowding the decks to look at the base from a distance. The old army amphibious ducks kept working – the floating vehicle with wheels figured heavily in the resupply process and we watched as it worked to bring in another load of drums. The crew working the ducks had to be careful. They had to play the engines to work against the swell to manoeuvre close enough for the ship's cranes to pull off the load. One bloke had already crushed his shoulder between the ship and the duck. Finally, well into the evening, the new wintering expeditioners picked up the duck crew on a zodiac and brought them to the rope ladder to join us. The duck was craned up, looking eerie under the ship's artificial lights, as water dripped from its wheels.

At 7.30pm, the ship's horn sounded three short toots. We gathered at the stern and lit flares, and through the red haze and smoke saw an answering glow from the base. One high flare exploded high above the station and we clapped and cheered as the ship started moving. We joked that hopefully Sprunky's fuel farm was safe.

When the last of the smoke drifted away, I heard someone say, "That's the finish, then". And it was. I didn't expect to feel so emotional, but as I watched the outline of the station become smaller, I knew that I would never see this again. And I'd really enjoyed my stay.

I signed the log on the AA, my second entry so far. I was hoping I'd be able to sign on again someday on my way to another base. My application for another posting had already been faxed from Macca. With the favourable reviews, I was quietly confident that I would be successful for another posting.

The swell increased and my friendly seasickness came back to visit. The other expeditioners would gather in the mess, the mood light, but I couldn't join in the fun as the Met bloke's duties didn't finish until we landed back in Hobart.

I managed to get a few weather reports out until the seasickness took hold. I admitted defeat and curled up in my bunk. The first or second ship's mate would do the report for me, code it and send it back to Australia via radio link. The next few days were a blur of sea spray but at least I had company with my cabin mate Tubby. An ex-naval man, even he was sick. Our other cabin mate Steve Lewis, the geologist whose rocks we'd lost in the boating accident, fared better.

Finally on the 22nd, five months and 20 days after we'd left, we returned to Macquarie Dock in Hobart. As the harbour pilot guided us past the multi-million dollar floating palace called *The World* and into our berth, I couldn't help comparing the luxury of those passengers, on their world tour, to ours. I think we ended up having a richer experience.

The crowd of people waiting for us at the dock was excited. Gradually, as familiar faces were recognised, the shouts and waving became frantic. I'd asked Deb and the kids not to meet me in Hobart, something I'd decided long before. Public emotional reunions aren't my style. When I saw my family I wanted the space and privacy to greet them properly. But I could still enjoy the sheer pleasure on faces as expeditioners reunited with their loved ones, especially those who'd been away for over a year.

I had a few chores to take care of before I could go home. That afternoon I tackled the first the official debriefing. Ian Hickmann and Graeme Taylor met me at the dock, and I went with them to go over the good and the bad of the past six months. They queried how I coped, how I found the island and if I had any outstanding gripes about the experience. I could quite honestly tell them it had been a brilliant time. We discussed the non-existent handover when I arrived, and the difficulties created by Ailsa leaving early. We discussed my application and they asked if I would prefer an OIC position. I was quite specific in nominating Casey as my posting of choice. She'd eluded me once and I was determined I would get to see her this time.

The next morning I left Hobart. The day was a blur of flights Hobart to Melbourne (accompanied by Jim Easson), then to Brisbane and Rockhampton where my family was waiting at the airport to take me home to Yeppoon. It was overwhelming to finally hold Deb, Michelle and David. I was relieved they were healthy and happy. As we caught up I answered questions about my experience, and in doing so reminded myself why I'd left them for so long.

The island is something special with its different animals, the ruggedness of the land, and the ever-changing climate. You see the documentaries on television, watch people doing what I'd just done, and think, "Maybe, someday, that could be me." And it had been me. That was the big buzz, the main highlight. I'd been there, I'd done that.

And the people. The experience and the atmosphere of the kitchen was what glued us together. My whole way of life was different. Instead of just work and home, footie on TV and mowing the lawn, we'd shared stories, pitched in to keep the station going, and learned about each other. I was going to miss that.

My other favourite memory was being involved in the fur seal program. That was something that all the Met training in the world was never going to give me, and the time I spent with Bec and the little pups was special.

Without the bad, the good can't be fully appreciated, and my time wasn't all smooth. The disagreement and falling out with someone I'd considered a mate still confused me. It had left me unhappy. I wasn't bitter. I just couldn't understand where the situation had come from. Still, it was a learning experience. You can't get along with everyone in life.

For now, I was home. That was all that mattered.

PART THREE
DAVIS STATION
THE RIVIERA OF THE SOUTH

"I will love the light for it shows me the way, yet I will endure the darkness for it shows me the stars"

Og Mandino (1923-1996)

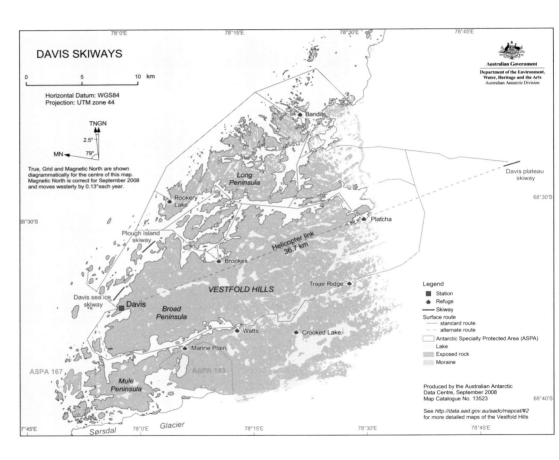

DAVIS SKIWAYS

0   5   10   km

Horizontal Datum: WGS84
Projection: UTM zone 44

TNGN

2.5°

MN   79°

True, Grid and Magnetic North are shown
diagrammatically for the centre of this map.
Magnetic North is correct for September 2008
and moves westerly by 0.13° each year.

Australian Government

Department of the Environment,
Water, Heritage and the Arts
Australian Antarctic Division

78°0'E   78°15'E   78°30'E   78°45'E

Bandits

Long
Peninsula

Davis plateau
skiway

68°30'S

Rookery
Lake

Platcha

Plough Island
skiway

Helicopter link
36.7 km

Brookes

VESTFOLD HILLS

Trajer Ridge

Davis sea ice
skiway

Davis

Broad
Peninsula

Watts

Crooked Lake

Marine Plain

ASPA 167

ASPA 143

Mule
Peninsula

Sørsdal   Glacier

7°45'E   78°0'E   78°15'E   78°30'E   78°45'E

68°30'S

68°40'S

Legend

■ Station
◆ Refuge
— Skiway
Surface route
— standard route
-- alternate route
☐ Antarctic Specially Protected Area (ASPA)
Lake
Exposed rock
Moraine

Produced by the Australian Antarctic
Data Centre, September 2008
Map Catalogue No. 13523

See http://data.aad.gov.au/aadc/mapcat/#2
for more detailed maps of the Vestfold Hills

Davis Station was known among ANARE expeditioners as the "Riviera of the South" due to the relatively mild weather as compared with Casey and Mawson. Temperatures vary little between day and night, but are vastly different between seasons. January the warmest month has an average temperature of 1°C, while winter is usually -20°C. The station was established as a strategic move to fend off interest in the region by the Soviet Union. On January 13, 1957, the station was opened and named for Captain John King Davis, a famous Antarctic navigator and captain.

CHAPTER 8
GETTING THERE IS HALF THE FUN

Home was a sensory delight – polluted air, freshly cut grass and musky earth. Though I'd only been away for a few short months, I found the business and commercialism of the "real" world overwhelming; shops overflowing with trendy overpriced styles and new electrical gadgets, queues, the unfriendliness of strangers in the street. Even stepping off the curb and having to remember to check for traffic felt strange.

Michelle and David were in school, the house was in its normal routine and I slowly realised that it was me that was different. I'd changed. For my family's sake, I tried to get used to this world again but struggled with the loss of the closed, safe confines of the station and the camaraderie of the other expeditioners. My family was happy I was home, but I noticed small differences, a self-sufficiency that had grown while I was away.

Once again, I found myself a changed man in a world that hadn't changed. The last time I'd felt this disjointed was when I'd left the pungent jungle and climbed on the "Freedom Bird" back to Australia. Work at the Rockhampton Met Office was beckoning, though I'd taken five weeks' leave to adjust before heading back. I wasn't looking forward to it. As the weeks ticked by, I waited for a phone call from Phil Littlehales or Ian Hickmann telling me when to come down to Brisbane for the obligatory exams for the next round of expeditions to Antarctica. One day I got a phone call from Cathie Saunders.

"Hey Dave, I thought you were applying for Antarctica."

I thought she was teasing me as she'd helped me with my application down at Macca.

"Yeah, I have."

"So what happened?"

"What do you mean? I'm just waiting to hear. Why?" There was a pause on the line, and then she dropped her bomb.

"All the Met staff have been chosen, Dave. We've all been interviewed and gone through our medicals and psych testing."

I froze. "You're joking."

"No. Notifications came out last week."

I hung up and stared at the wall. *What the bloody hell's going on.*

I rang Ian Hickmann, who was happy to catch up. His tone changed when I asked him what'd happened with my application.

"What do you mean?"

I told him about the phone call with Cathie, and that I hadn't heard anything from the ANARE program. We'd talked during my debrief about me going to Casey. I told him I'd sent off my application in February.

"If you can prove that, you've got a case."

I gave him the date I'd sent it and the number it'd been sent to, and Ian promised to look for it. He asked Jenny Coombes, the administrator for the Met staff in ANARE, to check. Jenny is the division's superwoman. If anyone could find it, it was her.

And she did in the bottom drawer in a pile of papers. It appeared that my application got shuffled into a pile of paperwork sometime between Graham's retirement and his replacement, Robin Thiema, starting. It had been put in a drawer and forgotten.

Ian rang back. "This is embarrassing. We've already selected the staff." I told him I didn't want to make trouble but I wanted a fair go.

Ian promised to get back to me. In the meantime, I talked to our union rep, who told me the Bureau would have to recall applications and resit interviews and exams.

An hour later, Ian rang. He'd seen the regional director, who confirmed what the union rep had said. They'd have to go through the process again.

I knew this would be a massive hassle, and would upset all the expeditioners already chosen. They would be preparing for their next tour. This was getting bigger than I wanted, and as I weighed up the options of pursuing my rights,

I wondered if I was cursed. Whenever I'd tried to get down to Casey, I ended up in the centre of a controversy.

Three or four days later, Ian rang. "Dave, I've just been talking to the regional director again. We've been thinking. For us to re-interview and re-exam would cost the Bureau a huge amount of money, and we'd like to avoid that if we can. Could we cut a deal with you?"

He told me it was more than likely I'd have been going to Casey as the OIC, but now it would cost too much to have that happen. Instead, they were offering to send me to Davis. And instead of being OIC, I'd go under Geoff Fulton (Beacon), and work with Cathie Saunders. In return, I'd be paid OIC rates even though the position was a grade lower.

No hesitation. I'd get to the Ice, and with the bonus of less responsibility for full pay. And I liked Beacon; we'd worked together years earlier in the regional forecast centre in Brisbane. He was a fun-loving character, always ready for a laugh. He'd got his nickname after once getting lost in the snow. The only reason they'd found him was someone spotted his bright red hair glaring against the white. Cathie was brilliant, and I knew we worked well together. I accepted.

The bloke originally chosen for Macca was told he'd have first priority for the following year. I felt bad for him. I later heard he was disappointed and I knew I was indirectly responsible. But I also knew he was young, something I didn't have on my side anymore.

Curse of Casey? In hindsight, I should have followed up when I hadn't heard from the Bureau. I knew I'd have to redo medical and psychological exams, but as I'd been promised Casey, didn't think I would have to sit an interview again. I assumed I had the job waiting.

The experience left a bitter taste in my mouth, but after a period I consciously put that aside. I couldn't afford to wallow in what should've or could've been. I needed to get ready.

June was busy with a medical exam in Rockhampton then a trip back to the army base in Brisbane to meet the psychologist. I was preparing Deb and the kids for another period on their own when I got another call. It was Robin Thiema asking about my Macca experience with the guy who'd fallen out with me.

"How'd you get along with him?"

I assumed this was part of the debriefing about an expedition and had to be honest. "Well, we went in as friends, came out enemies. But that's in the past. Why?"

Robin was quiet. "Guess what?"

"What?"

"He's going down to Davis with you."

"You have got to be joking, mate." *There was no way.* "If that's the case, the Antarctica Division will have to get us together and help us talk it through. Otherwise there's no way we can work together for twelve months."

Robin talked to the administrators at the ANARE Division. During this period, Cal (who I'd worked with at Macca) heard about the situation. He got on to them and voiced his opinion.

For two weeks, I tried not to let the prospect of working with this man ruin the excitement I was feeling. I was relieved, however, when Robin rang back and told me the guy was being sent to Casey instead.

I wondered how he'd got through the psychological screening. I wasn't the only expeditioner who'd felt this man's anger. I wondered how the Antarctic Division had let him through. Maybe they considered his problems insignificant when it came to serving as a successful expeditioner.

***

Once again I was staring out a small airplane window, trying to pick out my daughter and wife among the crowd of people on the observation deck. I'd driven David, by now a Year 12 student at St Brendan's College in Yeppoon, to school that morning and said goodbye, trying not to think about missing so much of his final year. Michelle, who was at university, drove Deb and me to the airport in Rockhampton to catch the flight to Brisbane.

Between the training and the time spent at Davis, I'd be away for 15 months, much longer than my seven-month stints at Giles and Macca. Deb was dreading becoming a "Met widow" again. She felt she was losing her husband. She worked part-time at the local school doing intervention work, helping students who were struggling with learning, but that still left a lot of solitary hours before the kids came home.

At least they have each other. I'd promised to try and get back for a few days, in the window between training and the ship leaving, in about three months. This wasn't the final goodbye, and I focused on that.

***

When the plane landed in Melbourne that night, I got into a cab and asked to go to my motel. Beacon had told me we were staying at the City Edge Motel in Gibbs Street, East Melbourne. However, when I gave the address to my taxi driver, he couldn't understand me. When he finally stopped the taxi and announced we were there, I looked around.

"Are you sure, mate? This doesn't look like a motel to me."

Nodding vigorously, he motioned outside. "Gibbs Street, yeah."

Fine. I grabbed my bags, paid the driver and watched him drive off before dragging my gear into the stark brick building. Inside, I realised it was a factory. A worker looked up and grinned when I asked if this was Gibbs Street, East Melbourne.

"Don't tell me – you're after a motel." When I nodded, he told me we were in Gibbs Street, Collingwood.

I cursed the taxi driver but the worker just laughed. "Don't worry, mate. Happens all the time." He rang for another taxi.

When I finally got to the motel, Beacon met me and showed me the two-bedroom unit we'd be sharing. His wife Margaret would be staying as well for a few days. It was good to see him, but I was tired, annoyed and emotional. It'd been a long day and I kept telling myself it would have to improve from there.

Beacon, Cathie and I spent the next few days at Broadmeadows Met training centre, studying report writing and on a team-building course to learn how to build morale and deal with conflicts. It was great to see Cathie again. I was chuffed when she told me one of the photos I'd taken of a roll cloud at Macquarie Island had made the 2003 Australian Weather Calendar put out by the Bureau of Meteorology.

From there we flew to Hobart for the next phase. I met up with Tubby, who was going to Casey, and Gerbil, who was heading with us to Davis. It was the first time we'd caught up since Macca. Tubby and I talked about Casey. I was sorry I wasn't going down with him as we get along really well. Being the same age, we had similar experiences and I always found him to be a solid bloke. On the other hand, I was excited that once again I'd be joining Cal, Cathie and Gerbil. I knew the food would be good, and the laughs guaranteed.

Training covered a range of outcomes. Basic ANARE training required fire fighting, manual handling and gymnasium courses (aimed to keep us fit and healthy over the long winter). I volunteered to be one of the hairdressers, and headed off to the Hobart TAFE (Technical and Further Education) to do a haircutting course, though I had serious doubts about my skills after hacking away at dummy heads. I was also on the hydroponics team and sat through an introduction course. Fresh vegetables were essential and a real highlight for expeditioners. We knew when we arrived we had to destroy the previous expedition's set-up and begin again from scratch to prevent disease. We had to do it well, as the morale of the crew would end up being influenced by our success or failure.

On the Met side, I spent quite a bit of time at the airport, training on DigiCORA sondes with Beacon. It was all new to him, and I was able to share what I'd learnt at Macca as we worked through the information. In between training sessions, I went out the airport several times to help out as the office was short of technical officers. I took on several shifts, pairing with Ian Grantham.

Ironically, after I'd spent a day at a harassment course, I saw my old "friend" from Macca heading back to his hotel, the Woolstore, as I was heading back to my room at Trinity House. We passed on the footpath silently, no small talk or reunion catch-up. I only saw him once after that, at Bronte Park, and all I got then was a cold stare. I knew then that my gut feeling was right - I couldn't see us spending an isolated winter together.

Social nights and time off broke the intensity of training. As training was for expeditioners heading off to all the various bases, we had station meetings where only the Davis expeditioners met as a group to bond, helped by good meals and drinks. I was sharing a unit with Col McIntyre, who was going to winter at Mawson as a Met tech. On weekends off we explored Salamanca Place, an area of Hobart with art galleries and restaurants in old merchant warehouses, and surrounding attractions.

One Sunday night, after spending the day visiting the markets with Beacon and geologist Steve Lewis, I was rudely woken by Col, who'd lost his key. Wide awake, I sat and turned on the telly to help me nod off again. Instead, I watched hell unfold once again, only this time it was people stumbling out of the wreckage of what had been the popular Sari Club and Paddy's in Bali. In all, 202 people died in the terrorist bombings, including 88 Australians. A further 209 were injured.

It was the second time I had turned on the television to learn that terrorism had hit hard, both times while I was in Trinity House training to leave my family for a remote location where I'd be unable to help if anything happened to them. Watching the chaos, it just didn't seem fair, and certainly didn't make any sense to me.

***

The Davis station leader, Jeremy Smith, had chosen me to train up as a scrub nurse. When he'd asked me to join the medical team, he wanted to know if I had any issues with the assignment. I was going to Antarctica to do a job, and didn't want my personal problems to be a concern. The doctors and psychologist had found me fit, and I didn't want to say otherwise.

In the days leading up to the start of the course, I started suffering anxiety about how I'd handle it. I'd seen all the blood and trauma I'd ever want to see in Vietnam; body bags and wounded Aussie soldiers being medivacked out. I was working on telling myself that this would be different sterile and controlled. Logically, I knew I'd be able to handle it, but emotionally I wasn't sure.

April, Nui Dat, Vietnam

I was in convoy on a weekly cipher run to various fire support bases and outposts to change the codes and secure radio channels. We were following an American vehicle when it hit a landmine and exploded, the piercing, shuddering noise telling us there would be no survivors.

Shrapnel fell around us, a wheel landing 50 yards away. When the air cleared, both Americans in the vehicle were dead. We sat, vulnerable, on the road for several hours until the Australian engineers and infantry could sweep the area with mine detectors and give us the all-clear.

***

The night before the course started, I sat up reading the ANARE theatre notebook: "A Guide to the Operating Suite". We'd be trained to perform a range of duties from cleaning and caring for instruments, performing the roles of scout or scrub nurse, understanding the medico's legal responsibilities, maintaining airways, to observing and monitoring the signs of a patient in a recovery room.

It was "identify and implement care to meet the physical and emotional needs of the patient" that gave me pause. Once down there, the station doctor would be solely responsible for keeping expeditioners healthy, and dependant on a small team of two nurses (Jim Milne and me) and two anaesthesiologists (Cal Young and Sean Wicks) to help in any critical situation. I'd have to learn to fill all the duties required of me in two short weeks.

Over the years there have been a number of major medical incidents in Antarctica. An American woman, Jerri Neilsen, the only doctor at the Amundsen-Scott South Pole Research Station, self-diagnosed breast cancer in the 1998-1999 season, and had to treat herself. Australian stations have suffered many medical emergencies, including the fatal heart attack of popular chief medical officer Frank Soucek during unloading operations at Macca in 1967. More than twenty people have died while on ANARE service, either at one of the stations or on ships chartered to ANARE.

I'd be responsible for helping our doctor in a similar situation. It was daunting, but I knew this was a tried and tested method and that I had to trust the system.

The next day the atmosphere in the Royal Hobart Hospital matched my mood (tense) but as I met the Perioperative Clinical Educator, Di Beamish, I forced myself to take deep breaths and focus on what she was saying. That first day was spent learning to scrub, glove and gown. It was just like on the TV hospital shows, but not as straightforward as it seemed at first. Maintaining a sterile atmosphere was critical, but the steps to each skill were drummed into us. The week included instrument handling, orthopaedic surgery, anatomy, physiology and positioning of patients, hand injuries, burns and skin grafts, and surgical count – a legal requirement of any operation, no matter how minor. Two people are responsible: the scout and the instrument nurse, and they count the equipment to make sure nothing is left behind in the patient.

We practiced until everything became routine. The week finished with a mock exercise: going in, washing, gloving up, gowning and ensuring sterility.

That weekend my brain became numb as I mentally reviewed all the steps and details. We were going to step into a live theatre on the Monday, and my anxiety was building. Besides it triggering my nightmare again, I was getting flashbacks about things I never wanted to remember.

Day 2, Nui Dat, Phuoc Toy Province, Vietnam

After lunch, all the new arrivals for the 104 Signal Squadron are ordered to report outside the admin building with our SLR rifles. We have to go to the rifle range to check out the sights on our SLRs and range them in. Then we take turns shooting the M60 general purpose machine gun. An American weapon, it has a rate of fire of 200rpm and is the main firepower of the infantry rifle section.

I'm in the line a few metres behind Bruce Meakins, who's lying on the ground lining up the gun, and while he's taking his turn, it jams.

"Bloody gun won't fire," he calls out.

The rifle range Sergeant comes over and yells, "Cock the weapon".

Bruce cocks the M60 and fires the action. No success. He tries again, and is enveloped in a huge explosion. Bruce starts rolling, screaming, his face bloodied and blackened. I kneel beside him while people are screaming for help. His face is covered in burns and shrapnel, especially around his eyes.

A group carries Bruce to a nearby Land Rover, which speeds off to the Nui Dat Regimental Aid Post. Later we find out he'll recover after a few weeks in hospital. Two rounds had got caught in the breech, causing the explosion.

That night, I couldn't sleep, the visions of Bruce rolling around the ground with his burnt and bloodied face jarring me awake every time I tried.

I didn't end up sleeping that night either. I'd previously told Di my background, needing her to understand where I was coming from before I set foot in an operating theatre.

"Don't worry. There've been blokes in the past who've fainted," she said. "And I promise I'll be there with you."

Telling her relieved some of the anxiety, especially as I now knew others had struggled, and that she'd be there. On the Monday, when we went into theatre to help with a real operation, I was numb. They scrubbed and gowned me, and when the surgeon opened up, I was amazed. I felt no emotions, no feeling whatsoever. I simply accepted the cut, the blood on the gloves. I'd built myself into such a state, but knew that I had to do this job. I was on automatic pilot, and got the job done.

The surgeon said to put my hand in the open belly and feel the intestines. It felt like a bowl of soup. No emotion. By the end of the morning I'd assisted in five operations. A further four were completed by the end of the afternoon.

That second week of training was all operations, and all under strict supervision. It's a very regimental atmosphere, from the instrument handling to the count. At one point, one of the surgeons pulled us in close, getting us involved. He said if we needed to do it for real, by ourselves in Antarctica, we'd better be used to it. He had us working inside the body cavity during a 4.5-hour operation for a bladder and prostate cancer removal. I was dog-tired but Di wasn't finished with us. She had us finish off by watching a video on instruments and patient handling.

The next day was spent assisting with electroconvulsive therapy (ECT) shocking to a brain-trauma patient, and later helping in the recovery, taking temperatures and blood pressures of patients fresh out of theatre. After lunch, I met up with Don Reid again, and was kitted out with my full ANARE gear followed by another weekly bonding session at the Good Woman Inn.

What ended up being, by far, my most memorable experience happened the next day. I scrubbed up and went in to help as the doctors and nurses delivered a beautiful baby girl by caesarean. I held the warm newborn in awe while they cut the umbilical cord. With the other operations, I could focus in on the part being worked on. In this one, the people were actively involved and the moment so humbling. I'd missed out on being at Michelle and David's births. Michelle had to be helped out with forceps and I'd been kicked out. David was born unexpectedly after I'd taken toddler Michelle home for a quick tea.

Two further operations followed, both to do with the brain. For the second one, I stood to the side, scrubbed and ready, as they wheeled in a frightened woman. The look of pure terror on her face before she was put under was haunting, and she looked straight at me. To this day, I can remember her eyes and how frightened she was resigned to what was going to happen but almost, I imagine, fighting it. I learned she'd been given a 50/50 chance of survival but I never found out if she did. That lady symbolised the responsibility I would hopefully never have to face.

Further operations followed the next day - carpal tunnel, removal of a piece of loose bone from an elbow, the removal of a screw from an ankle. Each time the scrubbing, gowning and preparation became easier, and I was slowly becoming more confident. After lunch, we visited the pathology museum in the hospital, which was completely different from anything I'd seen before. Different things that had killed humans over the years were stored in bottles, preserved to be studied. Before we finished for the day, we learned how to make and set plaster for broken bones.

The Royal Hobart Hospital, a respected teaching hospital, was the only one in Australia which trained Antarctic expeditioners, something they're proud of. And that pride was obvious to us with all the doctors, nurses and staff positive, helpful and supportive.

***

After another stint at Bronte Park where survival was drilled, and redrilled into us (field training is mandatory for each expeditioner heading to a station, regardless of when they'd last gone through it), it was time to head back to Yeppoon for a few days.

Lead-foot Robin Thiema drove me to the airport. A few hours later I stepped off the air-conditioned plane and into the mugginess of Central Queensland to find Deb, David and Michelle waiting for me. It was so good to see them again, but disturbing in some ways. I couldn't settle down at home, having already gone through the emotions of leaving. I'd thought when I left them weeks before that I hadn't yet said goodbye for real, but I guess I had. At least it would only be a 12-month absence, not 15-months.

In between domestic chores such as mowing the lawn, I scoured Rockhampton for a notebook computer. After Macca, where I'd had to go to the Met office in the cold to use the email, I decided to get one I could keep in my room. I'd be able to listen to music or watch DVDs, and stay in touch with my family.

I was interviewed by a journalist, Judy Wannop, from the *Capricorn Mirror*. The article, titled "Pupils can follow voyage", encouraged contact from schools involved in projects on Antarctica, something I fully supported. I know my own children, though nearing the end of their schooling, had found my stories about that challenging land interesting and I hoped that schools in my local area would get involved.

Before I left, I dropped into the Central Queensland Vietnam Veterans Support Centre to visit my friends. It had taken me a long time to originally enter the centre. A few years before, a mate had seen through my occasional shakes and had taken me there, thinking it would help.

I was still in denial about my post-traumatic stress disorder. Whenever Deb suggested I get some help, I refused to consider it. These blokes understood. Without having to say anything, they understood my battle with the demons that still haunted me thirty years on. I've been luckier than most, able to keep working and on the surface coping with life.

Most people don't even know I was in Vietnam. It's only at night, or when I hear a helicopter, that I cannot mask the terror. PTSD was slowly becoming accepted. It's the most common mental health disability suffered by Australian veterans and has been diagnosed in one in five soldiers who fought in Vietnam, and in later engagements in East Timor and Iraq.

A lot of people, including our friends, had questioned Deb about why I kept leaving my family. "Is it because he doesn't care about his family, or is he selfish and thinks only about himself and his ambitions?" I knew this was putting more pressure on her, having to explain to others what she was questioning herself. One lady said if I'd been her husband, she would've left me a long time ago, while another said that Deb, David and Michelle must be very understanding to tolerate a husband and father like me.

I couldn't fight about it. We'd already gone through the economic benefits of me taking these postings, and how it would allow us to pay for private school and uni fees, and have some for house improvements. More importantly, I believe that everyone has the right to pursue his or her dreams. I wanted that for my family, and for me. We had long discussions and decided on it as a group, but once the outside world started questioning, it made it hard. I wondered whether Deb was starting to think like the others.

At the airport I hugged them one last time, turned and walked away. *Don't look back.* One more look in their faces and I wouldn't have been able to go. During the long day of flights from Rocky to Gladstone, Brisbane, Melbourne and Hobart, I kept asking myself if it was worth it. I knew I couldn't handle having them see me off in Hobart with the moment of departure dragging on. I wanted the last time I would seem them to be at home in Yeppoon.

***

Once back in Hobart with the Davis crew, I felt more at ease. The next few days were uneventful. It was the calm before the storm.

The morning of departure, November 22, 2002, we boarded the *Aurora Australis* to go through safety procedures before gathering at the Fish Frenzy for a last meal. I took the opportunity to ring Deb, David and Michelle, promising to call again once I'd arrived. I also emptied the newsagency of newspapers. We headed to the ship and checked in our bags while customs checked my passport. Then it was time.

I joined the other Davis and Mawson crew on deck, along with 10 Chinese expeditioners we'd be dropping off at the Chinese base along the way, and 21 members of the Prince Charles Mountains Expedition, Germany and Australia (PCMEGA) program. They were going to join the others already at Davis. The 35-person international geological expedition was passing through Davis on its way further south to the remote and magnificent mountain range 500 kilometres south of Mawson Station.

This program was headed by Rob Easther, who had a long history in Antarctica since joining as a station leader in 1985. He'd be coordinating the operational support for station and field-based science programs, and would help the PCMEGA members as they investigated geological and glaciological histories and past climates in the southern Prince Charles Mountains. Robb Clifton, my old station leader at Macca, was the expedition leader.

On the deck, streamers linked families on the dock with the expeditioners on the ship. I joined Beacon, Sprunky and Gil Barton, and we talked about the weather. It was fine and sunny, and the wind had turned north.

"Let's hope it stays that way in the Great Southern Ocean, hey". All of us had done the passage, and knew what we were facing. I wished I still had the naïve excitement I'd felt before heading to Macca.

We watched as a crew member slipped the line off the bollard. The wind picked up and stretched tight the colourful lines of paper.

"That's it, then."

As the AA slowly pulled out, one girl at the front of the crowd on the dock became hysterical, screaming for her dad, begging him not to go, not to leave her. Streamers broke around her, the ends fluttering down as she continued to cry. It was gut-wrenching to watch. I imagine it was one of the low points in her dad's life. He was one of the tradesmen heading off to Mawson, and as the people got smaller, we could still hear her begging him not to do this.

I had to swallow a lump. I wasn't sure if it was for me or for him. I borrowed Sprunky's mobile. As we headed down the Derwent River, I rang Deb and had a quiet conversation. Conscious of the people around, I couldn't break down and cry, or talk about how much I missed them. I kept the conversation straightforward and talked about the weather and described what I was seeing. I kept telling Deb that if she needed me, to email. I could still be there with them, just not physically. The expeditioners handled the departure in a variety of ways. A few subtly wiped their eyes. My stomach was hollow, filled only with homesickness. This second departure was as hard as the first.

When I returned the mobile to Sprunky, he had a grin on his face. Except for his elderly mother, he had no family on the mainland, and he was excited about his next adventure. He was a true person of the Ice, never comfortable back in Australia. Antarctica was in his blood, and he would wait for the Ice to take him back. I think that's why he goes. Each expedition becomes home, each new expeditioner he lives with on the Ice becomes part of his family. He was heading down with us to refuel the various stations, but would be returning to the mainland afterwards.

The senior communications bloke, Ian Mclean, better known as Evil, came to my room and set up my laptop so I could stay in touch with the family by email. I was grateful. We had to pay for our phone calls, but ANARE subsidised internet usage.

The motion of the ship was constant as she fought with the waves of one of the world's unfriendliest oceans. Looking out the porthole windows, all I could see was grey interrupted by spray. I struggled up onto deck, the AA swaying from side to side. As I started my observations, I heard one of the other expeditioners mumble "Oh, Jesus" at a particularly violent smack when we hit the bottom of a wave. Quiet nervous laughter broke through mumbled conversations. The bridge was quite crowded, people coming up to get a good look at where we were going. They were standing, legs spread and braced, holding onto whatever solid piece of ship was available.

Before seasickness claimed me again, I joined the others in the mess where a training officer went over navigation. People were spread over the charts, compasses in hand, practicing. Out of the porthole, the seas were massive - blue slashed with angry white. As the AA swayed, the glass would go under water, give us a glimpse of sky before being claimed again by the sea. Everyone was hanging on, and as the lesson continued, the waves became more violent. Charts and compasses started falling to the floor as we clung to the bolted tables. Some apples and oranges had spilt out of a bowl and rolled back and forth with each wave. We were laughing, but never so much that we let go.

"Bit of rocking going on here," I heard. Talk about an understatement. I headed back to my bunk, holding onto the railings mounted on the walls and getting a few steps between each wave. As I vomited into the toilet, all I could think was "that's it".

There are three stages to seasickness. At first you feel it. Then you feel you're going to die. Then you feel you want to die, but can't.

I wasn't able to leave my bunk (known as bat caves as they didn't have any portholes) for a few days except for short periods. The bathroom was my new best friend, and I couldn't bear to be separated. I knew this was how I'd react and had loaded up with seasickness tablets, but they didn't help. For the next few days, I was in real danger of dehydration. I couldn't keep anything down. Dr John Cadden, "Cad", Davis's doctor and acting ship doctor, brought me dry biscuits and eventually gave me an injection to try and counter the dehydration. Nothing helped.

I didn't like being stuck in the bat cave. The lack of space was claustrophobic. Heading down the hallway towards my cabin always gave me the creeps.

During this time, I'd lie on my back on my bunk thinking of home and the 12 months I'd be at Davis. I had strange dreams, broken only by nightmares. They kept repeating themselves, time not moving, kind of a Groundhog Day meets Southern Ocean Hell.

Fire Support Base Julia, Vietnam

The pit holes, roughly 5 feet deep by 3 feet wide, were already dug, but needed overhead protection. I laid three iron poles across the top of the pit holes and covered these with iron sheeting to the corner of the hole, leaving a gap at one end just big enough to slide my body down. On top went two layers of filled sandbags and a tent sheet held by iron pickets. Still, it was better than FSB Jillian, where there were no pit holes. I was given an empty ammunition box for my bunk, which I could enter either head or feet first, but once inside only had enough room to turn on my side.

Sleep is broken, a couple of snatched hours in between clearing patrols, gun pit or Signal Centre duties, guns firing day and night, choppers coming and going all day and flares being set off all night. One night something wakes me and I listen intently. Torchlight reveals a fist-sized scorpion sitting at the end of the pit hole, and I scramble outside, chancing the VC and sleep on the top of the hole instead.

The VC preferred the dark cover of night to attack, and I'd peer out through the small hole in my pit as flares were ignited and tracer bullets lit up the sky. Loud cracks and booms would erupt as our armoured tanks and gun pits returned fire. Nerves would fray as the fights dragged on. On calm nights, sleep was troubled as my body was in full fight mode waiting for the attacks.

The food on the AA was brilliant and I was pissed off as all I could eat was Jatz biscuits and grapes. Beacon kept bringing me in water. I knew I was bad when Jeremy Smith, the Davis station leader, came to see me and said, "Dave, I reckon you'd be the only person on this ship who's losing weight".

Cad was a great help, visiting me a couple of times a day for the four days I couldn't leave my bunk to see how I was coping, poking me with more injections to counter the dehydration. He hinted at my nightmares, no doubt having been told by my cabin mates. I told him a bit just that I did suffer from them. He alluded to Vietnam, but that was it. Like every other time, I'd handle this like I'd always done, simply pretending it wasn't happening.

Gerbil came by, but this time he didn't mention my legs. He did, however, sum up perfectly how I felt: "Mate, seasickness makes everything you do an effort. You just don't feel like doing anything."

My laptop was my saviour in this time. I emailed my family daily, asking for news from the real world. Emails flew back and forth, and it was a blessing to have that to keep my mind occupied.

On day seven, the seas improved slightly. Winds were 30-40 knots, and the seas were above five metres in five to six metre sets. Believe it or not, that was good. I was able to eat my first meal in several days, devouring the roast turkey and vegetables we had to celebrate America's Thanksgiving Day.

A week later, I took my first walk back onto the bridge and the open deck, though I kept getting sick. The next day we saw our first iceberg. We were down far enough in the Great Southern Ocean now and close to our destination. Word spread, and everyone climbed out of their bunks and onto the deck, video cameras capturing the moment. At the beginning of the trip, we'd run a competition to guess the date and time the first iceberg would be spotted. All the expeditioners and crew threw their names in, but it was Martin Crowe, the other forecaster going in with Lance Cowled, who won. He'd guessed the 30th at 8am, and he was right on the money.

That night I saw my first decent iceberg up close. That was probably the moment that cemented where I really was. You can research, study and pore over books all you want, but the moment you realise you're really doing it is awe-inspiring. And it made all my misery worthwhile.

On the Sunday morning I was shadowing Beacon every three hours doing weather observations, interrupted by an emergency ship drill. I had to break to report to Jeremy and Cal (deputy station leader) in their cabin for an assessment, and we talked about the training in Hobart and Bronte Park, and the voyage so far. I assessed okay, and was starting to feel a bit more human. They told me once I got to Davis, I'd be one of the last to go out for field training as the summer scientists would have to leave the base first.

The next few days were busy as I took turns filling in for the other blokes who'd taken my shifts when I was sick. We finally reached the sea ice around 8pm on December 2nd, and the seas became calm.

Currents in the Southern Ocean circulate from west to east, with no land to interrupt the flow, helping to circulate the world's water. There are distinct bands surrounding Antarctica. Two of the most important are the Subantarctic, leading into the Polar Front, which encircles the continent between latitudes 40°S and 60°S. This massive flow of the Circumpolar Current is driven by some of the strongest winds on earth, making the largest waves. Sailors called the southern latitudes the 'Roaring Forties', the 'Furious Fifties' and the 'Screaming Sixties', for good reason. However, once we hit the ice pack, the sea started calming and the passage became more bearable.

Snow was falling, and icebergs surrounded us. The AA was starting to push through some ice, though it wasn't solid. I was fascinated by the sight of the ice being broken and pushed aside by the ship, and the light blue it took on under the water. The ocean was starting to become clogged with white chunks, and I spent as much time as I could watching them. It was another world. A leopard seal lay on an ice floe, lazily watching as the AA passed. I wondered how many other ships he'd seen before, and was intrigued by how calm he was. Icebergs now looked like massive land masses. More and more people were visiting the bridge, everyone waiting for a spectacular crack that would mean an iceberg was breaking up. At night the ship would switch on a massive searchlight to help try and avoid any large 'bergs.

Jeremy called us into the mess that afternoon for a station meeting and outlined what we could expect, and what we'd be expected to do, once we arrived at Davis.

The next day I joined the rest of the expeditioners on the trawler deck for the traditional 60-degree "South Crossing the Antarctica Circle" initiation. All virgins who'd never crossed the line were forced to front King Neptune (Beacon, fierce with his red beard framed by long fake yellow hair), Queen Neptune (deputy voyage leader Louise Crossley) and their two pirate helpers. One by one King Neptune would call us up, and the pirates, shirtless and painted green, would force us to kneel, pick up a rotten fish, which we had to offer to the sky before kissing it. Then they'd smear Vegemite through our hair and on our faces, much to the cheers of the onlookers. Gradually, the crowd became one big, Vegemite-smeared, fish-smelling mass. Once we'd all passed the initiation, King Neptune gave us our certificates proclaiming the event:

Let it be known –

That from the salty, salpy depths we stir.

Your ship makes speed, but time is ours.

And all that cross the veil of South

Must stand before the Ocean's Law.

That I, Australis Rex, Ruler of the Southern Ocean and its winds, shall take the right to cast an eye upon all those of sodden feet, who wish to cross the Southern realm, and land on icy shores.

It is declared that Dave Morgan has paid humble and due honour to this passage and is of sound, but watery character. So, if it pleases us that the holder of this certificate be now dubbed a South Polar Sea Dog, to take pride in the brine that will now course through their veins. And that the same South Polar Sea Dog be seen to be a true and trusted salt, respecting all, and will know the snaggletooths and sea devils as friends.

Dated 3/12/2002 on the Good Ship *Aurora Australis*.

I'd sat and watched everyone go through the initiation, but wondered why the odd person slipped away. I found out soon enough. By the time the event was over and I'd made my way back to my cabin for a shower, it seemed everyone else had too. It'd been cold and miserable above decks, and so it was in the shower too. With everyone hitting the showers at the same time, the water pressure on the AA couldn't handle it, and dribbled pitiful amounts of cold water down on me. Six hours later, it'd only heated to lukewarm. Those who'd been previously initiated were laughing.

That night we continued the fundraising with a Shave for a Cure night. Beacon fronted Di Beamish, my Hobart Hospital trainer, who shaved off his beard to the crowd's cheers. He'd had it for 30 years, and spent the night rubbing his chin, looking a different man. I fronted Beacon, who returned the favour by taking off my moustache and putt-putt, which I'd had for 34 years. It was all for a good cause, but all I could think that night when I looked in the mirror was it looked bloody strange.

The next morning, as I lay in my bunk, I could hear the steel hull grinding into the sea ice. We were well into the pack ice. Later we gathered on the trawler deck for a good old-fashioned Aussie barbecue, complete with steak, snags and beer.

As we sat around talking late that night, the AA pulled into Zhong Shan, the Chinese base not far from Davis, getting in as close as possible. Waking up the next morning, we watched as our Chinese friends and supplies were taken to their base by our helicopters. These Chinese expeditioners were the first lot going in, and they'd be joined by the rest coming later on their own ship. I watched one helicopter as it hovered over the ship for a minute and went to test the ice. Gingerly, it descended, its shadow getting bigger until they met. The chopper rested for a moment on the ice, testing the strength in case one of the choppers needed to land in an emergency.

This was my first glimpse of the mainland, and the coastline was stunning. Icebergs framed the area around the base. As I stared at the beautiful, stark sight, I knew I'd finally achieved my dream.

The ship's captain, Captain Peter Pearson, signed and stamped my ANARE Expeditioner Passport with "AA P&O Polar Australia". Mine was number A881, and looked like a real passport, complete with photo. These passports are intended to provide a historical record of ANARE service. The information contained was used by the Australian Antarctica Division as recognition of prior service, training and endorsements. While not legal, they are a great souvenir. I'd missed out on having one for Macca as I didn't know they existed; on the way back from that trip an expeditioner told me about them and I'd made sure to get one for this trip.

The AA was chewing through ice, easily breaking the seemingly solid mass. Behind us was a slash of blue ocean in the white. We continued moving forward, the grinding getting louder. As pieces of ice rolled past, we'd get an idea of their thickness. It was a sunny day, quite pleasant, but I knew the danger the captain would be watching for. If the winds picked up, there was the chance that the ice pack would close behind us, trapping the ship. I offered my face up to the sun for what little warmth it could offer.

As we got nearer, I couldn't focus on anything but the view the contrast of the white against the light blue sky, dark blue sea and high cloud cover. Everything was layers of blue or white, and contrasts of hard jagged icebergs and soft snow peaks.

More excited than I was, if that was possible, was Di Beamish. She'd always wanted to go to Antarctica. ANARE had asked her if she wanted to see what was in the hospital at two of the bases. She'd jumped at the chance to go to Davis and Mawson. We'd talked during the voyage about our dreams and what drew us down there, and she later gave me a letter that explained what she was feeling.

For Dave Morgan (5/12/02)

For 12 years I have seen ANARE men and women come to Royal Hobart Hospital to participate in the two-week operating assistant course.

The vast majority of these men and women are fun-loving, interesting modern-day explorers who seek new and interesting experiences, simply because they can.

I was invited as a round tripper to join Voyage 2 on the Aurora Australis *to enable me to visit Mawson and Davis Stations and evaluate the station operating theatres. To be on the ship for 2 weeks with 106 comparative strangers was to be a challenge, I thought. It has turned out to be a delight.*

The expeditioners and crew come from every imaginable walk of life, yet they have common traits. They are all expert in their particular field of work – botanists, carpenters, chefs, scientists, helicopter pilots, meteorologists. The list is as varied as our imagination.

The voyage is about friendship, camaraderie, patience, consideration of others, and having fun and enjoying new experiences. The voyage has been one of the most wonderful experiences of my life, never to be forgotten. The voyage will be re-lived by me for years to come.

The beauty of the Southern Ocean is almost beyond description. The friendship of 106 strangers, living together on the Orange Roughy, is almost beyond comprehension.

There will be a handful of people on the voyage who have become life friends. Dave is one of them.

I'd met this lady with apprehension, trusting her to give me the skills I needed to overcome my decades-old phobias, but when I said goodbye to her, I said goodbye to a mate.

The AA had to get in within a certain distance so that the fuel line could resupply the tanks. She had to force her way into thicker ice, ramming in until defeated, reversing and attacking again. The base was clearer now and I could see the communications ball and the different buildings, all brightly painted in various colours. All Australian stations are colour-coded.

"Here he goes, here he goes," someone cried as the captain again throttled forward, the hull clanging through the virgin ice. The crack of the ice countered the excited "oohs", people pointing as a line appeared in the ice, snaking its way forward. With a final clang, the AA stopped, solid ice surrounding all but the bow. We were there.

CHAPTER 9
SOUTHERN EXPOSURE

December 2002 weather details:

Max temp 7.5°C, min -5.8°C, monthly average -0.3°C

Maximum wind gusts 66 knots (122 kilometres per hour)

Average daily sunshine 9.0 hours.

I stood on the ice pack, staring at the brightly coloured buildings in the distance - my home for the next year. The scene was breathtaking. With the AA's engines off, the wind whistled eerily after the violent crushing of the ice pack getting in. I was standing on solid sea ice in Prydz Bay, gripped with a heady mix of exhilaration and isolation.

Davis station sits on the edge of the Vestfold Hills, one of the largest ice-free areas on the continent, an area of approximately 400 square kilometres of low hills broken by valleys and deep fjords and lakes. Those hills isolate the station from the icy plateau and the Sørsdal Glacier, protecting it from the icy blizzards the other Australian bases regularly experienced. The crispness of the air made everything seem sharper, and the icebergs in the distance, frozen in place by the sea ice, looked like mountains.

We were lucky enough to have been able to dock against a hard ice edge, still thick and strong enough to bear the weight of heavy vehicles, which would make for an easy resupply. The annual deterioration of the sea ice varies from year to year, and the summer resupply can be a gamble.

I watched vehicles inch their way across the ice to start transferring our gear to the base. Two penguins took off at top speed to get away from the monsters, and I grinned as they stopped and looked back before waddling off again, negotiating the little bumps on the surface.

Expeditioners, including the 21 members of PCMEGA joining their team, and visitors who were either going on to the next stop at Mawson or who were returning to Hobart, wanted to get ashore and have a look around, but that night we had to satisfy ourselves with stretching our legs on the ice. Vehicles drove in to the base loaded with cargo, then returned to the AA with rubbish to be taken back to Australia. A hose more than a kilometre long was laid on the ice surface to pump 622,500 litres of fuel to the bulk fuel farm tanks.

It was already an hour that would've been dark in Australia. Here, with the 24-hour summer sunlight, the resupply continued, and I knew it would take me some time to get my brain to recognise my body's natural cycle rather the unnatural brightness.

Before I went to sleep, I studied the landscape, scarcely believing that I was on the Ice. I'd been waiting for this for a long time. The majesty of the jutting icebergs fascinated me; their strength wouldn't be diminished by the thaw but would only be framed by blue instead of white. In the distance I could see two white crosses on another island's skyline. Those crosses, on Anchorage Island, two kilometres from the station, mark the memories of two men who died while working on Davis.

On October 28, 1995, the Department of Housing and Construction foreman working on the rebuilding project at Davis, Stephen Bunning, was badly burned when an explosion occurred while he was spraying sealant inside a storage tank. His injuries were so severe that the Americans took a risk with their LC130 Hercules and its crew, sending it from McMurdo to a hastily-built landing strip on the sea ice by Davis. Unfortunately, Stephen died of his injuries during the evacuation. The prominent bare hill which comprises the entire southern end of Gardner Island, four kilometres from the station, was named Bunning Hill in his memory.

The other cross marks the memory of Martin Davies, an archaeologist who died at Davis Station on November 25, 1995. Martin died in a cliff fall while taking an evening walk in the Vestfold Hills. Days before his death, he'd been part of a successful expedition that rediscovered the flagpole left in 1935 by Norwegian Caroline Mikkelsen, the first woman to visit, and land on, Antarctica.

She'd done so in a small bay now known as Tryne Island at the northern end of the region on February 20, 1935 with her husband Karius, captain of the tanker *Thørshaven*. Karius named the region the Vestfold Hills because of its resemblance to the province of Vestfold, south of Oslo in Norway. He also named a mountain in the region after her; Mount Caroline.

The party raised the Norwegian flag on an improvised flagpole and built a rock cairn to mark the site. This cairn was found by ANARE expeditioners in 1960 but was lost for many years until its rediscovery in 1995. Mrs Mikkelsen was still alive at the time and received word of the rediscovery of the original flag pole.

Unfortunately, since my time at Davis, a third man has also died there. Gold Coast building tradesman Peter Orbansen was found dead at the base on November 19, 2005, less than a fortnight after his arrival. A third cross now marks his memory.

Hope everything goes well. Excited, I was also aware of the power of Mother Nature, and after the voyage to get here, could appreciate the isolation.

The next morning, I gathered a small bag of essentials I'd keep with me for the next few days. Since the old expeditioners would still be in their rooms until the AA left, they'd made up beds for us in the comms room. Our gear was offloaded and brought to a storage shed. We were only allowed to bring essentials with us.

Cathie, Beacon and I walked the kilometre to the base where we found the Met building and the blokes we'd be replacing. I was working with Paul Wilson, watching as he showed me the ropes. The Met building was an AANBUS (insulated colourbond laminate) module container hut, built between 1984 and 1987, and was quite cosy.

That night, around 10.30pm, with the sun still shining, I stumbled towards the comms room ready to collapse into bed. There were tents everywhere and beds set up army-style in any available space. Davis is a busy station, with about 70 people during the summer season, and this overlap period stretched accommodation to the limit, although the new summerers were only going to be at the station for a day or two until they started their work in the field.

Walking through the bunks, I found my bed, or rather, the nicely made up frame. Some bastard had knocked off my mattress. Outgoing station leader Michael Carr helped me search, but it was gone. As winterers waiting until we could move into our rooms, we'd been given bunks with mattresses. Some of the summer expeditioners had blow-ups. It looked like one of those summerers had decided my mattress looked better than his. Michael said it'd probably been dragged off to one of the tents. He was really upset, but I didn't care. All I wanted was to curl up, and when I finally could, on a squeaky blow-up, I wished whoever was sleeping on my beautiful mattress a good night.

***

The re-supply period is chaotic, with everyone working long hours. Beacon went to Samson Island to provide Met reports for the helicopters resupplying the island. I kept dueling with Paul, working from 5.15am until 10.15pm. Michael officially welcomed us, told us the station rules and advised us not to be stressed by all activity. He warned us that the mess was stretched to its limits and to quickly get in and get out at meal times. Socialising could come later.

I was having trouble sleeping. The glare from outside was unbelievable. We had to pull down the blinds to try to make some darkness. My body still wasn't handling the continuous sunshine, and each morning I'd drag myself out of bed to tackle what felt like another never-ending day.

After a few days, the tractors and trucks stopped travelling the ice highway, and the sense of calm indicated the AA would soon be leaving for Mawson.

Mawson Station, named for the Australian explorer Douglas Mawson, who reached the South Pole with Shackleton's expedition, was Australia's first continental station and is the oldest continuously inhabited Antarctic station below the Antarctic Circle. It lies on an isolated outcrop of rock on the coast in MacRobertson Land, at the edge of the Antarctic plateau. Douglas Mawson first spotted the coast and mountains of MacRobertson Land from the ship *Discovery* during the British, Australian, and New Zealand Antarctic Research Expedition (BANZARE) of 1929-1931. The site for the station was chosen in 1954 by Dr Phillip Law for the large natural harbour (Horseshoe Harbour) and permanent exposed rock, and the station was built in 1955.

Before the Mawson expeditioners could start their journey, we needed to gather in the mess for the handover ceremony. Michael Carr handed over the responsibility of the running of the station to Jeremy Smith, and outgoing winterers were presented with medals for their service. After handshakes and toasts, we gathered at the edge of the sea ice and said our final goodbyes as the AA pulled out. This time it was us holding the red smoke flares and farewelling the expeditioners in the Antarctic tradition. The PCMEGA people left over several days by a Twin Otter piloted by a Canadian crew.

Once I finally got access to my room, I spent hours cleaning as the previous tenant hadn't had much time to do any before leaving. I was lucky to have a room on the coast side, with a brilliant view of the islands and the sea out my window. I tried to send an email to my family but couldn't get it to work. Sean Wicks (Wixy) took my laptop to the comms workshop and found I had a faulty cable. He gave me a new network cable and I was relieved to be connected. I surfed for some news and touched base with home. It was slower than I was used to back in the mainland, but amazingly efficient.

The facilities were better than at Macca: two big washers, several dryers and a heated room next door if you preferred to hang your clothes to dry. These were always being used and, just like at public laundromats, you'd often return to find someone had taken your clothes out and piled them beside the machine.

Beacon and I started dueling the next day. I was teaching Beacon his duties. As we tried to release a balloon, a wind eddy whipped the radiosonde into the shed, pushing the balloon too close to the door and bursting it in spectacular fashion. It was a lot harder to release balloons at Davis as the instant the doors were opened, the wind pushed us back. Obviously we'd have to refine our balloon-releasing skills here. Beacon and I weren't very good.

We released two weather balloons each day. Each one carried aloft a radiosonde that transmitted back temperature, air pressure, humidity and wind speed and direction as it ascended through the atmosphere. This information was collected and analysed, then sent via satellite to Melbourne where it was forwarded around the world to those who were interested in the atmosphere above Davis. We also took three-hourly synoptic observations that consisted of the surface conditions, cloud observations, visibility and any weather phenomena at the time. Turbidity readings were taken on days of direct sun from September through to late April.

Unlike the anxiety I'd felt going into Macca, learning the new routine at Davis was a fairly straightforward and relaxed curve. Partly it was due to the experience I'd had at Macca, but more than that was going in under an OIC, especially Beacon.

Though he was the boss and the Senior Met Observer, my seniority at the Bureau on the mainland didn't faze him one bit. He didn't care two hoots, and he said it meant he had a ready-made replacement for whenever he was to be away from the station. Like Gerbil, he's a larrikin and started a new tradition at Davis – Beacon awards. These were given once a month to fellow expeditioners for "deeds nefarious, grandiose, insane, foolish, kind and heroic, or any other reason Beacon may from time to time deem worthy".

I also spent time with the two forecasters working the summer season, Martin Crowe and Lance Cowled. They'd be working fulltime (5am until 7 or 8 at night) to assist the helicopters and light aircraft plan their movements.

With the departure of all the extra expeditioners on the AA, the station lightened somewhat but was still packed at Friday night drinks or Saturday night socials. With more than 70 people, everywhere I turned I'd bump into someone. Most were Australian but there were some expeditioners from Britain, Germany, Canada, Holland, New Zealand and the USA.

We also had visitors from the *Kapitan Khlebnikov* when she pulled in and brought ashore 60 tourists and nearly as many staff and crew who, for four hours, visited various areas around the base. They were undertaking a circumnavigation of the Antarctic continent, beginning and ending in New Zealand. I showed some through the Met office and spoke at length to an ex-Met bloke from the United States Navy. Between my travels through America and Met stuff, we had lots to talk about. "I wish I had the chance to spend 12 months down here," he drawled in his thick American accent, and as I watched the KK leave that evening and disappear behind the icebergs, I hoped he found what he'd come looking for.

The hydroponics team of Jeff, Cad, Malcolm, Beacon, Tony, Nanette, Chad, Paula, Jim, Paul, Jeremy and me started pulling out the old set-up and started again from scratch.

We planted seedlings in the new set-up, establishing a supply of lettuce, tomatoes, cucumbers, snow peas, chillies (a favourite for our chilli beer), basil, parsley, sage, nasturtiums and smaller amounts of bok choy, zucchini, eggplant, celery, spinach, capsicum and shallots. These would become even more important once our resupply of fresh veggies was exhausted, and if we didn't get a good start now, we'd be in trouble as we'd be running out of veggies and growing a new batch wouldn't be an easy task.

Though it was summer, snow had started falling mid-month and we recorded 0.8cm of snow in the gauge. Then the first 50-knot winds arrived, forcing me to struggle with the balloon release. Not only was the wind fierce, but it was throwing snow at me and while not graceful, I did manage to release it without it exploding. In between, I raced to the mess and grabbed some pizza for dinner before holding a radio sked with the nearby Chinese base. Twice daily we received weather observations and ozone readings from our Chinese colleagues at Zhong Shan and we'd input these into our communication network on their behalf.

Davis Station limits were from the southern shore of Heidemann Bay, Station Tarn, the transmitters to the southern point of Trigwell Island and to the northern point of Anchorage Island. From there they extend to the northern point of Gardner island and from the southern point of that island to Torckler

Rocks, and to the point at the entrance of Heidemann Bay. Any further than that and we'd have to carry our survival gear, which I picked up from Chris Gallagher (Psycho) that afternoon.

The fire drill was the same routine as on Macca - let someone know if you leave the station perimeters and turn your tag over at the muster point located in the hallway by the mess/kitchen and lounge/bar area, and a slab of beer on the bar if you start a false alarm. Apparently there'd been an incident during summer where one of the PCMEGA blokes slept through the fire alarm and had to be found and woken up.

***

Jeremy approached me a few days before Christmas, offering me a jolly (the Antarctic term for an excursion off the station, more for pleasure than for work). We needed ice for the upcoming Christmas and New Year's drinks, so we needed to collect pure virgin ice from the plateau.

My stomach tightened as I approached the helipad, the *thunk-thunk* of the low, heavy chopper blades vibrating up my legs. The trip to the ship at Macca hadn't been too bad, and I kept drawing deep breaths to slow my racing heart. *I can do this.*

We climbed in behind pilot Ward and as the chopper started its graceful lift, I focused on the window and as my panic started to clear, took in my first big-picture view of the station. A moonscape is the nearest description of the area surrounding our home no vegetation, dry, endless black rocks and cliffs. The chopper headed inland towards the plateau, and turquoise crystal clear lakes dotted through the rocks. We crossed into the Continental Ice Plateau, and where it joined the rock, pressure of the icepack had cracked the ice into "icefalls" with thousands of massive blue fingers of deep crevasses as far as we could see.

This was a region that would be impossible to cross on foot, and I knew if the chopper had to put down we'd be hard-pressed to find a safe area. Gradually the crevasses became fissures, then solid ice and the pilot warned us we wouldn't have much time a storm was coming and it was near enough to be a concern. He set us down and we hopped out, gathering chainsaw, picks and a crowbar and we negotiated the terrain on our crampons.

The chainsaw was supposed to do all the work for us, but we couldn't get the bloody thing to work. Normally we could've taken more time with it, but as it kept refusing to start and with the pilot keeping an eye on the sky, we resorted to picks to try and break out blocks of ice.

The featureless ice sheet stretched as far as I could see, though it wasn't as white as I'd expected, instead coloured with a slightly blue tinge. It was hard, frustrating work trying to pry out the ice. After we managed to break apart a piece, we'd take turns carrying it to the chopper. I was puffing heavily as I carried them back and heaved them into the rear seats of the chopper. Ironically, in the last few minutes we had left, we got the chainsaw going and managed to cut some decent chunks.

"Come on," Ward said, pointing at the sky. "Time to wrap this up. It's too dangerous to stay."

We'd worked up quite a sweat packing the chopper full, and as we rose I had to grin at the view below, and at the ice piled up beside me. This holiday period I'd be sitting down to a civilised drink, kept cool by pure almost virgin ice, something I definitely hadn't experienced before. We were about 10 minutes ahead of the storm front and as we crossed back over the glacier's crevasses and left the plateau behind, the Vestfold Hills' moon-like rocks started breaking through the white.

The station drew nearer, and we flew over the communications dome and various buildings as we headed to the helicopter pads. The choppers stay at Davis only for the summer season; they're brought in on the first ship to move scientists around for the season's projects, and they get loaded up to return to Australia on the last voyage.

***

Christmas morning greeted us with stark black rocks lightly hidden by falling snow. I rang Deb and the kids and, for a few minutes, lost myself in the familiarity of my other life. As always, special occasions intensified the feelings of homesickness, of being far away from them. I listened to their plans for the day and knew that mine would be very different.

And it was. During the morning the Davis Choir sang a range of Christmas carols before Santa's procession arrived on quad bikes. Reindeers led the way as we cheered, wind buffeting their green felt antlers and white chemical suits, and elves dressed in yellow overalls huddled and tried to keep their balance as they were pulled along behind.

Once inside the mess, Santa (Mark Maxwell) apologised that his suit hadn't arrived from the North Pole, and he stripped his parka to reveal red thermal underwear, complete with Lil' Abner flap. A skinnier Santa had never been seen, and as he sat down with a big "Aaahhh" and patted the arms on his chair, he asked, "Ok, who's the first kiddie to come and sit on my knee?"

Many of us received packages from home. Families had been able to secretly mail packages marked "Christmas" to ANARE in Tasmania, who'd organised them to come on the AA and then Jeremy had hidden them until today.

My twin brother Don and his family had sent a book on Shackleton and my family had sent a couple of packages. Beacon's wife Margaret had sent me a beanie with the BoM logo on it and my Secret Santa had given a framed photo of me standing outside the Davis Met office. I tried to remember anyone who could've taken it but couldn't. My second gift didn't give any further clues, though it would end up being a great joke for months. I unwrapped a 2003 Busty Babes calendar and amid much laughter, opened it up so we could check out Miss January. I decided then to never look ahead so that each Babe could be another surprise, and it caught. People started trying to guess what the next month's model would be like and came by after I'd flipped a page to check. Sometimes I'd wait until midnight at the end of the month to turn over the page. (Miss August ended up being my favourite, though Miss March was pretty good).

We burst out laughing when Beacon unwrapped his Secret Santa gift. Someone had taken his nickname literally and created a real beacon for him a red flashing light mounted on an orange safety helmet, complete with several battery packs mounted on a belt. He wandered around the mess, flashing, the orange helmet clashing with his red hair.

The meal, prepared by Gerbil and summer chef Meredith, was once again outstanding. I enjoyed the meal immensely, talking with various people. I couldn't relax too much though, as I still had to release an evening flight and needed my wits about me.

It was a quieter Christmas than at Macca, and I was grateful the dreaded Wheel of Humiliation had been left behind. I didn't think anyone was ready for another Dave Morgan strip dance.

***

The next day, I went with Cathie on a tour of the fire building. The fire team had done their training at the Cambridge Tasmanian Fire Training Centre prior to arrival at Davis, and went through various scenarios of crawling through burning or smoke-filled buildings, looking at clothing flammability and lots of practice with hoses, water and pumps.

No one had been keen on being Fire Chief, a role which ended up going to Cathie. Sean Wicks and Dave Power were her deputies, and they were all under the co-ordination of station leader Jeremy Smith and deputy station leader Cal Young. I was an acting BA controller, expected to turn into a full-time controller whenever one of the full-timers went off station. Like at Macca, I'd control air usage and times in the event of emergencies.

Along the way, Cathie also showed me "Fort Knox" – the secret storage (secure storage anyway) of all the drinks and chocolates. These were strictly rationed, and a constant bane for some. I wasn't much of a chocolate-lover so when I'd receive my ration, expected to last a month, I'd put it away.

Others, such as Jim Milne, were such chocoholics that try as they might, their rations would be gone in the first week and for the rest of the month they'd be scrounging. I'd know when he'd be bad, the look of longing on his face as he'd find me: "You don't have any chocolate, do you Dave …?" The pleading would be too much and I'd have to hand over my preserved pile.

I also was helping out in the brewery as we got various batches underway. The home brew club would meet once a week for a brew night, because of shiftwork, I'd end up helping out about once a fortnight. We all had different strengths Wixy and Mr Evil (Ian McLean) experimented with different combinations, one of the best results being the chilli beer, made with our own hydroponic chillies. By the end, when we were on full swing, we made a total of 5.2 tonnes of alcohol 1.6 of draught, 1 of lager, 0.36 of stout and 0.18 of cider, 0.48 of ginger beer, 0.8 of black and tan and 0.78 of special.

The old BoM building was pulled down by the chippies to be returned to Australia. Jim, Jeff Becker and Michael K were taking advantage of calmer days to dismantle various parts of the old Davis station, some of which had been built in 1957 and abandoned 20 years before I got there. The oldest parts were being left for now, but the more recent additions were being removed before they could disintegrate and blow away. They'd be loaded up on the end-of-summer voyage and be returned for preservation in a Hobart museum.

Then I finally came down with the dreaded Davis flu. One problem with visiting ships is they can often bring unwanted viruses and bacteria, and a particularly nasty strain of flu had arrived with us on the AA and gradually spread throughout the station. I'd watched everyone else come down with it and had thought I'd managed to avoid it, but it finally caught up with me. My throat was red raw, and coughing was painful. New Year's Eve I was in the worst of it headache, running nose. Out of ten, I had to rate myself zero but forced myself out of bed late that night to join the evening's activities.

The New Year was going to be celebrated in Davis-style, with a D Theme Party: "Please be dere for dinner den drinks den donga disco darlings. Da theme is D so dress down, dirty, doll up or do drunk dribble dancing. Delightful dull dude or dead delicious, demented devil or dashing duck do do". Say no more. When I managed to haul myself down to the mess shortly before midnight, the place was alive with a variety of doctors, Draculas, a devil and dentist, some dominoes and dice, many Dalmatian dogs, a dingo, a dominatrix, a Danish Viking, a drug dealer (and a drug addict), several diesel mechanics, a daisy, a deity, several drag queens (of course), a district nurse and a couple of dorks dancing to the live band. I was feeling so bad I didn't dress up, instead going only as Dave. I managed to cheer in the count of midnight and have a few drinks before leaving the fun behind to crawl back into bed.

CHAPTER 10
FIELD TRAINING WITH A VIEW

January 2003 weather details:
Max temperature 9.2°C, min -2.2°C, monthly average 1.9°C
Maximum wind gusts 61 knots (113 kilometres per hour)
Average daily sunshine 11.2 hours.

Days were, for the most part, fresh and crystal clear and temperatures cool without being cold. The sea ice was gradually disappearing from the front of the station, and as it thinned and melted, it'd break up and blow away. Each day further fragments broke and floated out, though sometimes they'd drift back to the beach, occasionally with penguins along for the ride.

Mid-month, the sea ice had melted far enough to leave clear water to the islands a few kilometres away, allowing boating activities to start. Each calm day or evening, boat trips were organised; some were for work purposes and others just for fun, a chance to photograph icebergs and penguins.

One night I lined up for an iceberg tour, and hopped in with Jeremy and Martin in one of the station's Zodiacs. Curtis, Lance and Sam were in the obligatory second Zodiac. It was a clear and sunny night, absolutely perfect, and as we left the station's shore, the daylight put sparkles in the water. We were rugged up against the cold but the movement of the boat make the temperature seem colder against any exposed skin, down to about -15°C.

For several hours we weaved around these beasts, each as individual as only the imagination could provide. Icebergs aren't made of frozen salt water but are the result of snow falling on the continental ice sheet, which accumulates and compresses over years as the ice sheet flows towards the sea. Once at the edge, the ice spills into the water when a glacier calves or floats on the ocean surface as an ice tongue or massive ice shelf.

We had to keep our distance as the well-known expression "just the tip of the iceberg" took on a realistic meaning. With less than 10 per cent of an iceberg visible above water, they are inherently unstable as they constantly melt above and below the water's surface, and get eroded by waves and wind. Smaller icebergs become top-heavy as they melt underwater and can roll when their equilibrium shifts, while larger icebergs can collapse into many pieces, creating large waves.

As we passed through ice floes, penguins stood on their ice rafts and watched us pass. We passed a tabular berg – an iceberg with a flat top and sheer sides. These can be enormous, sometimes hundreds of kilometres across, with an even bigger area underwater.

The jagged peaks and ice caves left behind after an iceberg rolls caught my imagination the most. We slowed beside one with two green peaks, the unusual colour caused by organisms captured within the ice layers. The green really stood out against the stark whiteness of other icebergs and the blue of the ocean. We passed slowly alongside icicles hanging down from one berg, the two boats manoeuvring so we could stretch and touch the drops falling down their lengths.

As we paused by yet another one, I was filming with my video camera when we heard a loud dreaded crack. It was just what we'd been trying to avoid, and Jeremy immediately floored the engine to escape. Martin and I flew backwards into the bottom of the boat, but in that crucial moment I had the presence only to cushion my machine and my good sunglasses went flying into the drink. Talk passed between the two boats that it may have moved and I heard one person mutter: "Don't trust these bastards". We paused a safe distance away, engines idling, and waited and waited. It refused to roll and we finally had to give up and leave.

Even though it was after midnight when we got back to the station, we still had to wash the boat and put away gear. I hopped into the Ute to reverse the trailer to the Zodiac. I didn't have much experience at reversing trailers but learned quickly, and I felt pretty good when I managed on the first try.

***

Mid-month, I had to pass a navigation walk through the Vestfold Hills as part of my field training. Gerbil had been named search and rescue leader with nearly half the wintering party members of the team, but we all had to go and learn field survival and comfort, navigation, quad driving, snow climbing, crevasse rescue and field first aid.

I was yet to go and do my main training as others needed to get off the station and they were a higher priority. A group of us Gil Barton, Wixy, Dave Power, trainer Psycho and I set off at 9am from base and had to navigate using a compass and local terrain to Lake Dingle and back, a walk of 14.25 kilometres. We started strong but it wasn't long before blisters formed. I kept shifting my full load as I negotiated the rocks, pebbles and steep hills, and eventually pulled the same calf muscle that I'd injured on Macca. Wixy also pulled a muscle, and the two of us struggled behind the main group, keeping each other company. We finally arrived back at the station about 20 minutes after the main group at 3pm, sore and tired but successful in all our tests.

In between shifts, I found a chance to practice my new-found, but as yet untried, hairdressing skills. Jim and I gave each other haircuts, putting our training to good use, and complemented each other on our skills. Mind you, it *was* pretty easy we'd just given each other crew cuts with the old clippers. After that, I started getting more customers, but never any females. They just didn't trust me, instead going to Cathie who'd brought dye and other items I just didn't understand, so possibly that lack of trust was justified.

The day before I had to head off to field training I visited Dr Cad with stomach pain around the old hernia site which had been aggravated on the navigation walk. He sat down with me for quite a while and then asked if it could be from nerves and worrying too much. He thought it was my fear of choppers, left over from Vietnam, and that I'd been building up knowing I had to head out in one the next day. He was a solid, compassionate man, who was amazed with what I'd been putting up with since I'd returned all those years ago.

He was my next-door neighbour in the accommodation block, and said later that at times he heard me scream in the night. Like Robb Clifton at Macca, I found him easy to talk to and easy to trust. An excellent doctor, he was always open to us for medical, psychological or dental problems, and would give us a regular medical check once a month.

Prior to Antarctica, he'd been sitting drinking a beer in New Zealand with fellow doctors when it occurred to him there was more to medicine than peering down throats and writing scripts in the suburbs. Listening to the other doctors talking about their adventures, practicing medicine in isolated areas, was an inspiration for Cad. As soon as his kids were old enough for uni, he applied for Antarctica, and after a round trip on the AA in 1999, got this posting at Davis.

My emotional state stayed with me the next morning but I took a deep breath and climbed in the chopper, greeting Ward, the pilot. We lifted off, and as we moved further from the station, I was in awe once again as the landscape below changed from dark rock with patches of white and deep rich blue lakes dotted among it all to the sheer white of the ice plateau. As we lowered on the edge of the plateau, Ward quickly checked how I was going. I was okay, but finally relaxed when we set down at Trajer Ridge and started hauling out our gear.

Even though there was a melon igloo satellite cabin, made out of red fibreglass, at Trajer Ridge, we weren't going to use it, instead having to chip the ice with picks to set our tents. The training equipment was waiting for us, having been brought out in the first days of the summer season, slung below helicopters, and which was left there until the last group went through their field training.

That was us. Once again I'd be taught by field training officer Psycho, along with Jim Milne (chippie), Curtis Avenell (sparky), Dave Power (sparky) and Matthew Rooke (summer photographer). The other group included Cathie Saunders, Gil Barton, and Gerbil, and they had their own field leader, Mike Woolridge.

We'd be using quads (Honda TRX300s), four-wheel drive cycles fitted with high-flotation tyres powered by a four-stroke petrol 300cc single cylinder engine. Once everything froze enough during the winter months to support our weight, these would be our ticket to explore the area around the station.

Gradually, I started to anticipate how my machine would react and I opened it up bit by bit as we charged along the ice from base camp onto the plateau. There was nothing to see but white surroundings, stretching out until meeting the blue sky, with only the odd cloud to break the line. Psycho pointed out different features like land formations towards the coast, and how to recognise clear ice. We had to keep an eye out for pot holes and clear ice, crevasses and thin ice.

Clear ice was one of our biggest worries. The quads lost all grip on it. If we were unlucky enough to hit a patch, we had to know how to get ourselves out of the situation. The ice surrounding us had a thin snow layer, wind moulding it into little ridges, and we kept to this.

Learning to travel over different terrain angles was a tense experience until we learned to compensate for the various angles. When driving across slopes, we had to shift our bums on the seat and angle our bodies to the uphill side. Going downhill, we had to shift our bodies backwards and use the rear brake. This motion took some getting used to as any brake used engaged all wheels. Going uphill, we had to lean well forward but remember not to gun it as that could make us flip backwards.

As it became easier to manoeuvre the quad across the land, I started to really enjoy myself. Everything went well until I hit some blue ice. We'd been travelling in a line, Psycho at the front, me at the rear following Jim. I thought I'd catch up with Psycho for a chat, and put the power on to catch up. As I was catching up, the group stopped at the top of the ridge. I realised too late. I sailed past them, over the ridge and down the other side.

I tried to stop, only to realise I had absolutely no control over the quad. On the biggest slippery slide of my life, I watched a drop in the distance come rapidly closer as I tried every which way to pull up my quad. I even contemplated jumping off and letting it sail off ahead.

Luckily I hit a patch of snow layer which helped to bring the quad to a halt, but found myself surrounded by clear ice. Psycho came to my rescue but was struggling to gain control of his own bike. He slid past me, yelling for me to stay where I was and that he'd come and get me. He worked the slide, angling over to a patch of thin snow which gave him the traction he needed to stop.

He started crawling towards me, using his ice pick to grip before each movement. When he reached me, he puffed out that I should do the same use my pick to crawl to his bike and he'd bring mine over. I wasn't wearing any crampons, and as I moved off my bike, I slid off my feet and felt my head slam onto the ice. The bike helmet I was wearing stopped any serious damage, but the thump had been enough that I literally saw stars. I crawled over the ice, clutching the ice pick, and cautiously got on the bike. Thank God for some snow.

"Aim for the white patch," Psycho yelled, pointing to a spot back towards where the others were watching the drama. "Don't do anything else, just aim for there."

Cautiously, I started the quad and did as he said, focusing on the spot. I was concentrating too hard to see how Psycho managed to get enough traction to do the same, but we managed to join the group.

Still shaken and with a throbbing head, I tailed the others to Platcha Hut, happy this time to follow the line. Kettle on and cosy from the cold, we did a radio check to the main base and debriefed on what'd happened. No matter how much you read, it's not until you're actually out there that it sinks in. I'd been extremely lucky. I watched Psycho sipping his cuppa and grinning, wondered how many other times he'd had to do something similar during field training.

After we'd warmed up, Psycho got us to do ice cliff climbs to learn snow and ice techniques. These were gruelling as every movement had to be controlled and gradual. I picked up my ice pick and started my climb. It was slow, each step a dig of the axe into the ice to support the hand, then a kick into the ice with the front picks of the crampon for the feet. I gradually got a rhythm, and slowly inched my way back up the cliff.

We learned how to climb by self-cutting. We were drilled on how to hold the ice axe, with the pick to the rear in the uphill hand, until it became second nature. Holding it this way meant if we ever fell on a slope, we could roll onto our stomachs as we slid, point our feet downhill and drive the pick into the snow to slow ourselves, holding it into the crook of our necks to protect our faces.

A few hours later, exhausted and cold, we climbed back onto the quads and headed to Sprunky's van where we'd be spending the night. We were in dangerous territory with some thin patches of ice around. I was following Jim when we heard a crack, the ice split and I jarred to a stop, sitting in water to my knees. *You have got to be kidding.*

Curtis, who'd been following me, pulled up in time and I saw the look of shock on his face before he climbed off his bike and gathered a rope to throw to me. I tied it on the bike and he used his quad to pull me back out. We could see the others in the distance and, once back on solid ice, we decided to take a longer route around the thin ice to join them. I steered the bike along slowly and wondered what else could happen.

When we caught up, Psycho said it was a good introduction to the afternoon lessons and showed us all how to get quads out, driving his into a thin patch. Working as a team, he showed us how use ropes, spikes and picks to get the quad back out.

He stressed that if it happened for real and someone fell into deep water, we'd have to fight the natural urge to race in to pull them out as we'd likely end up in the water as well. Instead, we had to throw a rope with a loop tied on the end so the injured party could make a noose around his body. We then had to lie down flat, to spread our weight out over the ice, and then pull. We spent the rest of the night practicing getting quads and people out of broken ice.

When we finished it was time to cook and get our bivvy bags ready. Psycho would be staying in the van, but the rest of us had to find ourselves some protection from the wind and bury ourselves into our bags. After watching me struggle all afternoon with my headache, he pulled me aside and offered to let me stay in the hut. I refused but did accept a few Panadol before hunting for a big rock to tuck in behind.

By now nature was calling and we took turns to pick up the dreaded black box, which we carried behind a rock in a vain attempt to get some privacy. Everything we did in Antarctica was dictated by the rule of never leaving anything behind, and that included our toileting. Everywhere we went, we had to carry two things: a can for liquids and a black box for solids. It had to be lightweight and close securely, something I was keen on as the black box sat on the back of my quad when we were moving about.

Jim had told me a story, while not acceptable today, showed how much of an impact we could have on this environment. In the early '70s, he'd been down at one of the bases and had gone behind a rock to do his business. When he returned 20 years later, it was still there, frozen solid. Since then, especially after the 1998 Protocol on Environmental Protection to the Antarctic Treaty (also known as the Madrid Protocol), all human activities have been subject to an environmental impact assessment process. At Davis, liquid waste is acceptable in a tidal crack, which is taken out to sea, but never any solids, which are always burned.

Curtis had chosen the top of the van to set up his bivvy. At that time of the year, the light doesn't fade but the sun does sink towards the horizon, disappearing for about 30 seconds before rising again. The Katabatic winds (coming from the plateau) were blowing 30-plus knots, and I knew it would be a long night.

It was. Not only was it bloody cold and windy, it was uncomfortable breathing in the confined space. The moisture in my breath froze, and icicles formed on my moustache and inside the bivvy bag. Once again I struggled with claustrophobia, but the little crack I left open didn't let in much light, and I managed to sleep in the darkness.

I was stiff from sleeping on rocky ground and couldn't get out and pack up quickly enough the next morning. Psycho made us a special porridge for breakfast before we loaded the quads and headed back for Trajer Ridge, meeting up with the other group at 9.15am and exchanging stories before they headed up to the ice plateau to do their own quad exercises.

We continued with further training, including self-saving while sliding down snow, how to walk in snow and ice, rope work and navigation. Some found the navigation tricky. The magnetic compass was affected by a magnetic variation of about 78 degrees in the area. Between that and taking bearings and finding recognisable features on a map, it made for interesting situations.

Climbing by step-cutting took some practice. In soft snow, we had to forcefully kick each foot into the snow, and then relax into it so the step could be firmed up before we put our full weight onto that foot. We had to learn the slight adaptations needed going up, across or down the surface. On ice, each step would have to be cut in with the pick before the foot could be put down.

We spent the rest of the afternoon practicing rope work, descending into small crevasses and learning how to climb out. If any of us fell into a crevasse for real, away from the station, we'd be useless unless we could get ourselves out. That night I shared a tent with Jim, who snored like a chainsaw.

The next day, our final one of the trip, the other group joined us. We put one of the quads over the ice cliff and, using pulleys and ropes, worked out how to get it back. After lunch and a welcome cup of tea in the Trajer 'melon', we set back out for a session of abseiling over the ice cliff.

We set up an anchor and were testing it before the first person went down when it came undone and exploded over our heads, taking all the ropes. Abseiling was the only way to descend an unsafe steep slope or crevasse. We tied off the rope to a belay so we could climb back up. One by one we took turns at stepping off the edge and lowering ourselves down the cliff. I was halfway down when I made the mistake of looking down. *Shit, this is high.* Still, it was one of the basic skills we'd need to get around during the winter if we went off base. Also, if we crossed crevasses in the coming months, we'd have to rope off and be comfortable getting ourselves or our team members out.

After a radio check back to the main base, we were finished. We packed up our gear and gathered by the helicopters where Gil was preparing slings for the quads. Sling loading can be very dangerous. If the load breaks free, the sling can flick up into the main or rotor blade. As much as we wanted to watch, we had to keep our distance in case the pilot had to suddenly jettison the load soon after lift-off. As we were the last group through for the field training, all the gear would be taken back to the station. The choppers worked for several hours, ferrying all the gear and us back to Davis.

One hot shower later and tucked in my soft bed, mentally and physically tired, I was happy to be home. When I woke after a good sleep in, I spent a few hours drying out my gear. The bivvy bag was the worst all that frozen condensation had been rolled back into it, but eventually everything was set for the next adventure.

***

Australia Day was a good excuse to have an old-fashioned barbecue, surrounded by something all us Australians hold dear: sports. We started with a friendly game of soccer, grouping expeditioners by nationality. Us Aussies were managed by Beacon, while Aldo headed up the 'Rest of the World' mob. We headed to Davis Beach and it was on. I don't think there were any rules. After much laughter, we debated whether the other mob, which scored two goals to our one, should have one of their goals knocked back for fielding 12 players.

We took the debate onto the cricket pitch outside the workshop. This time there was no contest. Much to some of the English expeditioners' disgust, the home side thoroughly thrashed the Rest of the World. Evil, Sharon and Neil had trouble keeping track of the run rate once the Aussie came to bat, cheered on by the crowd who'd gathered on the hill. We had 15-20 per team, so we would take five balls and then retire.

Cricket was followed by spear and haggis throwing, where competitors stood on an empty 44-gallon drum and threw our version of a haggis condoms filled with porridge.

Unfortunately for Gerbil, the fun of Australia Day was to be followed by some sad news. The next day the PCMEGA expeditioners, their project finished, returned to Davis on their Twin Otter aircraft which had a good ski-way on a snow ridge at the edge of the Vestfold Hills.

They'd brought Ming Lee back with them. Now, Ming Lee had decided to come to Davis with Gerbil, but as always, liked to have a bit of fun and had gone out with the German expeditioners on the project. When she came back, she just wasn't the same girl. I don't know what they did to her, but she was wrecked ripped and full of holes. She needed some surgical attention from Paul. An emergency operation later, she came back out to meet us with her new figure. She'd been stuffed with foam, and where before she was soft and pliable, now she was one solid girl. Those Germans must've been kinky blokes.

***

We spent a social evening on the last day of the month at an art show. For the previous two months, artist Steve Eastaugh and video-cameraman Matthew Rooke had been working on projects as part of the humanities program. Steve displayed his Antarctica-inspired art works inside the Davis Communications Satellite Dome and we wandered around sipping wine and eating nibbles while discussing the works.

I ended up buying one of Steve's paintings. His aim had been to "explore themes of human perception and depiction of the geographic world", and his painting of the BoM building had caught my eye. He'd used a piece of wood from the old Davis station, jagged to represent an iceberg, and had painted the blue building within, complete with icebergs in the distance and the dark Vestfold Hill rock in the foreground. I don't know much about art, but this was so unusual and was, after all, where I'd spent so much of my time. I decided that it should come home with me to Australia.

Outside, Antarctica was starting to hint at what was in store. Winds were gusting up to 61 knots, which at sea would be considered a violent storm on the Beaufort scale. I stayed indoors as often as practical, although I had to venture out to take weather readings in between my slushy duties. We all knew winter was closing in.

CHAPTER 11
FIRST OZONE LAUNCH FOR DAVIS

February 2003 weather details:
Max temperature 6.6°C, min −5.9°C, monthly average 0.2°C
Maximum wind gusts 71 knots (132 kilometres per hour)
Average daily sunshine 3.8 hours

We had our first medical emergency. The station received a call from a nearby Chinese ship, where one of the crew had fallen and suffered suspected broken ribs. He was brought in by Chinese helicopter and rushed to the medical building, where Jim and I were scrubbing up.

We helped Dr Cad with X-rays. He diagnosed that the bloke didn't have broken ribs, just a lot of serious bruising. Late that afternoon, Dr Cad cleared him of any severe medical complications and gave him tablets for the pain, and he was taken back to the chopper and his ship.

From our limited conversations, we thought he'd been drunk and fallen off the toilet onto the floor, although this was never officially confirmed. I was pleased it wasn't more serious, though it was a relief to know that all my medical training had kicked in automatically, and that I hadn't panicked at all. It'd been a great confidence booster. We'd worked together well and had a good result, and that made facing any medical crisis over the long upcoming winter months easier to think about.

Crisis averted, we headed down to the mechanical workshop for the evening's big event. We were having a large formal dinner and party celebrating the end of summer science program. With the return of the PCMEGA crew, the station had again swelled to its limits and the workshop was the only indoor space large enough for everyone to sit down at once. The mess can comfortably seat 36 people, and that night there would be 96. Most of the PCMEGA crew were sleeping in tents as there was no other accommodation, but on this night nothing mattered. Voyage 5 (*Polar Bird*) was due to arrive within a week to take back most of the summer scientists and we wanted to give them one last party to remember.

We used the celebration as an excuse to surprise Kathleen, a glaciologist who'd recently returned from camp on the Amery Ice Shelf, as she was turning 21 that day. Not many people can say they turned 21 on the Ice, and I couldn't help comparing the joy and happiness of hers with my birthday experience in the jungle in Vietnam.

Strong winds the next day pushed the sonde of my evening balloon release into the drink, but the second was problem-free. The increasing winds were making releases trickier, and I could only imagine how much fun they'd be when the winds really picked up. Unfortunately, that night we got the news about the Columbia Space Shuttle disaster. Every adventurer thinks of the possibility of death when pushing their boundaries but I could only imagine how devastated their families would be.

The search and rescue team staged an emergency scenario the next day, with a vehicle "crashed" on the only road out of the station, one person lying injured and the other suffering a blow to the head and wandering in a confused state. The medical team was called out. Jim and I joined Dr Cad and anaesthetic nurses Cal and Sean at the surgery and waited for the expeditioners to be rescued and brought in. We prepared instruments, donned full gowns and once they were brought in, cleaned and prepped them for surgery.

The scenario was a success, and a good chance for Gerbil and his team (Neil, Curtis, Tony and Chad as first responders, and Gil, Beacon, Sharon, Dave P, Jeff, Paul, Jim and Cad as back-up) to use their special training.

On the BoM front, Cathie, Beacon and I juggled our roster as Cathie needed more time for maintenance. Eventually, the *Polar Bird* appeared in the distance, and the tone in the station changed. This was the symbol that the end was near, and things got busy as the barge ship/shore operations started. The ship had already been loaded up with empty fuel drums and old camp gear from Samson Island, 200 kilometres down the coast, and was now moving onto Davis. The first barge brought fresh fruit and vegetables, and the most important thing: mail! Jeff Becker, a chippie, was our postmaster and we lined up at the bar area to see if he'd put anything on the pool tables for us. My family had sent me more film and newspapers, and I went off to read their words.

Visitors from the *Polar Bird* came ashore, some of them going to field huts to experience Antarctica. When barge operations were abandoned due to strong winds, some other visitors were stranded ashore. They had to find sleeping bags and mats to spend the night a bit more of an experience than they'd bargained for, I bet. That night, 105 people were crowded into the station.

Barge operations continued when the winds dropped. After three days, all the empty fuel drums, recycled materials and rubbish were loaded and we gathered at the beach as the summer scientists got on the last barge. At 11.10am the *Polar Bird* sounded her horn and we raised red flares, sending her and our friends off in the traditional Antarctica style.

That left 54 of us at the station. Suddenly there was room everywhere at the tables in the mess, in the laundry, for the showers. It was heaven. Another 30 were due to leave on the *Aurora Australis* in the coming weeks. Everything we did between now and then was setting up for the long winter ahead.

Though the weather was mild by local standards, we were starting to experience significant snow. Night was starting to become more obvious, each seeming to get darker earlier and last longer. As opposed to the mainland, the switch from summer to winter was much more rapid.

***

Cathie, Beacon, Tony Graham (part of the Light Detection And Ranging (LIDAR) program) and I prepared to launch the first ozonesonde. The launch date was set for the 20th.

We were taking part in the inaugural program of stratospheric ozone studies which had been established at Davis by the Australian Antarctic Division's Space and Atmospheric Sciences (SAS) group and the BoM. This was the first time that Australia was making in-situ measurements of stratospheric ozone in Antarctica, and was part of a larger investigation at Davis by the SAS program to investigate the composition, dynamics and climate of the middle atmosphere.

Ozone is a fairly sparse constituent of the earth's atmosphere. In fact, there are only about three molecules of it in every 10 million molecules of air. Most of the ozone is in the upper atmosphere, the stratosphere, anywhere from 10-50 kilometres up. This layer of ozone is what has protected, for the past 600 million years or so, all human, plants and animals from the biological damage caused by the sun's ultra-violet radiation.

Theoretical research from the 1970s that this layer was being damaged as a result of human activities became a reality in 1985 when the British Antarctic Survey discovered the Antarctic ozone hole. American NASA research confirmed in 1987 that the hole was caused mainly by the chemical destruction of the ozone by atmospheric chlorine, which they proved could not have been caused by natural sources. The culprits were shown to be halocarbon compounds such as chlorofluorocarbons (CFCs) containing chlorine atoms. These CFCs, designed to be chemically non-reactive with most substances in the environment, last a long time in the atmosphere if they escaped or were released.

In September 2000, the Antarctic ozone hole reached a record size of 29 million square kilometres more than three times larger than the land area of the United States.

We would be launching, on balloons, ozonesondes which were miniature chemical processing packages to profile ozone concentration from the ground to altitudes of up to 35 kilometres. The ozonesondes are not new. In fact, Davis was one of nine places in Antarctica where these were being launched.

These ozonesondes would be released monthly, increasing to weekly from mid-June to mid-October, the time of maximum interest in ozone levels. During this time we would also be involved in collaborative research with Chinese scientists who were operating a program of ozone total column abundance measurements using a ground-based spectrophotometer at Zhong Shan.

The morning before the first launch, we woke to find the Chinese ship *Xue Long* anchored in the bay, and hosted several Chinese expeditioners through the Met office. Though we couldn't speak a common language, they were polite, courteous, lovely people. The ship's summer season was coming to an end, and the visit to Davis was her last stop before heading north to Shanghai via Fremantle.

The Chinese expeditioners and crew returned our hospitality by inviting us to tour the *Xue Long* and to join them for dinner. Unable to attend as I was on the late shift, I envied the other expeditioners who'd gathered on the beach. I watched Jim, Beacon, Jeremy, Gil and Mark, carrying slabs of beer on their shoulders, join the others to climb on board the launch the Chinese had sent over. *Lucky bastards.*

The next morning, I had to laugh when I heard how the night panned out. They'd arrived just after 8pm, and after a tour, joined the others for a meal that included chook feet! After the meal, the karaoke began and our crew starting toasting the Chinese and singing. Just as they got into the swing of things, the captain said it was time to go to bed. Apparently our crew packed up the rest of the grog and the empties and headed back to the launch, arriving back at the station around midnight. They'd been prepared to go all night, all in the interest of cementing international relations, and certainly didn't expect to head back so early.

It's not often you see Aussies heading out with grog on their shoulders, only to return with almost as much. They carried their load into the mess and continued the party there, and there was more than one bleary-eyed expeditioner watching the next morning as the *Xue Long* pulled anchor and returned home.

That morning we launched the first ozonesonde. Cathie was kitted out in the safety gear, then working with Tony, released the large balloon. Tony had the LIDAR running, which sends a vertical laser-beam into the sky. The beam reveals atmospheric characteristics up to more than 60 kilometres away. The two devices recorded (in different ways) the same information over parts of their ranges, in effect confirming each other's measurements. It was an awe-inspiring moment. Not so much the releasing of the balloon with the sonde, which Cathie and I had both done at Macca, but launching the first one in Davis's history.

***

In the lull afterwards, we continued with the normal routine. I helped Dr Cad as he removed some of Beacon's cancer spots from his eye and elbow. It was a cut and stitch job and a good chance to practice my skills.

A team of physicists and tradesmen finished the erection and commissioning of an array of VHF radar antennas (nicknamed the "Ant Farm"), a project which had been running all summer. This research tool measured winds and atmospheric composition at altitudes higher than the upper limits of our Met balloons, and there was a subsidiary array that could detect meteorites.

Any meteorite that actually lands on the continent is sent to a division of NASA in Texas for examination. By 1999, some 16,000 fragments from space had been found on the Antarctic continent, which was more than everything gathered from everywhere else around the globe. The fragments were also conserved better due to the ice and cold.

Chippies were busy installing temporary summer accommodation units and a new potato store which had been delivered on the *Polar Bird*. We also had a powerhouse changeover, which luckily went smoothly. Once a year, the main powerhouse is shut down for maintenance, and our smaller emergency powerhouse, meant to carry the load if the main one has a problem, took over for several days. With the last ship of the season due shortly, all these projects were wrapped up and tools and equipment packed for the trip back home.

With the inevitable draw towards the end of summer, the elephant seals started returning to lie on the beach and moult. They were joined by moulting Adelie penguins. This period was a short one. As the sea started to freeze, they'd all begin to head back out again.

With the changing light, the sunsets were becoming more stunning, especially if ultra cumulus clouds were around to break up the colours. At night we'd watch the light purples and oranges take over the sky, and I'd often stop whatever I was doing to go have a look.

On the 25th, I rang home for Deb's birthday. By now I'd been away for three months. Deb had started volunteering at the Yeppoon Visitor's Information Centre when not working at the school. David had started university that day and I told him I was proud. It would be a hard road, but he would face the challenge well.

I promised Deb we would celebrate her birthday better next year and we hung up. The calls were expensive. I'd always try to keep them to five minutes, but they'd often go longer. In the end the cost was worth it to hear their voices.

***

Near the end of the month, Jeremy asked me if I wanted to go to Zhong Shan, the Chinese base in the Larsemann Hills (120 kilometres from Davis). Besides the Chinese station, there was also Progress 2 (Russian) and Druzhnaya A (Russian summer only) in the area at the east edge of the Amery Ice Shelf.

In January, the Chinese resupply ship spent several days off Davis, undertaking engine repairs in our anchorage. Courtesy visits were made to all these stations to re-establish friendly contact and to offer any help that might be needed in the future. Jeremy S, Geoff, Janine, Frances and pilots Rick and John G attended the banquet at Zhong Shan to celebrate the Chinese Spring Festival.

Jeremy thought it would be a good chance for me to take a trip there, especially as I worked with the Chinese Met officers daily. Was I interested?

Are you kidding? This was a chance to really get inland, to see a different part of Antarctica. Cathie, Neil, Cad, Al and Richard came along, and we split up into two groups for the helicopters. The timing had to be right to do such a trip — blue skies with little cloud. Helicopters never flew in heavy overcast skies for fear of whiteout.

We took off and passed the icefalls and crevasses on the edge of the ice plateau, on the way to our first stop an all-weather station (AWS) which needed repair. The pilots found the spot easily, with the help of their GPS, and we landed on the ice. These scientific stations, which measured temperature and the wind over the ice, are self-sufficient units generated by solar power. Occasionally they'd get damaged by bad weather or an instrument fault would force repairs. These two units had to be fixed before the choppers headed back on the AA.

As the repairs went on, I huddled against the bitter cold which was about -40°C with the wind chill. I was overwhelmed with the isolation. It truly was no man's land, remote and hostile, and I knew it would be impossible to survive on my own.

The bloke doing the repairs was digging into the snow and ice, preparing to hook up the solar panels. He kept on moving his hands to keep the circulation going while the rest of us held a tarp over him to keep away the wind. Light snow was drifting with the wind as far as the eye could see. This unit had been taken out for repair on an earlier trip, and he was putting it back. I kept wriggling my toes and stamping my feet. As I breathed against the wind, the condensation of my breath froze until I had icicles hanging from my nose, moustache and putt putt.

As soon as he announced the repair successful, we hopped back into the chopper, grateful for the buffer from the wind. The windows fogged up as we thawed out. By the time we started warming up, we'd reached the second AWS, about 60 kilometres from the first one.

I climbed out and was slammed by the wind. This AWS had a different probe and this time the bloke had to climb a pole to fix one of the instruments. It was anchored into the ground and I wondered what speeds it registered throughout the year. Snow was drifting and the wind was howling, making talking difficult.

When he'd finished, we headed off. Once out of the Vestfold Hills, the coast was sheer ice, with bergs, ice cliffs and ice caves. It was much more impressive than around our station.

The Zhong Shan base was fairly modern, and I was envious of their view. We were greeted by the station leader. The officer-in-charge of their Met program, Xu Cong, a smiling man with an open, honest face, acted as our translator. My Chinese was very limited, restricted to only hello and goodbye, which I put to good use as I greeted Xu's fellow Met workers, Lu Fei and Wan Jun, who couldn't speak English.

The Australian Met office at Davis received weather observations and ozone readings three times a day from Zhong Shan and fed them into our communication network on their behalf. Taking details from our Chinese Met counterparts was always an interesting exercise. Whenever I had Xu, we could have a decent conversation but if Wan or Lu was on, talk would be extremely limited. They'd call me up with "Mr Dave" and I'd answer, but they'd continue with "Good morning, Mr Dave, let's begin" and start giving me their coded figures. Their heavy accents were hard to understand, but as we never delved into further conversation, we always got our job done.

We followed Xu and the station leader inside, and sat around the table talking through Xu about Davis and comparing our stations and programs. After tea and biscuits, Xu took us on a tour of the station. He was especially proud of their new accommodation block under construction. Compared with their old block, this one had individual rooms and all the mod cons. While we were walking around, we heard a loud crack signalling an iceberg breaking off the ice sheet or breaking up. We jumped, but Xu said that happened all the time.

I noticed the Australian flag flying besides theirs, put up especially for our visit, something we would do in return whenever Davis had visits from other nations. Xu took us to their Met office, where Lu and Wan showed us a photo of Cathie, Beacon and me they'd put up over their radio link phone.

Cathie and I spent about an hour-and-a-half comparing instruments and set-up, and talking about expeditioners they'd met on the *Aurora Australis* at the beginning of the summer. The rest of the station was very well-kept, especially their fuel tanks, whose ends had been painted with dynamic unique faces. Their station was smaller, with only about 15 expeditioners, but they had a fresh water lake nearby which they could use.

While we caught up with our counterparts, the others had gone down the hill to the Russian station Progress, about a kilometre away, from where the choppers would eventually pick us up. After a gift exchange of spirits, Cathie and I headed off down the hill to join them.

What a difference. The Russian base was an eyesore, no other way to describe it. Rusting junk was piled up everywhere old fridges in one area, old tractors and machinery in another. With all the emphasis on protecting the environment, I couldn't believe that any station would be in this condition. We caught up with the others, who were talking to the station doctor. He was the only one around, and he looked uncomfortable. I wondered what was going on as he talked to Cad in his broken English and I heard Cad say, "Come to Davis, we have grog".

Their doctor offered to show us around his surgery, which Cad eagerly accepted. He proudly pointed out various bits of equipment. I was amazed because it dated back to the 1950s. It was like getting a glimpse into history, at what medicine used to be.

He was a nice man who had been down there for 18 months and wanted desperately to go home. Apparently he'd been scheduled to return, but the ship had been cancelled with no rescheduled date. Their shipping service was very unreliable and this was a common occurrence.

Neil rejoined us and we headed back to the choppers where I found out what the tension had been about. Neil had gone on an earlier trip to Progress to help the Russians with a problem with one of their parts, which he was going to have to bring back to the mechanical workshop at Davis. While there, he and some other Aussie expeditioners had accepted the Russians' offer of a drink, and so the good vodka had been brought out.

Apparently they managed to get through quite a bit of the good vodka. This time, when the Russians had seen Neil walking down, everyone had hidden except for the station doctor and the mechanic who had to come out to meet Neil. No station leader, no other expeditioners. It seems we'd worn out our welcome. It was funny but understandable as Russian supplies are very limited, and that grog probably represented a good supply of their stash. So instead, they'd locked up shop until we lifted off in the choppers. All of a sudden, we looked down to see about 20 Russians come out and watch as we flew away.

The trip back was spectacular. Our pilot, Ward, flew low to show us the crevasses and caves, huge jagged walls of white towering above the ocean, and followed the coast back towards Davis. A few times I jumped as the chopper suddenly jarred or shook with turbulence off the ice cliff, but the view was incredible. By now Ward and I understood each other. I had still felt apprehensive when we left the first AWS, but by the second one I'd relaxed, and now Ward was cutting loose and flying like he did best a controlled flying by the seat of his pants.

***

The month ended with strong winds, which were becoming the norm. I worked with Tony Graham to release a special 1000 gram balloon for data to coincide with his LIDAR research. It would only be a matter of a few days before the AA took the rest of the expeditioners and the real fun started.

A young Dave outside his tent at Nui Dat, Vietnam.

Fire Support Base Julia, Vietnam. Dave's pit hole, roughly 5 feet deep by 3 feet wide; once inside he only had enough room to turn on his side.

Dave's pit hole at Fire Support Base Kerry at bottom left. The VC preferred the dark cover of night to attack, and he'd peer out through the small hole in the pit as flares were ignited and tracer bullets lit up the sky.

Elephant seals basking in the sun. These massive animals were everywhere around base, and the sight, sound and smell wherever they gathered was unforgettable.

It was a virtual penguin highway—a parade of Royal penguins were heading down into the sea as a second parade returned with food.

A huge wave had flipped Dave's Zodiac boat into the dangerous rough waters leaving the boat wrecked and he and his fellow expeditioners shocked and exhausted.

This fur seal pup was one of the many being caught and tagged as part of the monitoring of the breeding population.

The view looking down onto the Macca base, the isthmus and the rugged coast line, was hypnotic.

Dave's photograph of a roll cloud at Macquarie Island made the 2003 Australian Weather Calendar produced by the Bureau of Meteorology.

The *Aurora Australis* would chew through ice, easily breaking the seemingly solid mass. If the winds picked up, there was the chance that the ice pack would close behind, trapping the ship.

A night-time iceberg tour in one of the station's Zodiacs. The expeditioners had to keep their distance, with less than 10 per cent visible above water, the icebergs are inherently unstable.

The green peak of the iceberg really stood out against the stark whiteness of other icebergs and the blue of the ocean. The unusual colour caused by organisms captured within the ice layers.

An explosive crack rent the air, boat engines idling Dave and his group waited a safe distance away hoping to see the enormous iceberg roll.

After a long day of field training, exhausted and cold, the site of Sprunky's van where the expeditioners would be spending the night outside of was welcoming.

A long night sleeping on the rocky ground in only a bivvy bag against the cold and wind of 30-plus knots. To block out the light, which didn't fade at that time of year, Dave buried himself inside the confined space of his bag.

Towards the end of summer and the changing light, the sunsets were more spectacular, especially if ultra cumulus clouds were around, as they would break the brilliant colours up.

This all-weather station, generated by solar power, measured the wind over the ice had to be repaired amidst drifting snow and howling wind.

Launching the first ozonesonde. These miniature chemical processing packages where launched on balloons, profiling ozone concentration from the ground to altitudes of up to 35 kilometres.

Icebergs looked like massive land masses and as the sun hit their sides, they'd start to glisten, a view both beautiful and stark.

Davis Station, pretty until a blizzard appears - a typical Antarctic phenomena where little snow actually falls, instead its blown along the surface, resulting in blinding conditions

Anzac Day; the snow fell softly on Dave's face as he recited the famous lines of the Ode.

The contrast on this tabular berg was intriguing —a smooth, perfect arch cut through most of its mass, with sharp jags sticking up all around its top.

A brand new berg tends to be white and they can as they age change colour like this azure blue jade berg discovered during the Rauers trip.

The Maggie "melon" was originally assembled in 1986 to support a long-term monitoring program on Adelie penguins. Dave had the opportunity to spend a night before it was dismantled.

Changeover. The sight of the *Aurora Australis* seemingly locked in the ice, was quite majestic.

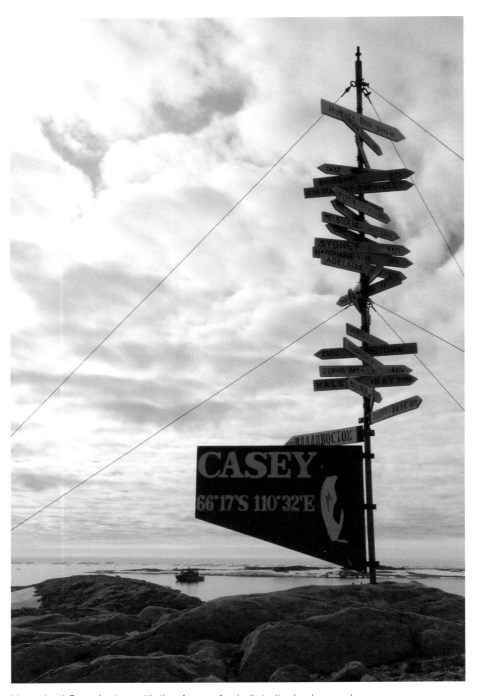

Never lost! Casey's sign, with the *Aurora Australis* in the background.

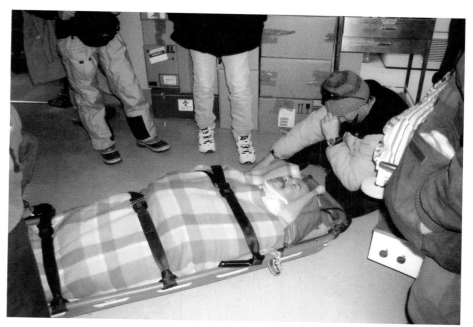

Dave lay on the floor surrounded by people, Dr Williams is nearby and Psycho (Chris Gallagher) rests a reassuring hand on him while discussions flew around. PHOTO: Kerry Steinburner

Casey evacuation. Expeditioners gathered around the door and called out various messages: "We'll miss you, mate" and "Enjoy your winter". PHOTO: Kerry Steinburner

Aurora Australis at Casey base.

The only time Dave allowed his son David and daughter Michelle to meet him at the ship.

CHAPTER 12
FAREWELL TO THE *AURORA*

March 2003 weather details:
Max temperature 0.2°C, min −13.9°C, monthly average -6.5°C
Maximum wind gusts 74 knots (137 kilometres per hour)
Average daily sunshine 3.0 hours.

One morning we woke to find the *Aurora Australis* anchored near the shore, the official symbol of the end of the summer season. It would be a quick turnaround. She'd arrived at 7.30am and would leave later that day with the rest of the summer expeditioners. She was likely to be the last ship to visit Davis until next November.

It was an eerie feeling, one all of us winterers had prepared for. For three hours, luggage went to the ship, essentials were transferred to shore, and except for two items of luggage falling from a pallet being sling-loaded out to the ship (later retrieved in a very sodden state), it all went smoothly.

We hugged and farewelled the summer expeditioners at the helipad and made our way down to the shore. The helicopters took the last expeditioners to the ship and were strapped down before the AA finally sounded her horn. The sound raised the hairs on my arms; it was such a mournful sound. We lit red hand-held flares and cheered as she pulled out, elephant seals lining the shore burping their own goodbyes.

"Farewell to the *Aurora*," one person yelled. Among cheers I heard "this is it" more than once and chuckled as one cheeky bloke called "don't go", naming each of the women who'd just disappeared from sight.

This was it. No way out for at least eight months. Excitement built as I watched the ship grow distant, and knew this was what I'd come down here for. This feeling. Though it was dampened slightly by the worry, always in the back of my mind, that something might happen to my family while I was unable to return quickly. I talked with the others; sipping the champagne we'd cracked to celebrate the beginning of the winter season, certain they'd have similar thoughts about their own families. Nobody voiced it though, for today was about something bigger.

As the AA left, another expeditioner showed herself for the first time. Stay, the famous dog, sat on the shore staring out to sea. We were honoured she considered us worthy of her company, having spent years at some of the best places winters at every ANARE station, various field sites, including the Prince Charles Mountains, Mt Brown and Bechervaise Island, even remote Heard Island and Spitsbergen in the Arctic.

A full-sized golden retriever Guide Dogs collection box, quite correctly named Stay, had honourable beginnings in Antarctica but her presence soon disintegrated to a bold tug-of-war among stations. Originally collected from the Guide Dogs Association in Hobart in late 1991, she was only meant to spend one year on the Ice. Mawson station leader John Wilson had the idea after hearing the real dogs were being sent home from Antarctic stations. Under pressure from other signatories to the Environmental Protocol, who'd said they could spread distemper to the seal populations, Australia promised to pull out their dogs by 1993. Many thought this was a political stance taken in retaliation for Australia forcing smaller nations to clean up their stations under that Protocol.

So the dogs came out and Stay went in to Davis, both as a way to raise money but also as a protest. The intention was she'd come back in with the returning winterers. During that year, other stations heard about Stay and the tug-of-war began. Someone dognapped her and took her to Mawson where the real dogs peed on her. In later years she appeared at different stations once the final ship disappeared.

Once she'd even jumped in between two Mawson expeditioners in a mock fight and sacrificed her leg, which was then sent to Davis with a ransom note (not to the amusement of the Davis expeditioners, who'd thought the Mawson crew had taken her leg off on purpose). After a few legless years, a summering Mawson carpenter named "Smoothie" fitted her with a new Huon pine leg which is with her today.

Her travels included the rest of the Australian stations and even the *Aurora Australis'* bar. The Guide Dog Association had asked several times when they'd get Stay back. They were not impressed to be told "never", and efforts to raise funds began in earnest. Thousands of dollars have been raised since and many fundraising events continue in her name every year.

As the AA disappeared over the horizon, so did all the expeditioners. We seemed to all need a bit of solitude and space. The reality of where we were and what we were facing gradually began to sink in.

***

There was an immediate difference in the station. With only 24 of us left, there was room in the mess to move around and we soon established a new routine. It was getting colder and blown snow transformed the station from the dark rockiness of the summer by laying a soft, white blanket on the ground. The strengthening winds pushed it into drifts which Curtis shifted with heavy machinery so we could move freely.

The radio link to the outside world felt more important. A challenge to play darts came from the American station at the South Pole. Stations in Antarctica are usually in different time zones. Our designated time for the match was 10am on Sundays. Our three teams would be pitted against three teams from the South Pole, one from Casey and one from New Zealand's Scott Base.

For the first match, a crowd gathered by the bar, after walking across my freshly mopped floor. Sean set up the HF radio on the bar near the dartboard.

A brilliant start by Jeremy meant we were looking good before one of the South Pole teams won. Teams had to start and end the second round with a double. The Davis teams struggled while Casey finished quickly and won.

We continued the tradition of Friday night drinks with an informal meal, and dressing up for formal Saturday night dinners, complete with tablecloths and candles. Every Tuesday night I joined a group in the green store for Volley Gin a friendly game of volleyball followed by gins at the bar.

Around the middle of the month, Jim hosted Friday night drinks in the old station, bringing history alive with stories from the time when he lived there. Jim was about my age, a soft-spoken bloke and a man on the road. He'd travelled the world and wintered in Antarctica about six times.

We started the night with a game of carpet bowls in the former powerhouse, one of the largest of the old Davis station buildings. It was a struggle to keep the balls going straight on the skewed floor which in several spots had been lifted by ice. It was cold and damp, but Jim kept us entertained with stories such as living there and using the "gas crappers" (two outside toilets in a yellow shed) whose solid contents would be incinerated with the occasional explosive accident. The site for the old station was the sixth one explored. It was originally considered a last resort, but fears Russia or another nation would build in the area forced Australia's decision. It did have some advantages a sandy beach with a flat terrace about 9-12 metres beyond for buildings. On the downside, elephant seals covered the beach and vehicle access to the terrain was difficult. The station's location in the prevailing wind on a leeward slope meant most doors filled with snow up to the roof-line, allowing expeditioners to open windows and excavate holes to use as fridges. Water, made from melted snow, was in short supply. Each expeditioner could have a weekly shower provided he didn't use more than a bucket. One bloke went seven weeks without a shower to conserve water.

Work began on the first station building on January 13, 1957. A week later, when the *Kista Dan* departed, Davis station had seven buildings a sleeping hut, community hut, an auroral observatory, a store hut, a balloon-filling hut and a theodolite shelter. The main complex buildings were interconnected with porches and corridors. By the time the station rebuilding program started in 1978, it had grown to 27 buildings.

The most recent time anyone had lived there was about 12 years before our visit. The old station has sat abandoned ever since. Considerations are being made on its historical significance and its future, most likely to be removed back to Australia.

It was a brilliant Friday drinks night, our imaginations fired by stories about the living conditions of earlier expeditioners as we returned to our modern, warm beds.

***

One day I decided to videotape my daily routine for my family. As I stepped out of the accommodation building, I had to control my breathing so it wouldn't dominate the sound. Walking out from the warmth of any building was always a shock to the system, the cold cutting hardest when it hit my lungs.

Heading towards the north of the station, I passed Gerbil's ute parked behind the kitchen. The chef always gets a vehicle. It's essential for transporting the huge quantities of food from the green store to the kitchen, but others often borrowed it to do chores. My boots crunched in the soft snow with each step towards the green store.

Pipes and wires around the station are enclosed in protective conduit and laid on elevated tracks criss-crossing around various buildings. This stops them from being buried in the snow, and helps keep the wildlife off them (seals especially like to lie on the hot water pipes).

I slipped and nearly dropped my camera. Navigating off the main roads can be tricky, with snow and ice hiding uneven ground. Before the green store I turned left towards the Met building, with the old powerhouse and old Davis station to my left. I crunched my way past the new portable accommodation block on my left and then the science building on my right.

A few manoeuvres through the snow and a short climb on a bridge over more cables brought me to the Met building. A group of Adelie penguins were hunched down outside the office with their backs turned against the wind to conserve heat and energy. At the rear of the building, with the Ant Farm visible in the distance, were our Met instruments the wind dines, Stevenson screen, sunshine recorder and snow gauge which were checked daily. We took daily readings at 9am and 3pm, and at 6pm would head out to the sunshine recorder to change its recording paper.

I was rugged up with my new Essendon beanie, fur boots and gloves, but when I took off my glove to work the buttons, I couldn't stop a "Bloody oath it's cold" being recorded.

***

A few days later the wind was howling through the station and making the buildings shudder. I peered out the doorway, through the limited visibility, mentally picking the path I'd have to follow to get to the Met office. Gale-force winds were gusting to 74 knots but I needed to get to the office if I could.

Rigging lines are permanently hooked between each building, allowing expeditioners to follow a path to safety whenever visibility dampened normal senses. I gripped my hand into a circle around the line and leaned into the wind, following it to the safety of the green store, then past the emergency powerhouse and finally to the office.

When I released my first balloon, it burst on the old Davis station, but the second one made it over before bursting in the water. I had to give it away and admit defeat. Anything over 58 knots was a hard release. In 74 knots, it wasn't going to happen.

Conditions had deteriorated during my shift, and looking towards where I knew the accommodation building stood, I felt uneasy. We had food and water in the Met office so if conditions were so bad we didn't think we could head out safely, we could bunk down until the worst passed. However, I didn't want to spend the night by myself, and didn't want to consider spending several days there if conditions worsened. It was my first blizzard visibility less than 100 metres, temperatures below zero and winds above 34 knots over one hour.

I shut the door against the wind and went back to the phone to ring Gerbil. "I'm going to try and make it back, mate. Give me 10 minutes".

Once he knew I was heading out, he would allow me a certain amount of time to arrive before sending out a search party. When I opened the door again, I had to admit I felt tense. Even with all the training I'd had, this was Mother Nature at her crankiest. The snow was thick, blocking what little light Antarctica offered.

The pressure pushed into me until I could hardly breathe but I forced my body into the wind, fumbling for the rope and gripping it, refusing to let go. Cold seeped into every tiny crack in my clothing, and I kept gasping to get air into my aching lungs. Gradually I started inching my way forward, burying my head in my jacket to hide from the assault.

The relief at reaching each building along the way was tempered with the knowledge that I'd have to keep going. The fury of the wind was humbling; this wasn't the worst that Mother Nature could throw. I peered ahead, trying to make sense of vague shapes in front of me before leaning back into the wind and forcing myself onwards. I was worried about any loose objects that could be lying around – they could become deadly missiles just waiting to take off my head.

When I finally shut the mess door behind me, the change was instantaneous. The outside roar was muffled, and the laughter and warmth of Gerbil's kitchen and the people gathered made a mockery of the experience I'd just had. As scary as that had been, I couldn't imagine being where it was worse, though I knew such places existed. Russia's Vostok station had experienced the lowest temperature ever recorded on earth, -89.2°C (-128.6°F) recorded on July 21, 1983.

***

With the sun dipping further below the horizon and the air temperature falling, the sea was now freezing over. It had started early in the month, first as ice needles and tiny ice plates known as frazil, then into a thin sludge known as grease ice. Finally it formed an ice skin but this broke up and was blown out by gales or waves. It would freeze again and break into soft, round pancakes rather like pale waterlily leaves and as they collided with each other, they developed raised edges. When the temperatures stayed low for a few days, these pancakes thickened and firmed.

Just like a few short months earlier, when we waited for the ice to melt so we could start our boating activities, now we were waiting for it to freeze so we could use it as a road. It was growing at a rate of up to 60 square kilometres a day, and it wasn't long before it became a flat surface stretching out as far as we could see.

It was still too thin to walk or travel on. Sea ice was measured religiously, with set minimums for travel: 100 millimetres for skis, 130 millimetres for walking, 300 millimetres for quads and 500 millimetres for Hagglunds. Sunsets would tease us peeking over distant icebergs in the frozen sea covered in snow. It looked solid, but was still only fragile.

Adelie penguins had started leaving Davis in a follow-the-leader formation. They were headed to the pack ice for winter. The air temperature was higher there than on land. While at Davis, they'd moulted their old feathers and grew clean, sleek, new plumage to last them through the coming winter. We wouldn't see them again until the spring breeding season began in October. I was going to miss seeing them clustered in groups, sheltered in the rocks, under steps or besides buildings. I'd become used to them surprising me with a sudden squawk as I headed to work. Now only the odd penguin still remained, but in the coming days they too would follow the group.

Elephant bulls were still gathered on the beach. It wasn't a breeding area and it was rare to see any cows. They normally went to Heard Island or other areas to breed. These guys were going through their moult and took over the area; one big wriggling smelly pile of testosterone lying close together to preserve body warmth, alternating between sleeping and picking fights.

All seal colonies have one dominant bull which is occasionally challenged for supremacy by a younger one. Whichever one lost was exiled. The exiled bulls formed their own group with a pecking order. Fights would break out as they sorted themselves out. These fights were part of the young bulls' training. Some of them, when old enough, would grow to challenge for a colony. Some of the older bulls had deep scars, testament to earlier failed challenges.

While I watched them, they'd let out the occasional belch while keeping a wary eye on me. We kept at least five metres away to avoid upsetting them.

***

One night the buzzer went off in my room. It signified an Aurora Australis in the sky; a natural phenomenon of swirling and pulsating coloured lights. Different gases cause the different colours. Oxygen atoms give off red and green light and nitrogen molecules give blue and violet light. It could be quite intense where we were, fairly close to the south magnetic pole, as charged particles from the sun get trapped by the Earth's magnetic field and flow towards the pole. Expeditioners could have a buzzer connected to the LIDAR put in their rooms which would be activated whenever an aurora appeared.

Around this time Paul and Cal told us that our water tanks were finally full. In the warmer months, fresh water is made from the brackish water of a natural tarn by a process of reverse osmosis which produces about 18,000 litres every 24 hours. In the summer, with so many people, it was hard for production to keep up with the usage. Now it was full and this was expected to keep us comfortable until next spring when the fresh water production would again start. To celebrate, we relaxed in hot baths rather than the two-minute daily showers we were normally allowed.

On the 20th, as I was busy with slushy duties, we heard that the US and Coalition forces were at war with Iraq. At home, I would've been glued to CNN on but here I was peeling carrots and potatoes. We were never isolated from world news. Our communications blokes, Evil or Sean, would put out a daily newsletter with headlines and details from the Tasmanian newspaper, *The Hobart Mercury*. I'd surf the internet at night, reading up on the day's happenings. I never felt like I missed out on what was happening. What was different was how absorbed I was by it.

The world had narrowed down to our little community, with its rules and dependency. Even though Evil and Sean had set up a webcam for the station so anyone around the world could see what was going on in real time in Davis via the Australian Antarctic Division's website, the reality was that our group of 24 expeditioners lived an alternate life where little things took on significant meaning.

Our hard work in the hydroponics shed was starting to be rewarded as we were able to bring Gerbil more and more vegetables. My turn in the hydroponics shed, on Thursdays, was a welcome relief from the harsh outdoors. As soon as I'd opened the door, the warmth and the smells would assault me and I'd happily shut the outside behind me and potter around. It was the smell of the plants that got to me; with no vegetation around, tending to a delicate growing plant became important, a way to keep my feet grounded, so to speak, and the bright lights, greenery and warm, moist atmosphere made me feel I was doing something important for our little group.

By now we were harvesting lettuce, cucumber, basil, zucchini, silverbeet and rocket, and Gerbil would make a special side salad for our Saturday dinners. I'd watch everyone dig in even the expeditioners who never really liked veggies and feel proud for helping provide for them.

CHAPTER 13
THE BOYS ARE LEAVING TOWN

April 2003 weather details:
Max temp -3.5°C, min −24.0°C, monthly average -13.4°C
Maximum wind gusts 48 knots (89 kilometres per hour)
Average daily sunshine 2.0 hours

The beginning of April was a pleasant time; the temperature still fairly comfortable (for Antarctica) as long as the wind wasn't blowing and we were rugged up in the proper clothing. The sun's angle painted long shadows and pink tones on frozen sea ice and trapped icebergs.

Still, the wildlife was recognising the signs longer periods of darkness and the colder temperatures and the remaining stragglers made their way out to the ice pack. The last of the moulting Adelie penguins headed out, as did the scavenging skuas. Gil and I went to check on the remaining elephant seals on the shore.

Out on the sea ice, we spotted a Weddell seal poking his head up through a hole to breathe. A second Weddell was moving across the ice, throwing his weight forward over and over again. He'd lift his tail and slam it down, the movement arching through his body and taking him forward a few feet. Then he'd rest before starting again. It was hard work. The ice wasn't very thick yet, and we watched waiting for it to break. All of a sudden, he found his fast gear, his massive body one big wave of blubber as he trucked across the ice. He spotted a hole, hesitated, belched, and then gave one more massive flop to bring him to the edge. He must've known we were waiting for him to dive into the water so he turned coy and played games at the edge, studying it and poking his head in the water to blow bubbles, before lifting his head up again to study the hole once more.

I'd been hoping to see a Weddell close up. The most southerly breeding of all mammals, they tend to inhabit areas of coastal ice (ice connected to land) rather than the moving pack ice. They breathe and enter the water through holes in the ice which they need to make or maintain, cutting the ice with their incisors and enlarging and maintaining the openings with their canines. They won't begin to cut a hole in ice more than 10 centimetres thick, but once they've made a hole, they'll maintain it until the ice is up to two metres.

Apparently these seals are particularly noisy under water, producing a varied range of whistles, buzzes, tweets and growls. The sounds the males make can be detected up to 30 kilometres away. They have a short life span for seals about 22 years - possibly because the practice of maintaining holes breaks or wears down their teeth, or causes abscesses.

We waited until he finally put his head in the hole and let gravity take the rest of his body. The wind was howling and I imagined the water enveloping him would feel a whole lot warmer.

It was getting colder, -20.2°on the 3rd, and Jim and four others went to check on the sea ice thickness. The rest of us waited to hear the results. Until Mother Nature decided to thicken the sea, we would be trapped at the station. With my quad training behind me, I was waiting for the official green light to grab one and explore the region around the station.

The remaining elephant seals on the shore were grunting and flopping around as they played within their pecking order. Two young bulls, probably cranky with the itchiness I imagined the moulting created, fronted each other. They reared back, balancing on spine and tail and flared their noses back before chest-butting each other. They rocked back and forth until one flopped over, and the victorious bull collapsed on top, both catching their breath. These young bulls liked to challenge each other but still fell prey to sunshine and laziness to lie back and relax. Two further down the line picked up the fight, but one bull chose to use his head instead of his chest, poking the other bull's chest until they both gave up and flopped down.

They gradually kept heading out during that first week. Like the penguins, they went in a line, their fat, lumpy bodies flopping across the sea ice, instinctively seeking out the edge of the water where they could spend their winter. Dr Cad was the official elephant seal counter and had recorded 134 at their peak. Now there were less than 50, with more heading out of town each day.

***

One of the biggest days on the Davis calendar was the famous fishing competition. Jim and Sharon had organised it, drilling holes through the ice and supplying chairs and tackle. A group of us went onto the sea ice, about a kilometre off base, and set up stools next to the holes. It was overcast but pleasant, about -12°C but with little breeze.

At 2pm the competition officially started and we lowered our hand lines baited with mutton trimmings and weighted with nuts and bolts through mushy ice into the water. We'd been told to make sure these hit the bottom, which was where the fish fed.

Now I don't mind throwing out the odd line with friends but can honestly say I'm not the world's greatest fisherman. After a while I got bored and got up to chat to the others. Nanette was rugged up in her yellow suit, beanie pulled down and she glanced up briefly to say "hi" before returning to the task at hand. I asked if she'd had any luck. In her crisp English accent she said, "Oh yes, one nibble. I reeled it in as fast as I could but it took the hook, sinker and all. Now I've got stronger line."

Meanwhile, Jim circulated with cups of tea, delivering reading material and offering to take photos, the small fee for each service going to Stay. Then Jeremy called out victoriously and I heard "oh bugger" from someone behind me. Our fearless leader was showing his troops the way with the first fish, a tiny 15 centimetres long brown Antarctica cod. "That's a winner," he insisted as he held it up for us to see.

I went to talk to Cathy, set up next to Cal with Stay keeping them company. The entry fee into the competition went to the Stay fund, and I guess she was checking to see how we'd do. Cal was drilling a new hole, saying the other one was all fished out. He was using an old-fashioned hand-held drill and with about two feet of ice to get through, I knew he'd be a while.

I chatted to Richard, who was enjoying his Easter Sunday with a few stubbies and his rod, getting a few nibbles but complaining they wouldn't stay on and Tony, who had one bite and had opened up the top of his hole with his ice pick ready to finish any beast unlucky enough to suicide on his line. As Jeremy kept pulling fish out, I decided to pay five dollars to get another hole drilled next to him and try my luck again.

At the end of the day, the others had caught 15 fish. My prediction had proven correct: I had none. Jeremy caught the most (nine) as well as the largest, and Tony was the runner-up. Jeremy lined up with his winning fish with Stay to pose for photos. The fish were so small they didn't even register on the huge scales, but as a reward he had to scale, fillet and cook them as an entrée to dinner.

***

A few days later, I walked with Richard to Garden Island, 2.2 kilometres from the station. It was a magical day, though the wind was up and it was quite cold, -17°C. My moustache became encrusted with icicles as I walked, condensation from my breath freezing instantly.

Along the way, we checked out the different locked icebergs towering above us, the moon occasionally peeking out. Edges of trapped icebergs are notoriously dangerous, with ice ponds between the berg and the fast ice. During the night, icicles would form at the base only to melt away during the day. I'd brought my camera with me, but only managed to get quick shots as my hands would start shaking with pain and cold after about 30 seconds.

Once at Garden, we managed to get onto the island, though we had to watch the unstable edges, and had an unbelievable view Davis in the distance, Iceberg Alley all around one big white mass interrupted by various peaks. I remembered the iceberg trip and wondered how many of those bergs were now trapped, and how many of them would manage to leave the area next summer.

Thicknesses were checked again the next day by the sea ice monitoring team with a maximum of 750 millimetre and minimum of 240 millimetre recorded. Unfortunately, an offshore storm had generated enough swell to crack the ice which blew out, leaving behind some open water.

***

Anzac Day (April 25) is probably Australia's most important national occasion, marking the anniversary of the first major military action fought by Australian and New Zealand forces during World War I. The pride they took in the Anzac name (formed from Australian and New Zealand Army Corps) endures to this day, and the importance of the day far overshadows other military remembrance days.

Several weeks earlier, Jeremy had approached me regarding the service. He wanted me, as the only veteran on base, to be involved, and I struggled with my thoughts before I could answer.

So many bittersweet emotions. I'd joined the Citizens' Military Force (CMF) in my late teens, drawn to the adventure offered. I'd never had a dad growing up. He died when Mum was pregnant with Don and me. I'd watch my friends go off fishing and camping with their dads, and always felt I was missing out. The CMF offered that, with the navigation and bushwalking exercises, and the group of like-minded people.

I'd started flying in my teens, sinking all my money from my milk run and postal run jobs into lessons. When I finished school, I knew my marks wouldn't get me into the air force so I joined the army instead, with a plan of working my way into the army aviation program through the back door.

I still remember the time Australia sent its first troops to Vietnam. I was sitting in the classroom in Caloundra when the troop carrier *HMAS Sydney* passed the coastline through the windows. Everybody, students and the teacher, crowded to watch the big grey ship disappear around the headland. It was exciting. Our troops were heading out to war in Vietnam, foreign to us Aussies. It was the first time that troops were leaving our shores since the Korean War.

Four years later, I would join other soldiers. I'd never imagined I would, but had been deployed to Vietnam as part of the Signal Corp. I was a normal 19-year-old, worried about my mum's health issues and what the future held. By the time I headed over, the television was starting to show negative reports. The war wasn't positive, but I was young, I was trained, and I believed my duty was to fight for my country.

My mum, older relatives and my brother supported my decision. I wasn't scared. I knew I was properly trained and somehow knew I'd survive. I wonder now how many others thought the same, especially those who didn't return. Back then I believed what the government was saying. If "they" took Vietnam, it let communism in through the back door to the rest of the world.

It wasn't until I returned that I realised that everything I'd gone through, and my belief in serving my country, wasn't appreciated. TV was telling me I was a killer though I'd never killed anyone.

I'd arrived home around 0100 hours to a hot and humid Sydney and headed to a hotel with Bill Scott, a tank driver in the Cavalry Regiment who'd been a rookie with me at Kapooka and on the same flight to Vietnam a year before. At reception we asked for a couple of rooms, but when a group of rich American tourists arrived a few minutes behind us the desk clerk told us to step aside as "there are customers more worthy of being served first". We were stunned into silence. Too tired to try and find another hotel, we waited and finally got into our rooms at about 0230 hours.

That morning we headed back to the airport, me to fly onto Brisbane and Scotty to Melbourne. At the TAA terminal, we saw a large group of anti-Vietnam protestors waving placards. As we got out of our taxi, they rushed us, yelling obscenities and calling us child killers and murderers who should be in jail. Scotty and I tried to make our way towards the terminal entry while the crowd jostled and heckled us. A hippie lady spat at me. I wiped the spit from my face and continued inside, struggling to understand what was going on.

Never before in Australia's military history were returned soldiers psychologically attacked by their own people.

A few weeks later the postie delivered a small package. In it were my Vietnam Medal and the South Vietnam Campaign Medal, mailed rather than presented on the parade ground. I was insulted.

It became obvious why the Australian Government brought their diggers back at night. It seemed that these demonstrators, traitors in our eyes, were targeting Australian service uniforms.

Girls, seeing my short back and sides in a period of long hair and free thought wouldn't talk to me. My hair, my demeanour, was evil. Lost, I'd headed to the local RSL to talk to like-minded people. The RSL wasn't interested. Vietnam wasn't a respected war like Korea or the World Wars. It didn't matter to Civvy Street if you were a Nasho (national serviceman) who'd been drafted or an army volunteer. They hated us both.

One of the lucky ones, I found a wonderful girl, married and started a family. Others weren't as lucky. One of my mates suffered for years with nightmares before blowing his brains out in Thailand. Others sought to numb themselves with drugs and alcohol.

I'd marched in two Anzac Day parades: Brisbane in the '70s and Longreach in the '80s. Both times I felt uncomfortable. Crowds would cheer the Korean vets, and then fall silent as we passed. I walked away from it all.

Now, Jeremy was asking me to read the Ode to the Fallen. We gathered outside the comms building near the flagpoles at 10am for the dawn service.

Sean raised the flag to half-mast in the weak sunlight and it hung limply. For once, no wind was blowing. The silence was total, interrupted by Jeremy with a few words of introduction before I read the Ode.

They shall grow not old as we that are left grow old,

Age shall not weary them nor the years condemn.

At the going down of the sun and in the morning,

We will remember them.

Lest we forget

Snow fell softly on my face as I recited the famous lines. I'd only agreed to participate because I felt it was my duty, but it ended up being more personal than that. I felt warmth and respect from the other expeditioners.

Tony played the Last Post on his trumpet and a minute's complete silence was then followed by the flag fully raised to mast-head. Once back in the warmth of the mess, we followed the ceremony with a traditional game of two-up, Anzac biscuits and drinks. We all started with a million dollars in play money but within an hour no one had anything, except Jim, who'd won it all.

***

The world got bigger the next day with the news that the ice was finally thick enough for us to leave base. It was cold, down to -24°C. Seven people left the station on jollies, and there was a rush to put names down on a roster so that, weather permitting, we could head out on quads to check out the surrounding areas.

By the end of the month, the ice was thick enough in most places for quads, though Malcolm and Paula were anxious as we were still banned from Ellis Fjord, where a tidal race slows down the formation of sea ice across a critical channel. Their study site at Crooked Lake lay beyond the channel. Until they could cross it, they couldn't set up their electronic equipment to start their lake environment experiments.

Station maintenance, a never-ending process, brought surprises and frustrations for some of the expeditioners. Gil, Neil and Sharon spent several days rebuilding one of the powerhouse generators which had dropped a valve into one of the cylinders, causing considerable internal damage.

Their work seemed non-stop. While the rest of us had stepped off the AA and worked our way through changeover, they immediately started pumping

622,500 litres of fuel across the sea ice into the bulk fuel farm tanks. During the winter, they serviced all the machines not required that season while also keeping the quads going, unbogging Utes and other machines, and clearing snow after blizzards.

Sharon was the first female mechanic to winter with ANARE. From a small town in Queensland, she left her farm and animals behind to work as a diesel mechanic at Davis. I'd talked to her in Brisbane at the psych tests at the Army Recruiting Centre. She got the job in her late twenties and returned to Davis in 2006 for another winter. In 2007 she was awarded the Antarctica Medal for her work as an Air Ground Support Officer.

CHAPTER 14
JOLLY TO THE BANDIT

May 2003 weather details:
Max temp -7.0°C, Min −29.2°C, monthly average -17.8°C
Maximum wind gusts 71 knots (132 kilometres per hour)
Average daily sunshine 0.7 hours

Another blizzard had its grips on the station. I tried going to the office but had to turn back, crawling along the rigging lines to the safety of the accommodation block. It cleared long enough for me to go outside for an aurora, which was the best I'd ever seen. Intensely green, this sky painting would continually change with fingers of light flowing like a waterfall which lit up the area.

The winds finally died down and conditions cleared enough for a jolly. Spontaneity is not an option down south, and it took quite a while to pack my bag, bivvy, food, water, medical kit, comms radio and check the quad bikes. Finally, around midday, Mark, Gil and I took off towards the Law Cairn, about five kilometres from base.

It was overcast and about -20°C, and I was balancing keeping the quad stable gear loaded in the front and dreaded black box strapped securely behind with the excitement of being released from the base to explore the surrounds. We headed north on the sea ice, keeping the coast on our right and passing by Flutter and Lake Islands before turning into the coast again.

We found the cairn, now legally registered on the Australian Heritage Council's Register of the National Estate, packed under rocks. A tin box holds copies of historic documents at the site of the flag-raising ceremony conducted by Philip Law in 1954. The then director of the AAD, he was also the leader of the expedition on board Kista Dan which landed in Vestfold Hills. It was the first ANARE landing in the area and an important precursor to the establishment of an Australian presence.

After signing the book, we headed back on the quads and took off for Bandit's Hut. Established in 1983 on the north-west side of Tryne Fjord to support seal research, it's the furthest spot away from Davis (about 26 kilometres north-east) and can only be accessed via sea ice or helicopter. Because the trip is so long, we planned to break it up with a cup of tea at Brookes Hut in Shirokaya Bay. We made steady progress, with Mark manning the GPS while Gil and I used the map. It was completely different from anything I'd seen while exploring Macca. White, blue and black were the only visible colours besides our bright clothes.

At Brookes Hut, we parked the quads on the edge of the ice and went inside to warm up. It's a good set-up which is used mainly for seal and lake research. It was a good day for travelling, but the motorised speed really intensified the wind chill factor. A quick cuppa later and we headed back into the bay and travelled north-east past Soldat and Partizan Islands before turning east into Long Fjord. We found Pioneer Crossing before moving north into Tyrne Fjord and arriving at Bandit's Hut at 3pm.

Once inside Bandit's, Mark immediately got the gas heater and stove going to counter the damp cold. We sat down to a well-deserved cup of tea before Gil and I went to start the generator. We struggled with it before eventually realising we'd failed to turn a knob to let the fuel through. As the generator finally cranked over, we felt like fools.

Mark and I sat in our freezer suits, waiting for the hut to warm up from its -25°C ambient temperature when Gil returned from a trip outside to use the black box. He sat near the gas heater to warm up, and Mark and I noticed clouds of steam rising from his back and an acrid smell. Apparently he'd managed to pee on his freezer suit while trying to sit on the box. Mark and I pissed ourselves laughing to the point where I had to leave the hut to catch my breath. It was a good chance to get to know these blokes better.

Mark was the optical physicist but also the electoral officer, sea ice monitor and fire team relief. A few years younger than me, he'd earned the nickname "Midnight Special" for his habit of rolling up to the bar in the early hours after work to have an afternoon beer, just as others were enjoying the final moments of their long nights. He was a top bloke, as was Gil, and we spent the evening eating Gerbil's stew and rice, toasting the experience with a few gins and Baileys.

While waiting for the sun to rise the next morning, I cooked sausages and bacon on bread for breakfast. The floor, filthy from our boots the night before, was made spotless and we emptied the slush bin before filling up the sauce bin with snow, ready for the next mob. Meanwhile, Gil refuelled, checked and started our quads.

At 10.30am we went to the top of the hut, ready to film the sunrise. The tracks we'd left the day before were all that marred the pristine surface of the sea ice looking towards Barrier Island. *Spectacular.* For that short moment, I imagined what someone standing on Everest would feel isolated, nature challenging your view, simply on top of the world.

After a final toilet stop, freezing hands not making the exercise any easier, we packed our rubbish and headed off. We were going north, past Mikkelsen's Cairn on one of the last islands to the north in the Prydz Bay, before turning back to the northern edge of the Vestfold Hills and to Sir Hubert Wilkins Cairn in Walkabout Rocks. It was here that Sir Hubert declared the area in the name of England, and a cairn with a flag and a copy of the declaration is at the site.

We climbed the steep hill and studied the spot before signing the book and heading back down. It was a good opportunity to practice ice stops sliding down then turning and putting your ice pick in. Gil took a bum ride instead sliding down on his behind and locking his heels in to slow down.

Our plan was to go return via the coastal route through the icebergs, but we kept encountering rafted ice (sheets of sea-ice piled one against the other) so opted to head back via Tryne Sound. Along the way we stopped to drill into the ice and measure the thickness (even jollies have duties). We followed a GPS route which took us out into Prydz Bay. The snow was thick with heavy drifts and areas of rafted ice, but Mark led us out until we found a clear route.

In the afternoon we stopped at Rookery Lake apple, about halfway back to Davis, for a cuppa and lunch. Mark was complaining about his feet, something we were wary of because of the danger of frostbite. After a rest and warming of weary bones, we separated. Gil headed back to Davis while Mark and I took the scenic iceberg route home. We made good time. On the smooth ice we could travel about 55 miles per hour, while the rafted ice dropped us back to about five kilometres per hour. We got back to the station in fading daylight at 4.45pm after a 138 kilometre trip. We refuelled the quads, signed off and went to turn our tags back over in the mess hall.

I was desperate for a hot shower, but when I took my helmet off the look of horror on Mark's face told me something was wrong. I felt a fist-sized lump below my chin and knew I was in trouble. Frostbite. *Bad frostbite.* It had swelled out my chin and neck area and was seeping blood, forcing me to visit Dr Cad. The tingling started as soon as my body thawed out.

The tissue had frozen while I'd been out exploring the icebergs. When I put my helmet on it pushed down my neck warmer, allowing air to flow below my helmet and under my chin. While Mark and Gil had been wearing balaclavas, I had just the neck warmer and beanie. Since the air always seems bloody cold on a quad, I hadn't registered that something was wrong.

Dr Cad treated the worst of it and warned me that I'd need treatment for several weeks. I would end up with a small scar the size of a 5c coin. A few days later Dr Cad took several photos of my chin to send to the AAD's Polar Medicine Unit in Hobart. He'd never seen such severe frostbite and thought the pictures would be a good example for the unit. I'd expected some pain but didn't feel anything. After that experience, Jeremy issued me with a balaclava.

***

Back at the station, nothing much marred the routine. Every day the hydroponics team checked water and nutrient levels. We also had to take on the job of insects (which could not survive so far south) to pollinate. The month was busier than most as we were running an inter-station tomato-growing competition. Seeds couldn't be sown earlier than May 1. The station producing the best tomatoes by the end of July would win. So far our baby plants were little, but we were confident Davis would win its rightful title of best tomato growers.

Cathie had tested the hydrogen and pager alarms in the Met building and found them faulty. Because the Met team worked hours when few expeditioners were up and about, and because we used hazardous hydrogen gas, the Met building was set up with alarms. One was supposed to go off if there was a hydrogen leak. A pager alarm was to notify us if the person wearing it had fallen over or was in trouble. After much investigation, she found the fault.

Dr Cad came in to replenish the medical kit in the Met office and I took the chance to dress him up in our safety gear so he could release the evening balloon. It was cold, reaching -28.1°C on the 20th, and a cause for concern for all at the station.

Whenever anyone left the base to go into the field, they had to carry a hand-held VHF radio which relied on a repeater on a high hill, Tarbuck Crag, to handle signals from around the Vestfold Hills. Now it appeared that the repeater would no longer function when the temperature fell below -20°C.

Tests suggested that the repeater, powered by a small wind generator and solar panels, was the problem rather than its batteries. Ian led an expedition (with Neil, Cad, Dave P, Wixy and Sharon) up to the peak with a new repeater. Successfully restored, field activities could resume again with full confidence.

Gil invited me to tour the main powerhouse, and at midday I headed to his workshop. It was overcast and cold. I crunched through the snow, skirting around snowdrifts past the petrol bowsers, tractors and graders to the red doors of his workshop. Snow here was creeping up the doors and walls. As soon as I opened the door I was greeted by familiar mechanical noises. I found Gil working at a bench, welding a hydraulic fitting.

The tour had to wait as he manufactured a part for a loader bucket. He held up the offending part before returning to his welding.

"Normally I'd just put in a new one, but as we don't have any, I just have to make one up," he said. Antarctic ingenuity! Gil made sure it was fixed the best he could before motioning at me to follow him.

As we left, Gil grabbed a shovel to clear the doorway of drift and then led me towards the powerhouse. We had to tread carefully among the sharp rocks and cable pipelines.

As we approached the blue building, the hum of machinery was audible. We went into the control room where Gil checked all the instruments and took readings of KW and power factor, pressures, water and oil temperature and updated logs. These checks were done four times a day 8am, noon, 5pm and 9pm. For Gil it was simple: "Everything's got to be right, or we have to get out of bed to fix it".

He handed me a set of earmuffs and opened the door to the deafening noise of the generating plant with its four 165KVA generator sets. Power is generated by diesel-driven alternators which consume approximately 700,000 litres of Special Antarctic Blend distillate annually. A modular oil-fired boiler (five stepped burners with a 427kilowatt total) supplements the heat recovery system and acts as a primary heat source if necessary.

Waste heat is used to warm water that is pumped around the station through the site services to heat buildings. The services to station buildings provide the heating, hot water, potable water, fire-fighting water, sewage, electrical services and communications in an above-ground pipe system that is heat-traced to prevent freezing. It's all controlled by computer which operates unmanned around the clock.

Power generation is the major consumer of fossil fuels, so in recent years the Antarctic Division has been investigating the use of alternative power sources, including solar and wind. Mawson uses wind generators, which provide over 70 per cent of its power needs.

As part of a research project, a solar hot water system was installed at Davis and has supplied one hundred per cent of the hot water for personal and laundry use in the summer ablutions block. Similar additional units could mean that, at least through summer, all the hot water and heating for Davis could be supplied by renewable solar energy.

For the winter, though, the generator plant still rules. I watched Gil check the oil and give me the thumbs up at the dipstick readings. During the year he, Sharon and Neil had two major jobs in the main powerhouse: rebuilding the No.2 engine when a valve hit a piston, and then changing out the old No.1 engine and fitting in a new one.

***

For Friday night drinks that week Jim and I ran a barbeque, something I love doing. It gave Gerbil a chance to prepare for the big night planned for Saturday *Priscilla comes to the Ice*. In true ANARE fashion, cross-dressing was at its best (Jim teetered around in a tight miniskirt while Cad made quite a queen). Luckily I was on the evening shift and grateful for the excuse not to don a dress. Peer pressure or not, I couldn't imagine myself walking through the snow in a frock to release a balloon.

I got the chance to go with Jim and Richard for a sea ice observation trip, one of their weekly duties. There was barely a cloud in the sky when we set off on quads around dawn (somewhere between 10-11am). We were headed to various established spots up to six kilometres offshore, marked by bamboo canes, to drill through and measure ice thickness and snow cover. These measurements serve two purposes. Early in the season they monitor whether the ice can support people and equipment. But they are also part of a long-term glaciological research program.

They found the first spot and I stood ready to record, my breath making white clouds. Jim and Richard worked the petrol-powered drill, countering the vibration as the drill dug slowly into the ice. Once through, a quick pull up and down the hole cleared it so measurements could be taken. I pulled my glove off for short periods to record the details, each time enduring seconds of painful exposure.

In the background the sun was reflecting off the surrounding icebergs, bathing them in soft pinks and oranges. We packed up and headed to the next location, with a small detour to visit ice caves. No two winters are the same. The summer thaw brings in new bergs and ships out the old. With expeditioners going out on various field trips, it wasn't long before this winter's favourites were identified and locked into the GPS.

We pulled up at one cave and got off the quads. Richard and Jim stood at the surface, dwarfed by the massive opening, before going inside. I could hear their voices echoing while I studied the smooth opening, itself dwarfed by the impressive size of the iceberg. I picked my way inside, choosing my steps carefully among the ice chunks scattered around the floor. Crampons would've been handy. It was incredibly slippery and the shards very sharp. I accidentally knocked a piece and it shattered with a sound much like a glass breaking.

We truly were in another world. The feeling was overwhelming. The cathedral of ice demanded respect. Through the opening we could see the blue reflection of ice with a pink tinge of low sun along the bottom third. Slight popping and cracking reminded us that there was movement below, but we knew it was safe.

Jim remarked to us: "We could live in here."

"We could," I agreed.

Then Richard piped up: "When banished from the station, this could be the place to be."

I sat in awe of what nature could create and absorbed the moment, realising that it was this feeling I'd been imagining when I dreamt of Antarctica. Of being overwhelmed by beauty, of yearning and unfulfilled desire. Of the extreme joy and satisfaction at seeing the gifts Mother Nature could give after testing us with hostile and extreme conditions.

We had to go. I broke away from my thoughts as the others headed out. After one last look around, I followed.

While we weren't supposed to enter any caves, the temptation had been too great and we'd only gone in after fully assessing all the risks. You have to use your knowledge and common sense. I'd say we weren't the only ones to have done so over the winter, but we didn't talk about it once we got back.

For the rest of the afternoon, we went to the various sites and continued to take measurements. More drilling, more dropping of the plumb on a weight to gauge distance to the water trapped below, more bursts of freezing fingers as I duly took the recordings.

As the sun set behind an iceberg, throwing long streaks of colour into the clouds, I took a turn with the drill, struggling to keep the shaft straight against the vibration and shaking. Planted legs helped, but the drill kicked as it dug in, the whine of the engine sounding just like a lawnmower which was quite out of place in this environment. Ice was crushed into a fine powder which we brushed out of the way with our boots before attacking again. A sudden give and we were at the water. Jim dropped the plumb and announced 713 millimetres.

Last measurement done, we headed back to base to finish our 20 kilometre trip, the angle of the sun seemingly setting fire to the icebergs.

***

Supplies were running low at the Met office, so Beacon and I went to the green store to get more sondes and balloons. Of course, they'd been stored on the top shelving, requiring a forklift to get to them not a problem for us with all our forklift training. That is, until we actually tried to do it. I had a shot but reversed into something so Beacon took over. He too crashed into the compactors and handed the wheel back over. Anyone passing by would've wondered what all the banging and crashing was as we fumbled our way around. Eventually we got our gear and loaded it into Gerbil's ute for the trip up to the Met office, leaving behind, I'd imagine, a few dings in the remaining gear.

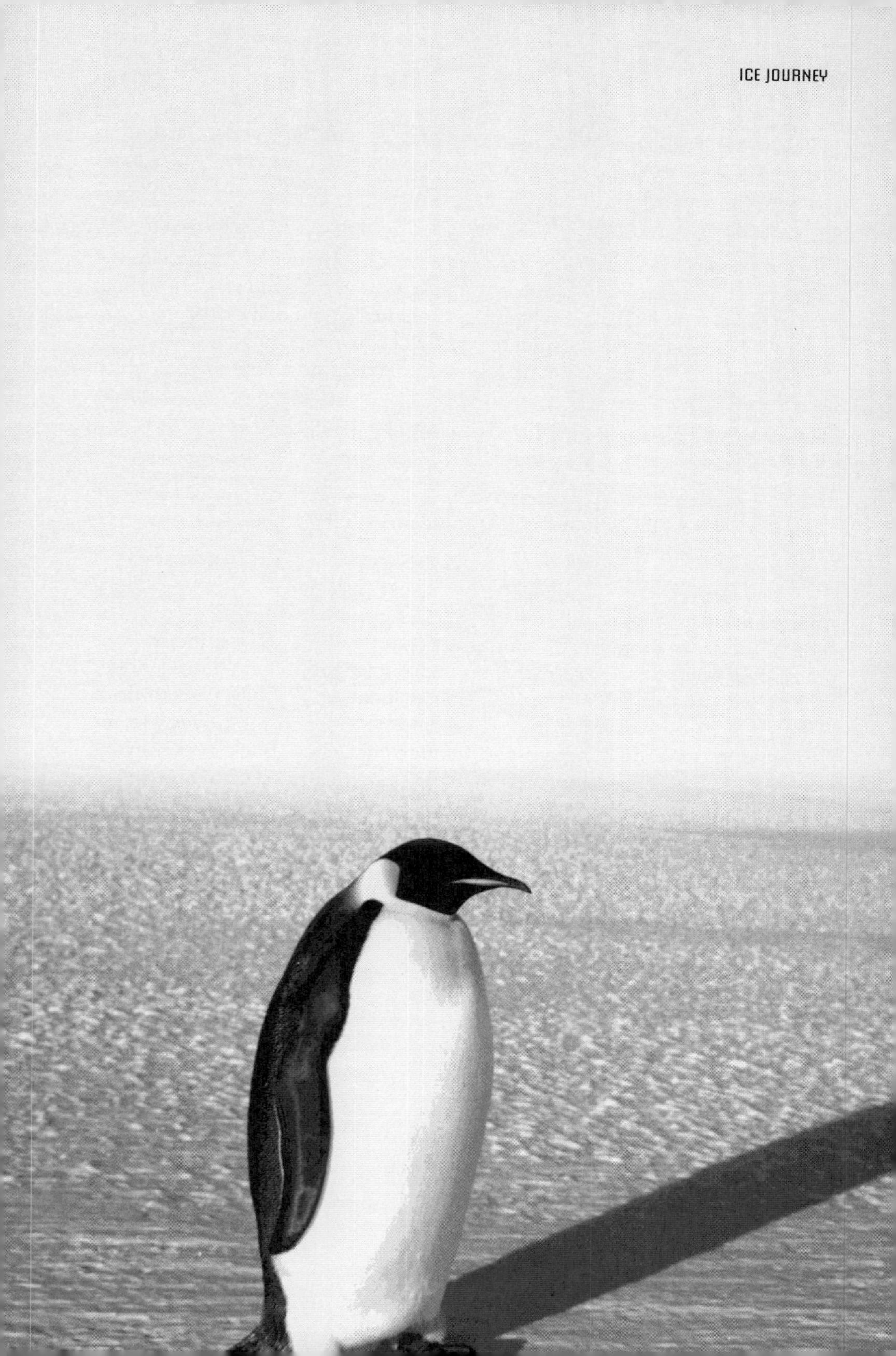

CHAPTER 15
DARKNESS, DARKNESS EVERYWHERE

June 2003 weather details:
Max temp -2.8°C, min −26.0°C, monthly average -14.4°C
Maximum wind gusts 72 knots (133 kilometres per hour)
Average daily sunshine 0.0 hours

The second day of June was the last day the sun would rise above the horizon for a while. It stayed above from 1320-1411 hours, a final gift of 51 minutes of sunshine. The pole has 24-hour darkness for several months. Further north, Davis (only a few degrees beyond the Antarctic Circle) still gets twilight for a few hours during the six or so weeks before the sun again peeks over the horizon.

Midwinter is often blamed for problems like sleep disorders, depression and conflict between expeditioners, especially as it's only the hump in the year. There's still half a year to go, and the excitement of being in Antarctica is waning after the highlights have been explored.

I didn't find this to be true with our group. Everyone handled the experience differently. Some chose to spend their downtime in their rooms, but back on the mainland, this would've been true too. With the official disappearance of the sun, we focussed on indoor activities, planning outdoor activities around the limited light, and leaving other projects to be tackled when the sun returned.

I was taking guitar lessons from Tony, the LIDAR physicist. Although he was about 40, he appeared a lot younger with his long scruffy hair and unshaven face. If someone had told me when I first met him that this bloke was a physicist and a brilliant musician, I would've laughed. Instead, he left me in admiration at how talented he was, and how kind and patient he was as I fumbled along.

The Met team and Tony worked closely together, especially during this period with the combination of our ozone balloon flights and his LIDAR beam. He didn't live in the main accommodation building, instead occupying a couple of old mobile containers about 20 metres away. He had it set up with all the luxuries you could imagine, and was quite happy in his own company, writing music or drawing in his spare time. At times you wouldn't see him for days, so someone would have to go and check on him to see if he was okay.

Volleyball was a popular escape. One night it was boys versus the girls, although no real girls were playing. Instead, we had a selection of ugly, hairy-legged, fake-breasted girls, including one in a bright yellow wig with Priscilla wide-bottomed fluorescent pants. I felt very masculine in my Essendon beanie.

As I headed out on the cold porch before the match, I hadn't realised who was playing. I passed a girl wearing glasses, calling out "G'day, Paula, how're you going?"

"I'm not bloody Paula," a deep male voice bellowed back and Chad turned around with a frown. I burst out laughing at the look on his face and tried to explain I'd just seen his long hair and glasses and assumed it was Paula, but I don't think I convinced him.

The "girls" ended up walking all over us, and though we made up some ground, they beat us 3-2.

If I wasn't learning guitar or playing volleyball, I'd be at the movies. Movie nights were a popular part of the social scene and at most screenings a group would gather in the comfortable seats. Gerbil provided ice cream, popcorn or chips and Cathie would load up baskets with lollies or chocolates.

Although we had recent VHS and DVD movies, it was the old films that we adopted, going through classics such as Paint Your Wagon and Seven Brides for Seven Brothers.

Monday nights were reserved as musical nights. We went through all of our musicals before switching over to westerns. Friday nights were Bond nights and for 19 weeks we watched every one.

Many of the movies in the extensive library were 16 millimetre films, and Evil, Sean or Malcolm would man the projection booth. Often the old movie flickered or stopped part way and they'd have to leap up to rescue film from spooling on the floor or to make a quick splice and feed it back as we'd heckle and shout. The only thing missing were Jaffa's rolling down the floors.

***

One day I left for Ace Lake with Chad and Nanette to help with their project studying viruses in saline lakes. For a number of years it had been evident that viruses were common in the sea and lakes, and were threatening the bacteria and phytoplankton (single-cell organisms which form the basis of the marine food web and play a key role in the exchange of carbon dioxide between the atmosphere and ocean).

By killing these, the viruses were having an effect on local climatic patterns by affecting the cycling of carbon in the lakes. They occurred in concentrations of tens to hundreds of billions per litre, and Chad and Nanette were checking weekly three lakes surrounding Davis Ace, Pendant and Highway for concentrations of micro-organisms.

Chad and Nanette were a solid team, both academically and personally. They spent their first year of married life working together in the Arctic. Nanette was a postdoctoral research fellow in limnology and Chad was a biologist studying the role of viruses in saline lakes.

We headed north at 12.30pm on quads to Long Peninsula, which held all three lakes. It was cold with strong NE winds blowing about 15-20 knots. Our quads were loaded up with gear, and I'd been warned we'd have to man-pack it a fair way as rocks would prevent us from driving onto the lake. As we headed up the coast past Powell Point and through Zvuchzyy Island to park in a cove, the wind chill cut into our gear. I kept moving my fingers inside the protective pockets around the handles to keep circulation moving.

Once at the lake, Chad and Nanette unpacked before drilling through the thick surface. They'd be taking water temperatures, water samples and radiation readings at various depths from two down to 14 metres. The water, packed in sample containers, would be taken back to base to be checked for organisms using a microscope.

The wind had picked up and I kept moving around, waiting to record statistics. "She's a cold one," I complained as the wind whistled. Chad could at least keep warm with the vibrations of the drill, but once he'd finished and was collecting samples, he screamed and started dancing and jumping across the ice in an effort to warm up.

The water collection system was intriguing. Chad would cock the top of the tube and drop it down the hole on a stick. Once he was at the right depth, he'd release the trigger to snap it shut and lock in the water at that level.

Nanette glanced up from her samples and I saw her eyes widen. "You've got a really white patch on your cheek."

I couldn't feel anything, but she dropped her gear and came over, rubbing the spot. "Oh, Dave," she said, pulling down the warmer covering her mouth. "Cover it up straight away."

She went back to work and I kept rubbing the spot, trying to encourage more circulation. We continued, Chad pulling out samples and Nanette taking the samples to bottle them, occasionally studying me again and telling me to keep rubbing. After the damage to my chin and neck, I certainly didn't want any more frostbite, which was especially dangerous at that time of the year.

Once we were finished we lugged all the gear, heavier now with all the water, back over the rocks. Chad had an amazing strength and stamina. While only average build, he carried the lake packs, drills and equipment effortlessly, like a pack horse, while Nanette and I struggled to carry a full container with water samples between us.

***

I'd completed my Hagglunds theory with Gil, and now faced the practical part of the training before being allowed off base in these machines. The Swedish-made dual-cab over-snow vehicles are equipped to carry four people in the front. They can travel over most terrain, including sea ice and soft snow, and have a range of 250 kilometres, depending on speed, load (they can tow up to two tonnes on sleds) and terrain.

Gil took out Curtis and me and put us through our paces. I was in the cab with Curtis, a veteran on the machine, and being the only rookie I figured I was in for a long afternoon. I drove while Gil explained the steering and how it affected the articulation of the front and rear cabs.

"Use the knob to steer – it's not like a car where you can actually go straight ahead and it can centralise the wheels."

It took a while to get used to it; four rubber tracks reacting differently to wheels. I concentrated on aiming where I wanted to go while Gil coached us about where to keep the revs over different terrain.

It was like being in a yacht trapped in big seas straight up over tidal cracks and then nose down while the rear cab, used for gear and equipment, followed. I was feeling confident until Gil took us to a flat patch and made us reverse between bamboo sticks and cans. I concentrated on the back section, using my mirrors, and managed to finally get through. I was pleased I wouldn't have to keep hearing the annoying alarm which came on when reversing. We worked through a zigzag pattern until Gil was satisfied we could manoeuvre the beast and finally headed home.

***

The winds had picked up again. I'd lie in bed at night listening to the wind train howl past outside. I'd grown to hate the walk in the dark from the accommodation building to the Met office; the only one out there at that hour, holding onto the rope and forcing myself forward.

Before heading out, I'd assess the situation to see if it was even worth trying. If the wind gusts were around 70 knots, I'd see if I could get to the main store. That's providing there wasn't a total whiteout, otherwise it was no go.

But for once I could sleep soundly, knowing I wouldn't work the next day. It was Mid-winter, the biggest date on the Antarctica calendar. Not only is it the winter solstice, it's also the approximate mid-point of the expedition and the celebration is a tradition going back to Scott's first Antarctic expedition in 1901. Plus it was a holiday no one on base would work that day, except Gerbil and waiters Jeff and Jim.

Activities started with a chicken and champagne breakfast, followed by successive dips in cold and hot spas. It was traditional to swim in a hole in the sea ice, but this year they hadn't been able to make a big enough space. Gil and Jeff used explosives to break through, but the chainsaw hadn't worked when they'd tried to enlarge the hole.

A few of the younger expeditioners were disappointed but I was never going to swim there myself. Dr Cad had warned a few of us older blokes that the shock could cause heart problems.

Plumbers Paul and Cal built an outdoor cold spa and an indoor hot one in the tank room. Throughout the day we took turns, sipping on champagne and relaxing in the hot water. Then we gathered in the mess for the feast. Every place setting had a decorated menu featuring photos of all of us. At the front, Gerbil had placed a massive iceblock about two metres wide and one metre high with 'DAVIS' in bright green letters. On the walls hung a range of flags, including the Australian, Aboriginal, ANARE, various other countries and even Australia Post. At the back of the room was another huge block of ice on a table, this one with "Davis 2003 Antarctic Mid-Winter" on it.

Once we sat down, Jeremy took the floor and welcomed everybody to the celebration. His thanks to Gerbil were met by huge cheers and claps, and Gil and Jeff were thanked for their valiant attempt to make a swimming hole, as were Cal and Paul for the spas, Mark for the planning of the evening's entertainment and Pauline for the costumes.

Stations traditionally exchange greetings to celebrate Mid-winter, and Jeremy read out some of the 40 or 50 Davis had received, including those from Ministers and from ANARE.

Then we started the feast a range of seafood, ham, salads from the hydroponics shed (including the first ripe tomatoes of the year) turkey, various soups and entrees and several sorbets and desserts. The food was so substantial that one buffet was barely touched, and I doubted that any meal I'd have in the future would ever match what Gerbil produced for us.

Entertainment followed with Malcolm, Wixy, Evil, Chad, Cad, Beacon and Mark taking to the stage for the pantomime Jack and the Beanstalk (with an ANARE slant). Cal and Cathie rounded out the cast as the front and back ends of a cow and Tony accompanied them on his guitar. Mark organised the stage and Jeremy was the proud producer. The group left us in stiches, especially with the veiled ANARE twists to the old much-loved storyline.

It was our day. Mid-winter on the Ice is the closest a lot of us southern hemisphere residents get to the climatic feel of a northern Christmas, but this was more than that. We're all outsiders here, with national boundaries less defined than in our respective home countries, and on this day we celebrated the genuine humanity and feeling of cooperation.

***

A few days later we were back to blizzard conditions, with visibility well under 100 metres and wind gusts to 65 knots. It was around this time, when the weather improved, that the sea ice team went to do their weekly ice-thickness measurements and discovered winds had broken and blown out the offshore ice, taking with it the two furthest sites and leaving only water where the bamboo canes had once stood. They put markers along the new sea ice edge and monitored as it reformed to make sure it was thick enough to bear normal movement. They also reported seabirds flying past, the first animals sighted for many weeks.

On the 26th I joined Chris Lawson of ABC radio (Rockhampton and Central Coast) in a live radio broadcast, talking about what it was like living down at

Davis. We managed about five minutes before we lost the connection, but it was fun, especially as I knew my family back in Yeppoon was listening.

It was snowing steadily, but the winds started to ease back to a more reasonable 20 knots. I managed to release an ozonesonde into a clear night, which later produced some magnificent auroras. I sat, chilled but not caring, wondering if I'd ever get bored with the sight. Somehow the sense of awe never left me, each show being so unique.

The snow continued through to the end of the month, which required continuous digging out from doorways, especially the big steel doors in the balloon shed.

On the 30th, I went with Wixy and Cathie to the wind direction recorder which had iced up with blown snow during the blizzard conditions. Strapped into their fall-restraint gear, they climbed up the wind Dines mast through the falling snow while I manned the radio below. Beacon in the Met office would give directions, which I'd relay up the mast and Cathie and Wixy would adjust the recorder according to Beacon's instructions. Then I'd relay back and Beacon would check before giving further directions. This went on until the two matched.

One of the highlights for the month for some of the others was moving a melon hut (brought back from Brookes Hut in May) from the station to Crooked Lake for Malcolm and Paula to use as a refuge and field laboratory. Nine people (Malcolm, Paula, Neil, Sharon, Jeremy, Paul, Jeff, Jim and Richard) moved the melon on a steel sled towed by a Hagglunds (with four people in it, the rest on quads) to set it up. Apparently three rocky crossings between frozen fjords and lakes made for slow going.

We were now on the downward run of the year. Our social activities and routine continued, and we looked forward to the sun breaking the horizon in a few weeks.

CHAPTER 16
FIRST SIGHTING OF THE SUN

July 2003 weather details:
Max temp -5.3°C, min −30.8°C, monthly average -19.3°C
Maximum wind gusts 69 knots (128 kilometres per hour)
Average daily sunshine 0.2 hours

For years, a lone mysterious face, roughly carved from a squared length of Oregon timber, had stood behind the Met building, its inscrutable face looking past the usually frozen sea, past icebergs towards Australia. Nobody knew its history; all that was known was it was the work of an expeditioner sometime in the late 1980s and it had been moved there in 1993 due to construction work.

During the summer, artist Steve Eastaugh, had taken inspiration from the face and developed a unique Antarctic sculpture garden, creating four other works to join it. His hope was to create an Antarctic sculpture garden by tempting others to construct more totems. The idea was to create some other vertical structures in the environment besides the antennas, flagpoles and windsocks situated all about the station.

Establishment of the sculpture garden was given official blessing by the environmental preliminary assessment process earlier in April, and would now be open for additional contributions from inspired expeditioners, providing they liaised with the station leader and the Operations Branch Environment Adviser so that environmental assessment guidelines could be followed.

The publicity generated by Steve's sculpture garden led to a request for information about the original head sculpture in the ANARE Club's journal Aurora, and nearly 30 years later, the puzzle was solved while we were there.

Hans Van der Sant, a plumber who wintered at Davis in 1977, told of the head's origins: "The wooden head has survived! Wow, pity about his name though, the head had a title, 'Man sculptured by Antarctica'. The head was carved in wood to be sculpted by the elements to become a token of our humanity in an environment that we have only just arrived in.

"The head holds my spirit of that stay. He looks out to the forests I left behind me, when I stand on the coast and look for auroras in the southern sky he was there to look back at me."

The Australian Antarctic Division said a meteorological technician named Bernie had been at Davis late in 1996 and found the carving when cleaning up around the office. Before returning home, he took it out and placed it in a stone cairn he'd built to hold him up, and aligned him so when sighted along a line from the nearest corner of the Met office, he was due north and aimed his face in that direction.

***

The sun finally made an appearance on the 9th, two days before the official sunrise of the 11th. Davis is supposed to have the sun below the horizon for 38 days but many factors can affect that definition of the horizon, how much of the sun should be above it, weather conditions, etc. Mark was the only one to spot it, but that might have had something to do with the fact he was standing on the roof of the Space and Atmospheric Sciences Building just after lunch, and his extra height gave him an advantage.

Regardless of its early showing, we would celebrate the official sunrise on the 11th with a golf afternoon organised by Jim and Jeff. The opening of the Davis Golf Day competition was an official event, complete with fireworks (well, detonations which needed to be tested for reliability due to age. Jeff set them off, three small explosions a safe distance out on the sea ice). Then the games began.

We were sharing clubs and working on Davis's five-hole top golf course, mostly over sea ice whose rough surface played havoc with our well-planned shots with the pink and orange balls.

As with fishing, I don't mind having the odd swing at a golf course, but wasn't holding my breath for anything impressive. The Davis golf course required more luck than skill, and while we laughed at each other's sad attempts, Cad toured the course in a caddie's cart (a dressed-up quad) delivering refreshments and spare balls.

I watched Jim take a shot, concentrating furiously, while someone in the crowd kept tossing a glove to distract him. For all his effort, it was a terrible shot, travelling only a couple of yards, but the crowd's "oooohhhh" provided sympathy.

Then it was my turn. I'm a complete hack and couldn't even manage that. Beacon was on his third hole and as he swung, the crowd's heads turned as one to follow the graceful arc of his club as it went flying instead of the ball.

On the third hole, I took a mighty swing and sent my ball about 10 feet sideways. Unfortunately, Jim was in that direction, bending down for something and my bright orange ball connected squarely with his bum. He shot up in shock while the crowd laughed, and I yelled out "Sorry, mate".

The surprise was on me the next night at dinner when they handed out awards such as "Best Handicap", "Best" and "Worst". I got called up to accept my trophy "Closest Shot to the Hole" with my orange ball sitting on top of a wooden block, my name written in black.

Anyway, on our first official day of sunshine, we ended up recording it from 1331-1416 hours.

***

Mid-month, one of our water pipes broke and we lost 16,000 litres of water, which was one week's supply. The problem was 20-year-old plastic, but the loss was serious and became the talking point that night. We were told to be even more cautious with our water use. Already restricted to two-minute showers, we were encouraged to limit usage wherever we could. Cal and Paul found the break under a two-metre snow drift and spent some very cold hours completing the repairs.

We cracked the -30°C mark, recording -30.8°C just after lunch. The wind chill factor was high, and Cal showed us a trick outside the kitchen. He brought out a pan of hot water which he threw into the air and it instantly froze into steam, drifting off in the breeze. Several people didn't seem to believe it, so he went in to fill up with hot water again. Apparently it's the Mpemba Effect, which states that hot water changes its state from liquid to solid or freezes faster than cold water. This doesn't seem to make sense but has been discovered to be true. I could honestly say it was the first time in my life that I watched boiling water instantly become steam.

My ozonesonde release failed a few days later, and I assumed the string broke as I was receiving a signal on the computer but it wasn't going anywhere. Cathie and Paula later found it in the aerial farm and Beacon gave me a Red Face award for forgetting to do up the string. Everyone spent the day laughing at me, and even though I know I did tie up the damn string and the knot didn't come undone, no one would listen.

Beacon Awards were a highlight around the station and teasing was rampant. Jim got his share for the Great Toast Episode. He was making a pile of toast in the kitchen and had his back turned as he was talking footy with me. Suddenly the toast caught on fire, flames licking up and I'm trying to tell him there was a fire behind his back. He was miles away, so intent on the footy that he must've thought I was waving my arms in agreement.

My favourite award was Mark's, given to him for the Great Davis Flood back in May. He was soaking dirty gym towels when, distracted by preparations for an upcoming jolly, he left the water running in the laundry tub.

"Even when an agitated communications technician entered the mess with wet feet and trousers rolled up, looking for a plumber, the penny didn't drop," he told me.

"It did eventually, but not until someone came in and said that some idiot had left the taps running in the laundry. When I went up to the laundry to clean up the mess, I could see that the floor waste drain was sitting quite proud of the surrounding floor, causing water to exit under the laundry door and possibly over the edge of the concrete slab to bedrooms below.

"So, off I went to see which rooms might be affected and to my horror discovered that the Doc's surgery was situated directly below the laundry. On entry, I found the Doc and Cal up a ladder looking for a non-existent leak in the pipe work in the ceiling of the surgery," he said sheepishly.

Mark had to wear his Beacon Award – a laundry plug attached to a chain – at all times when he used the laundry for the rest of the season.

***

As well as having winter expedition photos, it's also an ANARE tradition to have a winter plaque placed on the lounge walls at each Australian Antarctica base. For our 2003 winter plaque we had trouble choosing between two – one with a map of Davis and surrounding areas, and the other created by Nanette capturing the Antarctic winter.

I had trouble choosing between the two but decided to vote for Nanette's which won in the end. It was a very unusual piece of art work, nothing like the other previous plaques at Davis. It also became the logo on our tee-shirts and polar shirts.

Nanette described how she came up with her idea:

How dark really is the Antarctic winter? Winter is the sun's time off and in its place the moon shows off in all its glory. One morning a luminous moon was found surrounded by a glittering halo, which took up half the sky and seemed to almost skim the surface of the sea ice.

Often on those winter mornings, green glimmerings of the southern lights could be seen. The growing dominance of the moon, amidst a fast disappearing sun, offset by streaks of veiled colour in the sky, came to be the hallmarks of an Antarctic winter, with not a penguin in sight! All these winter impressions were distilled into a painting, which then formed the basis of an idea for the Davis 2003 winter plaque.

The creator's undictated intention was to represent the disappearing sun with the onset of winter as a series of decreasing yellow dots, ending in a large silvery moon suspended in the darkness, surrounded by stars (the Southern Cross) and a halo. Out of the perpetual night stream green auroras.

As the sun starts to return, the yellow dots continue on from the moon, getting larger and larger, signalling the return of spring and summer.

A lot of people formed their own interpretations as to the meaning of the design. Ideas ranged from the green auroras representing the greening up of spring, to the ever increasing sun appearing to be a string of Chinese love beads each to their own.

It is hoped that everyone will add their own slant to the plaque, making it unique and applicable to each individual.

***

By now, we were getting about five hours of sunshine on clear days and little wind meant outdoor activities were more comfortable than the previous month. The first Weddell seals were spotted beside their breathing holes on the sea ice. All the signs were there that we were slowly approaching spring.

CHAPTER 17
THE MIGHTY SØRSDAL

August 2003 weather details:
Max temp -5.5°C, min −32.7°C, monthly average -18.6°C
Maximum wind gusts 76 knots (141 kilometres per hour)
Average daily sunshine 1.3 hours

I started my month with another visit to Dr Cad after work, this time so he could remove a growth from the corner of my left eye. He'd been monitoring it during my monthly checkups. As it wasn't going away, he decided to cut it out. Seven stitches later and I looked liked I'd been through a boxing match. After he finished with me, I helped him with some dental work for Jim, who needed fillings.

Strong gale force winds continued, and the next day the 70-knot winds shredded my balloon. I was planning to leave for Watts Lake Hut the following day with Gil, Tony and Mark on a field trip and I hoped the winds would drop.

Luckily conditions were good: overcast and lightly snowing. But at -17°C it wasn't as cold as the previous few days. We were travelling over the sea ice and were halfway up Ellis Fjord when the quads started struggling to keep their grip on the blue ice. Tony started putting little bursts of power on, skidding in a circle and even Gil was struggling. I wasn't game to get off my quad to film without crampons. While putting my camera away, I told the others to start and I'd catch up. But I struggled too, trying to find a balance between enough power to go, and having too much and skidding.

Fortunately it wasn't far and the whole trip took only about half an hour. I was the last to arrive and stood on the quad's pedals to absorb the bumps where the ice pushed up against the coast. The view was magnificent, a gentle landscape with the long, seemingly smooth fjord behind, the red hut nestled in the saddle between the north eastern shore of Watts Lake and Ellis Fjord. Placed there to support biological programs in the fjord and nearby lakes, it was the ideal spot for us to pass the night.

It was bloody cold though, and the first priority was to get the heater going. With my outer gear left on the cold porch, I stood by the heater thawing out when one of the blokes yelled out, "What's that smell?"

Slowly realising it was me, I jumped back just in time. I had got too close to the heater and hadn't noticed my thermal wear had become too hot. Damn. At least I'd only suffered a few holes in my footwear woollen boots would cover that.

Once warmed up, we rugged up again and went to explore the surrounds. I headed off to film Watts Bridge but when I started the camera it died due to the cold. Gear had to be protected and I learnt my lesson. From then on, I put all my gear inside my yellow freezer suit between my singlet and thermal gear. The lump was well worth putting up with.

Dinner was beef stroganoff with garlic bread, calls of "bloody beautiful" sent back to Gerbil. We spent the rest of the night in the cosy hut, snow and ice gracefully piled up in the windows, playing poker for matchsticks something, unlike fishing or golf, I was really good at from my years in the army. As we joked and talked, I kept going until I was the recipient of all their matchsticks.

We woke late the next day at 10am. Days off were always a chance to have a sleep in. At 11.30am we headed back out towards Trajer Ridge and the ice plateau.

We had a clean run until we hit our first narrow ridge. We would have to cross several of these, and our centre of gravity on the quad would be important to avoid the huge drop-offs. The first one was nerve-wracking, and I fought my butterflies, concentrating on putting my weight over and taking it easy on the power. Like everything, once you've done one, the rest get easier.

It wasn't until I saw Tony stop ahead that I realised there was more to come. The narrow ridge ahead had massive drop-offs on both sides. It was an awesome view, but all I kept thinking was whether I could do this one. One by one, we carefully went over, relaxing once on the other side.

We stopped at Pauk Lake to take pictures, before pushing on through Trajer Ridge to stop at the apple. Its cheery painted happy face was a welcome sight. I'd been there in January for my field training and it was incredible to compare my memories with its current frozen state. Unlike at the station, where changes were gradual and seen on a daily basis, here it was dramatic. We walked around talking about the changes the panoramic freshwater lake now stark blue ice, with long white crack scars marring the depth.

We went onto the ice plateau. The barren landscape appeared endless, making distances impossible to judge. Clouds stopped the sun from fully exposing itself, letting only soft pastels of light through. We followed the edge of the plateau to Sprunky's Van, where we'd bivvied for the night during the summer training. We wanted a last look at the van, which was scheduled to be moved in the next few weeks back to Davis. It'd been home to two summer scientists working on the Sørsdal Glacier.

On the way, just past Trajer Ridge melon, Tony pulled up sharply and stopped the rest of us following. Cautiously we got off the quads and went to see what was wrong. Massive holes the largest a four-foot wide crevasse had split the ground, making it impossible to travel over. In shock, we studied it, looking down the seemingly endless depth. We'd travelled over this exact spot on the way to Sprunky's Van and the ice had obviously collapsed behind us as we'd driven off obliviously. And I was the last in the line at the time.

It was a reminder that nothing is certain out there. We were living and working in a fragile environment. What seems solid and stable can change in a minute.

Subdued, we went right around the area back to Watt's Hut, headlights cutting our path on the last stretch.

Morning came quickly. We cleaned up, loaded the black box onto the back of one of the quads and left at 11.30am for Crooked Lake. Cal, Cad and Beacon were there in one of the Hagglunds, helping Malcolm with his research, working with automatic weather sensors to investigate the temperature of the water and wind speeds, as well as drilling and checking for organisms. After catching up, we headed to the east side of the lake to climb Boulder Hill, a 10-minute trek which offered superb views.

Our goal that day was to get onto Sørsdal Glacier, which is accessed by the far western side of Crooked Lake, through the rapids, Mossel Lake and Chelnok Lake, but we couldn't find the path. It was clear on the map, but we couldn't get across ridges. There's only a narrow entry to get to the glacier and we missed it several times as we went up and down the area.

Finally the gap revealed itself and we made our way to the glacier, but by then it was heavily overcast and we couldn't make out the line between glacier and sky or see its true colours. In the heavy light, it looked quite angry, with a scarred edge. It was quite disappointing as others had raved about this massive slow-moving glacier, but for us to see it at its best wasn't to be. Even so, we walked along the glacier for a while in wonder at what stretched out beyond what we could see.

The Sørsdal is considered to be one of the key polar outlet glaciers that contribute to the drainage of the East Antarctic ice sheet. The year before scientists from Geoscience Australia had planted a DORIS beacon (Doppler satellite tracking system) to identify and monitor zones of fast-flowing ice so they could relate them to the development of crevasse fields.

Then it was time to head back, via Watts Hut to pick up the rest of our gear and the rubbish, going down Ellis Fjord to arrive at Davis at 5pm. It had been an exhilarating few days 133 kilometres of some of the best Antarctica could offer but after the scares with the crevasse and drop-offs, I was quite happy to curl up in my bed.

***

The 10th was a new low for us. The temperature reached -31.6°C. I didn't think it could get any colder, but the next day it did, down to -32.1°C. I stayed inside and started putting my flying rat together in preparation for the upcoming competition.

Cal had bought a pile of balsa wood planes powered by long elastic in Hobart and brought down to Davis, envisioning a period where we might need some excitement. So the birth of the "hangar rats" competition was announced and about 24 of us were to meet in the green store later that week for our first fly-off. The temperature kept dropping, hitting -32.7°C the following day. I was making slow progress with my flying rat, putting it together and taking it for test flights.

Finally, on the Friday night, we gathered in the green store for the big fly-off, a pig on a spit for dinner providing sustenance. One by one, we wound our rats up and set them free. I wound mine up, let it go and it crashed straight into the wall. I picked up the pieces, ready to rebuild for next week.

***

I had another chance to venture out with Chad and Nanette on one of their expeditions, this time to Pendant Lake. Light snow was falling and we headed off after morning tea, parked the quads on the edge of Highway Lake and walked the 1.5 kilometres across Highway Lake and then over rocks to Pendant Lake.

Chad and I would work the drill, motor straining, until we reached its limit when we'd have to pull out for Chad to put an extension on the shaft. The ice was thick but so clear it was deceptive, seemingly going on forever something the blue-grey ice of other places couldn't offer. Here large bubbles had been trapped and large white rounds perfectly preserved, only the odd white scar running through the ice ruining its canvas.

With the approaching summer, Gerbil had progressively resupplied the various huts around the region, bringing back accumulated old food items to be sorted, eaten or burnt. I went with Gil and Gerbil a few days later in a Hagglunds to the Rookery Lake apple and then to the Magnetic Island melon, located on the south western side of the island, about five kilometres from Davis. This was used by expeditioners involved in the long-term monitoring program on Adelie penguins but was closed to jollies during the penguins' breeding season.

At Rookery Lake, we swapped the supplies and took off on the sea ice through Iceberg Alley towards Magnetic Island, looking this time for arched bergs and stopping at some of the more impressive ones. The sun was out, making the entire landscape sparkle. We stopped at one tabular berg whose perfect arch almost cut it in half, the smooth edge of the arch contrasting with the sheer, jagged sides of the outside. The sun was behind and lit the inside with orange. Absolutely brilliant.

Along the way, we stopped to watch a solitary Emperor Penguin on the ice. It was a long way away from the edge of the sea ice. We were puzzled. These animals are incredibly social creatures and are usually found in large groups. The males are the "mothers", spending a remarkable 115 days of courting, mating and incubating of an egg without eating a single meal. Once the female has laid her egg (usually around the middle of May), she heads off to spend the winter at sea, leaving the male to spend the next 65 days with the egg resting on his feet, covered by a fold in his abdomen which envelops the egg.

While the female eats and stays in the warmer water, all the males huddle in a group with their backs to the wind, each with an egg on his feet. They take turns in the worst weather to move to the outside of the pack, each shuffling with his egg, so they can all take a turn in the warm centre.

In mid-July, the female returns to her mate, having memorised his call. He transfers the egg to her and the baby hatches soon after, leaving him to start the long trek to the ocean for water and food, the first in nearly four months.

What this one was doing so far from the ocean, by itself, we didn't know. Magnetic Island was calling so we headed southwest, got the Haggs to the edge of the ice and started carrying the new food in while Gerbil sorted through the old stuff. From the apple we could see sea ice and frozen bergs out to the horizon. When Gerbil had packed the old food, we slid the boxes down the hill to the ridge, heaved them into the vehicle and took off.

Friday brought an opportunity to break from routine and attend Jeremy's weekly blah-blah meeting. The heads of each section gathered in the afternoon and discussed the week, sharing any highlights and tabling any problems. Beacon usually attended these but he had slushy duties and asked if I could go in his place.

Afterwards, I headed to the green store for the second week of the flying rats competition. I was optimistic and cheered with the others as one by one we gently twisted the rubber bands to load up the propellers and sent our rats in the air. The crowd was verbally willing each on its journey. Dr Cad's lifted smoothly and stayed in an effortless circle above our heads.

Mine crashed, of course. At least the crowd gave a sympathetic "ooh" as it did. I winced at the bang and went to pick up the pieces, studying the wings which continued to defy me. Cathy took pity on me and gave me a new set to try.

Nanette and Sharon organised a brilliant Japanese night for the formal Saturday dinner, and I got into the theme by becoming a Japanese businessman

As the winter wore on, these social nights were becoming more important. Davis had a room full of makeup and costumes for theme nights. I wasn't very clever with a needle, but some of the others would adapt or create new costumes to add to the collection.

After Gerbil's creative feeding of the masses, he needed a break and that Sunday it was my turn to be chef for the day. Well, chef for lunch and dinner anyway everyone made their own breakfast. Cooking for 24 people by myself would have given me pause in my former life, but down here we were quite forgiving of whoever got the relief chef duties. Lunch was toasted sandwiches and leftovers, and I spent the afternoon creating the Bomber's Banquet night. Never one to ignore a chance to talk up the Essendon Bombers, I was celebrating the fact they'd beaten Fremantle by 60 points the night before to get into the finals. As I wrote out the night's menu on the whiteboard I couldn't resist adding "Go Bombers!" underneath.

We were still bottling beer in the brewing cellar, sampling our goods as we worked. A specialty was chilli beer, made with the chillies we'd grown in the hydroponics shed. As I drank, I could feel the liquid burning the lining in my stomach but the others liked it. We'd also preserved the chillies and Beacon urged me to try one. He'd munch on them endlessly, so I was game and popped one in my mouth. At the first chew, my mouth started to burn and I staggered to the water fountain in the mess, eyes full of tears, coughing and cursing a laughing Beacon.

For the next ten minutes, I poured in the water but nothing helped. Beacon may have had an iron gut, but I didn't. Shortly after, I got the runs and spent hours on the toilet with a burning ring of fire.

**

We ended the month with the third and final flying rats competition. I was ready new wings glued in place. This time my rat would fly. It crashed. I came to the conclusion I was never going to be an aeronautical engineer. Richard Groncki won with a top flight of 64 seconds.

Adding insult to injury, Essendon lost to Collingwood by 16 points that night. Wixy and I had a bet going that the loser would have to wear the winner's colours, and I never wear Collingwood colours. My team let me down, however, and I spent Saturday walking around in Wixy's Collingwood socks and scarf. Traitor!

Some of the others went off in two Hagglunds to retrieve Sprunky's van from the Vestfold Hills. The trip back down a steep snow ramp was a tricky testament to the skills of all involved, with one Hagglunds pulling the van down on sleds while the other Hagglunds anchored them from above.

Research in Davis's old logbooks found an answer to something that had been puzzling us. Early in the year, forecaster Lance Cowled had discovered a rusted old gas cylinder at a beach at the head of Long Fjord and put the location into the GPS. In July, Beacon, Wixy, Cad and Jeremy brought it back to the station for Cal to vent the residual contents. Analysis found it was hydrogen, which puzzled expeditioners. In the Met we use hydrogen every day to fill our balloons, but this is done on the base, while the cylinder was found about 24 kilometres away.

Jeremy found an answer in the logbooks. The cylinder was found a kilometre from the oldest field hut in the area Platcha hut, established in 1961 as a remote weather station by Norwegian-born meteorologist Nils Lied.

Lied was one of the founding Davis wintering expeditioners of 1957 and wanted to establish a remote weather station near the edge of the ice plateau to study katabatic winds, which he achieved in 1961. The van was established with great difficulty and persistence, assisted by expeditioners shovelling and pushing as Lied pulled with a tractor.

The weather station was manned by two men at a time in shifts of two to four weeks until January 1962 when it was shut down. Another hut was erected in 1982 and Leid's original hut was restored in 1988.

It was a reminder that August was over. The sun was shining longer and longer each day. In a few short months the peaceful routine we'd settled into would change with the arrival of the first ship of the season.

CHAPTER 18
EXPLORING THE RAUERS

September 2003 weather details:
Max temp -4.9°C, min -27.8°C, monthly average -14.3°C
Maximum wind gusts 65 knots (120 kilometres per hour)
Average daily sunshine 3.2 hours

Spring brings the best of Antarctica together longer days, improving weather and still solid sea ice to travel on. We'd planned to use the period to get off the base to explore a new area and prepare for the incoming summerers. Large-scale planning started for two teams of expeditioners to go to the Rauer Group of islands, about 40 kilometres south of Davis.

While not far, the Sørsdal Glacier lies in between and the sea-ice in front of the glacier frequently blows out, making that route unreliable and dangerous. To get there, we'd have to go up to the ice plateau and across the glacier, avoiding crevasses along the way.

In a few months, a group of biologists would be working in the area investigating pollutants in sea birds. We were charged with checking the condition of the huts and stores as the last time they'd been used was two years before. We gathered in the mess for a planning meeting and were assigned jobs. I'd be going with the second group near the end of the month, and was assigned to work with Gerbil on food rationing.

One afternoon I joined the others on the edge of the sea-ice near the field hut for our group photograph. An ANARE tradition, photographs were taken of winterers each year to hang in the lounge/bar area. Beacon set his digital camera on a tripod and was rushing to join us but hit a patch of slippery ice. He was frozen in slow motion, body frantic but no forward movement, when the camera went off. I yelled out that surely that qualified for a Beacon Award. The group cheered but we had to refer to rule No.1, Beacon is not eligible. We did manage to get a photo and it was a special feeling to know that I would hang on the wall for future expeditioners to look at a piece of Antarctica history.

***

On the 15th, the first group headed to the Rauers. Chad and Ian headed the group, Malcolm was in charge of logistics, Gil of vehicles and generators and Paula, Jeff, Richard, Nanette and Jeremy all piled into the Hagglunds and left soon after 7am. This group would have the additional job of placing 30 marker canes across the glacier for the return journey and for our group to follow.

Back at work, we started dipping our 1500 gram balloons in ATK petrol to harden them and prolong the time they'd spend in the air. I'd dip the balloon by hoist into a large can full of the stuff and hang it up to dry for use the next day. This made a big difference to our releases, giving us about another 15 minutes of flight time before bursting.

Curtis used a lull in the wind to try a first for Davis. With Beacon and Cathie's help, he used a modified camera suspended beneath a balloon to take the first aerial photograph of the station in winter, a time when there are no aircraft there.

Four days after leaving the first Rauers trippers returned to base, expeditioners full of stories and enthusiasm about what they'd done. Listening to them made me excited about the days remaining until I could go out myself. We left the next day at 5pm. The 25-30 knot winds buffeted us as we headed north across the sea ice to the western island. The Maggie "melon" had rested there since 1986, when it was assembled to support a long-term monitoring program on Adelie penguins. Traditionally, the hut would be closed during the breeding season, but the decision had been made to close it permanently, dismantle it and return it to Davis to be shipped back to Australia. Many people had marked the upcoming closing of an era by spending one last night there, and Gil, Mark and I decided to do the same.

We settled in the cosy melon to stew and rice, a couple of beers and poker. Once again I managed to clean them up throughout the night before we retired to a cold, damp sleep. A clear, sunny day greeted me when I crawled out at 9am the next morning, but the inside of the melon was thick with steam and fogged my camera as I tried to take a few final shots of the hut.

Jumping on quads, we headed further west towards the edge of the sea ice. We were about 19 kilometres away from base, and I knew in a matter of months that water would gradually claim back the distance.

About 20 metres away from where we stood, a leopard seal was playing at the water's edge and we gave it a respectable wide berth. They have a reputation for being aggressive, and I knew its placid face hid exceptionally long canines and unusually sharp molars. Females can reach lengths longer than three-and-a-half metres and can weigh over 500 kilograms, larger than their male counterparts.

An Emperor penguin was also roaming around the edge, also giving the seal a wide berth. As penguins are the leopard seals' favourite food, I couldn't blame it. Typically the seals chase or grab penguins in the water and thrash any poor captive back and forth until the skin peels away before it is consumed.

The Maggie melon was finally removed near the end of the month, Jim and Jeff emptying it with the help of Beacon, Jeremy, Richard and some others before untying its anchors. It was eventually manhandled down rocks and onto a sled and brought back to base. At the same time they removed the helicopter landing pad for use at another hut site.

***

The snow cleared to leave a sunny and clear morning and just after 7am, Gerbil, Wixy, Dr Cad, Mark Maxwell, Tony Graham, Sharon, Neil, Paul, Dave Power and I found our spaces in the two Haggs and left Davis behind, early enough to make the most of the day for the long run to the Rauers

We picked our way over snow and ice through the Vestfold Hills until we hit the Breid Basin at 8.40am, where we had to get out and walk up the steep ramp to put us on the plateau. The Haggs were loaded and pulling sleds, and for safety reasons we weren't allowed to ride in them up the ramp in case they tipped over.

Neil and Sharon, both experienced Haggs drivers, had the task of inching the giants slowly up the sharp gradient while we struggled up well behind. It was hard work, taking the better part of a quarter of an hour. We joined the vehicles at the top, climbed back in and followed the edge of the ice plateau south.

Two hours later, we arrived at the old Russian fuel dump. Rusted drums littered the otherwise pristine surface, a reminder of man's ability to blemish the land. From here, we continued on, passing over plenty of slots on the Sørsdal Glacier, feeling the Haggs as they dropped into the indentations.

At 1.30pm, something embedded in the ice stopped the first Haggs. Neil got out and peered at the object before calling us out. In the middle of thousands of square miles of empty ice was one of our Met radiosondes. We all climbed out and watched as Neil worked the ice pick to pry it out.

"Bloody Morg," someone yelled out. "Polluting Antarctica with your balloons and radiosondes."

I smiled as Neil held it up. It was like the proverbial needle in the haystack, but we must have been meant to find it. According to the GPS, we were 24.6 kilometres from Davis. I often wondered what happened to the ones that made it out of the big blue steel doors but didn't successfully reach bursting height.

A few hours later, we reached Rauers ramp where we refuelled the Haggs. The first expedition had dropped off fuel supplies and quads for us and after checking the decline, two people went ahead on quads while the rest of the group piled back in for the ride down. I took over the driving going down the ramp and an hour later we dropped from the ice plateau to the sea ice and to Hop Island.

There we unpacked and put up tents before heading to the melon (on the island itself) to boil snow down and to heat up some pork stew. We'd covered 87.7 kilometres in five hours, from Breid Basin ramp to the island. The night was quiet just food, card games and conversation in the cosy hut.

I knew I'd have a nightmare that night. New locations and changes to the routine often triggered them, and I knew I'd feel claustrophobic in the tent. Back in Vietnam at some of the fire support bases, we'd have to dig a hole and drop down large ammunition boxes. Skinny blokes would climb in the boxes, piled high with sandbags, while the bigger blokes would sleep in cut-down water tanks.

Mark and I were sharing. We made our way from the warm melon into the 35-knot winds to our tent. Once inside the cold porch area of the polar tent, I took off my boots and freezer suit, leaving only my thermals on and crawled through to the dry area where our bivvys and mattresses were. Quietly, I tied a rope around my ankle and attached the other end to the sleeping bag, not trusting myself not to run out of the tent in my sleep. At least if I managed to get out, I'd still be attached to my bag.

It was cold and the night only granted me a broken sleep. Once in my bivvy, I put on a dry pair of socks and tracksuit and curled up but the chill found its way in. Like most of the others, I had a pee bottle with me and, last thing before trying to sleep, I'd used it and tucked it down by my feet to warm them up. By morning, it was frozen. Even hot water bottles were of limited use. We'd use them for a short while and then kick them out of the bivvy bag before they too turned to ice.

Still, the winds buffeting the tent were an exciting change from listening to them from within the sturdy walls of the station, a reminder of the fact that only a scrap of material was protecting me in this beautiful but harsh environment. I loved it.

Some of that joy wore off the next morning when we opened the tent to find blowing snow and 35-40 knot winds. The other expedition had been given perfect weather. Obviously we weren't going to be given the same. Porridge in the melon to cheer us was the first priority and then off at 11am to Filla Island, a short 30-minute trip. Here we dropped off supplies, a gas bottle and sleeping bags at the temporary hut before continuing to Winterover Bay at the edge of the plateau. There we took photos of the spectacular ice cliffs before heading back to camp via Sloan Island.

Throughout the day we were looking for a canister, a piece of lost Australian history. We'd been asked by Jeremy to search for flags and records left in the area by Sir Hubert Wilkins in 1939. Many people had attempted to find the historic artefacts in the Rauers over the years, but none had been successful.

All we had to go by was an excerpt from Wilkins' journal:

> 8/1/1939 "On January 8th, with Pilot Lymburner, Wilkins landed on the highest and northernmost island in the group; at the southern end of the island. Near the highest point and close to the topmost nest of a penguin rookery Sir Hubert flew the flag of the Commonwealth of Australia and then deposited the flag and a record of the visit in a small aluminium container at the foot of a rock about three feet high. The container was covered with small stones and a small cairn was erected about 25 yards to the South."

Sir Hubert Wilkins, pioneering Australian polar aviator and explorer, was manager of Lincoln Ellsworth's private US expedition which departed Cape Town late in 1938 aboard the *Wyatt Earp*. After departure, Ellsworth informed Wilkins of his intention to claim for the United States any land that he might visit in Antarctica despite a pre-departure joint statement declaring no such intention.

Wilkins resolved to reassert Australian sovereignty over the areas claimed by Mawson. On January 8, 1939 he and fellow pilot J. H. Lymburner landed on the northernmost of the Rauer Islands, flew the Australian flag and deposited it near a rock cairn with a record of the visit in a small aluminium container. He repeated this exercise on the following day at the south-western end of the Vestfold Hills, and again on January 11, at what is now known as 'Walkabout Rocks', because of the copy of the Australian magazine *Walkabout*, which he deposited with the Australian flag and record of visit. The latter, the only one of these three Wilkins sites subsequently located, is listed as an Antarctic Treaty Historic Site (No. 6).

We, too, had to admit defeat and left the area empty-handed. Back at camp at 3.30pm after 40 kilometres, we had a late lunch of ham and cheese sandwiches in the deteriorating weather. Heavy snow was falling and visibility was less than 1000 metres but at least the winds had dropped down to 10 knots. We satisfied ourselves with a look at the outside conditions from the comfort of the hut. Conversation was lively over a lamb and veggie stew. After packing that away, I lined up a group of victims for poker before bed.

CHAPTER 19
THE START OF SUMMER

October 2003 weather details:
Max temp -1.3°C, min -23.5°C, monthly average -11.8°C
Maximum wind gusts 61 knots (113 kilometres per hour)
Average daily sunshine 5.8 hours

The next day was fine, the sun trying to break through high cloud. We headed off to Macey Peninsula in the Haggs to drop off a food box and a drum of fuel as an emergency stash for future expeditions. The trip was tricky and we carefully picked our way across the ground. At one point, there was no visual definition between land and sky and with a number of large drop-offs around, we slowed to a crawl. Several people got out, tied themselves to the Haggs and led them through the difficult areas.

We stopped at several different islands and features on the way back, continuing our search for Wilkins' records, but despite the 60.7 kilometre trip we had no luck.

Chores done, the next day was reserved for sight-seeing. We explored the nooks and crannies of the islands, taking in a few stunning jade bergs and stunning ice cliffs while still looking for that elusive canister. The jade bergs took on surreal qualities. One looked just like the cartoon character Snoopy and another resembled the castle at Disneyland.

Unfortunately, the weather wasn't holding and started to deteriorate. Heavy snow and 40-knot winds closed down visibility. By mid-afternoon we were back at camp and didn't think much of our chances for a safe return. Visibility was down to less than 1000 metres. If we left, we wouldn't be able to see the plateau nor get up the ramp. A call to Davis confirmed our suspicions. Beacon checked the satellite picture and declared the conditions had set in and would get worse. We'd have to stay.

It gave us a chance for a rare lazy day of chess, card games and reading. I slept a fair part of the day away, occasionally peering out the tent opening to check the conditions. I quickly zipped it back up when I realised I couldn't see the melon even though it was 25 metres away.

I ventured to the hut later that afternoon and found Gerbil and Paul had baked scones. If you're going to be stranded in a blizzard, make sure you get stranded with the chef, I say. We quickly knocked off the scones and spent the evening playing cards before heading back to the tents. I envied the blokes in the hut as I curled up tight in an attempt to preserve body heat and cursed the cold, freezing, bloody night.

In such cold conditions, simple things such as getting dressed or undressed in a tent are a challenge. What would normally take only a couple of minutes now took a good 20 or 30. Off came the damp freezer suit, boots and clothing and on went the dry clothes two pairs of socks, normal underwear, thermal pants and top, track suit, dry beanie and fur cap. Then I crawled into my cold but dry sleeping bag insulated by a blow-up mattress. Mark and I had to take turns dressing as there wasn't enough room in the tent for both of us to get ready at the same time.

Even with all this clothing, I never felt warm during the night. The only time my feet were warm was when I peed in my bottle and pushed it to the bottom of the sleeping bag, but this only lasted about 15 minutes. When the warmth had gone I'd chuck the bottle out of the bag. What got me was how the contents would be frozen solid by the morning. That's how bloody cold it was.

The howling wind had changed from an exciting reminder of our adventure to an ugly, fear-inducing threat. Many times during the long night I feared the tent would not survive its assault.

We gathered in the morning to discuss options and I urged the group to take advantage of the break in the weather to head back to Davis. We radioed Beacon, who confirmed the satellite showed conditions improving. Gear was quickly stowed in the Haggs and the melon cleaned before we headed off just after 8am, arriving on the plateau at the top of the Rauers ramp an hour and a half later. We had to pick up the sleds from behind the rocks where they'd been tucked away for protection and it was a struggle in the snow and 40-knot wind which cut easily through our protective clothing.

One of the Haggs had a broken coupling which forced us to leave one of the sleds loaded with fuel behind the sheltering rocks for a future expedition to collect. Luckily the second Haggs was fine and we packed the quads onto the remaining sled.

It wasn't quick work. We played a game of tag, hiding behind the Haggs for a few minutes to get out of the wind before ducking forward to work. My breath froze instantly on my moustache, forming icicles and making my face stiff.

Finally, we headed back along the plateau until we hit the badly slotted and crevassed area of the Sørsdal Glacier. Gerbil and Wixy got out and tied themselves to the Haggs to lead us cautiously through. At one stage, while the vehicle was stopped, I opened the door and stared down into a large crevasse. I quickly grabbed my camera. By 5pm we were back at Davis and I savoured my first shower in six days.

***

The high of the trip didn't last. The next morning I was putting my bag and tent into the fuel store when I learnt of the death of our friend Paul Saxby. "Sax" had summered with us at Davis, a chippie who was a tireless and skilled worker enthusiastic in everything he tackled. He'd spent several summers on the Ice, at both Davis and Mawson, and had just been awarded his dream of a winter stint. In Tasmania to train for the upcoming Mawson winter, he'd taken the opportunity to go diving during a weekend off and had accidentally drowned.

His death hit the team hard. He was a respectful, gentle and kind man. Many of the winterers had kept in touch after he left with the other summer expeditioners. The fact that he had been so cruelly denied his long-awaited and well-earned winter was something we found hard to deal with.

***

We'd been running a competition to predict the day the first penguins would return. On the 15th Paula and Tony took the prize when the first few birds struggled in across the sea ice to take up summer residence at Gardner and Magnetic islands. The return of wildlife was a clear signal winter was over. The birds rapidly built up their numbers until thousands were quarrelling over breeding sites on the bare rock of the island slopes.

Activity back at base continued to increase in an effort to finish jobs before the really busy season, especially the main store. Beacon had volunteered to be winter storeman and was now organising all the paperwork for the return to Australia of accumulated rubbish, our gear, old equipment and recyclable materials. Paul and Cal had started water production, drilling through the ice covering the tarn before pumping out the salty water beneath and starting the reverse osmosis desalination plant.

Every available space around the base was being prepared for summer accommodation. The only lamp pole at Davis was removed, its intended use no longer required as it interfered with the optical program, and it too was packed ready for return to Australia.

Three-quarters of the way through the month we received a call that Dave P and Jeff had been stranded on a hut maintenance trip. Their Hagglunds had overheated, forcing them to abandon it a couple of kilometres from Bandit's Hut where they spent the night. Early next morning Gil and I went out on quads to give them a hand. The wind chill meant we were driving into -50°C temperatures. Ten kilometres out from Davis, we found the Hagglunds and Gil quickly found the problem – a coolant hose had exploded.

It didn't take Gil long to replace the hose but we couldn't get the coolant through. By the time we cleared the air blockage we were severely cold. Once the engine was running, we abandoned the quads and took the Hagglunds to Bandit's Hut to pick up the stranded expeditioners before returning to get the quads. Gil took Dave P with him in the Hagglunds while Jeff and I set off on the quads back to Davis.

We took the chance to head back on the sea ice through Iceberg Alley, where we spotted a Weddell seal pup tucked up out of the wind behind its mum. It fed quietly as we took pictures. I took my quad up to an azure blue jade berg. Incredibly clear with deep white scars, its colour was more intense than the sky framing it. The blokes in the Hagglunds had continued on into the distance, an insignificant speck beneath the towering icebergs. Seventy-five kilometres later, we arrived back at Davis at 3pm.

***

That Saturday was a special one. We had another attempt at a 2003 expedition photo before the End of Winter dinner. We had all been asked to contribute our thoughts, highlights and humorous moments to Paula for a yearbook which was handed out at the dinner.

CHAPTER 20
AN END TO THE ISOLATION

November 2003 weather details:
Max temp 0.6°C, min -11.4°C, monthly average -3.6°C
Maximum wind gusts 44 knots (82 kilometres per hour)
Average daily sunshine 8.9 hours

I was working when I got an unexpected visitor Father Barry Allcock (Jim) in a formal black suit top with clerical collar and a short black miniskirt revealing black suspenders, black stockings, several inches of hairy thigh and white high heels. He'd come to the Met office to fill me in on Ming Lee's memorial service.

Ming Lee, the famous blow-up doll, had the day before been pronounced fatally ill and unable to return to Australia with the rest of us. Gerbil was understandably upset, considering their years spent together, but recognised what had to be done. He arranged her coffin to lie in the smoker's hut across from the kitchen and accommodation block for viewing. One by one, expeditioners made their way across for a few final words before her funeral.

"How'd the service go, Reverend?" I asked.

"Can I sit? These heels are killing me," he said, gracefully lowering himself into a chair and crossing his legs, further exposing his thigh.

"Beautiful service. Lots of tears and sadness."

He moved his mock Bible from one hand to the other and a girlie picture fell out onto the floor. Sheepishly he picked it up and tucked it back in before continuing on.

I'd only been able to go to the beginning of her funeral service because I had to work, but the video captured the mood:

Father Allcock: "Ladies and gentlemen and friends ... we are gathered on this very sad day. Ling Mee ..."

Mourners: "Ming Lee!"

Father Allcock: "Ming Lee was a friend of all. Had two winters with ANARE. Well known to us all."

One of the mourners: "Some more than others."

Father Allcock: "... some more than others. Paul, Gerbil, Geoff, Dave, Tony ... and Gil."

Loud guffaws from mourners at the significant pause.

Father Allcock: "So I'd like ... can we have one minute's silence?"

The crowd was quiet except for the occasional sob or nose being blown.

Father Allcock: "Thank you ladies and gentlemen, and now we'd like to have a few words from station leader Jeremy."

Jeremy: "Thank you Minister. Today is a sad day when we farewell our good friend from the past winter, Ming Lee. She has been a tireless worker and a constant companion. We have all appreciated her openness, her tolerance and her silent presence at all hours of the day and night. We have watched her as she has gone through various changes of life, aided and protected by her special friends Paul, Jim, and of course, her original best mate Gerbil who has been with her now for three years. Sadly, her pregnancy revealed at mid-winter came to nothing, and it may be this experience more than any other that has completely broken her up, though it was not until late last weekend that she totally lost her head. She has been a real member of our winter community, as in Warren's warm embrace (gesturing to the incinerator, where Ming Lee lies in her coffin, photos of her in happier times propped on top) she slips into her last passage into the unknown, a little bit of each of us goes with her."

The crowd paused, then Gerbil sniffed. Dark sunglasses were hiding his eyes and he peered out from beneath the woman's black mourning shawl over his head.

Gerbil: "I'd like to say a couple of send-off words for Ming Lee. I won't speak of Ming Lee loosely, being a loved team member here at Davis after being uprooted from Macquarie Island in 2001. A wonderful woman, who always had time to fit you in her busy fast-paced life. A girl filled to the brim with the zest of life, she could always turn the other cheek and show the world a little or a lot of love. You were deep in us, we were deep in you, my little Ming. Our Miss Lee, Godspeed, may the rash of your love haunt us forever."

More sniffs came from the crowd and Cal was asked if he wanted to say something.

Cal: "I can't speak, sorry."

Father Allcock: "Well, at this point, if you'd all like to say goodbye and light the flames. God bless you Ming Lee."

Jeremy pulled away the ANARE flag draped through Warren the incinerator's entrance.

Father Allcock: "Could we get the man with the matches, please?"

As Warren tried to start, the odd call of "Ming Lee" came from the mourners. Finally Warren jumped to life and everyone peered in with their cameras, trying for that final photo.

Father Allcock: "Ashes to ashes, dust to dust."

Warren intensified and Father Allcock warned the others: "I think we should stand back at this point" just as someone yelled out to him to watch his legs, the stockings an invitation to disaster. Finally, as the coffin caught fire, a voice came from the crowd in a heavy Elvis accent: "Thank you very much, Ming Lee." And everyone cheered.

After he filled me in, he stood and excused himself: "I have to go back to the bar" and left. I watched him head back towards the living block, his suspenders straining his stockings as he gingerly stepped across the ice, calf muscles bulging with the effort of walking in heels. It was the world's ugliest sight. As he headed around a building, a quad whipped around the corner, nearly clipping him.

In all seriousness, it was important to have characters such as our "good father" and situations like Ming Lee's mock funeral to break up the monotony and inject some humour during the long winter. Poor Jim. When he reached the bar, the fire alarm went off. As part of the fire team, he had to kick off his heels, jam his feet in boots and race off to the fire station. When the alarm went off, I ran from the Met office to the muster point and caught sight of him racing along, the mini riding up his legs as he went.

***

Shortly after the "funeral", our solitude officially ended. At 5pm, three Canadians landed their fixed-wing Twin Otter C-GCKB on the sea ice outside Davis. They'd left Calgary, Canada, and flown through America, South America and onto one of the American Antarctic bases before arriving at Davis. They were our first visitors in the eight months since the last ship had left in March.

Captain Blair Morphet, Flight Officer Josh Bauming and Aircraft Mechanical Engineer Robert Bealey joined our group. As good blokes, they brought a freshness to the station, but it also signified that our close-knit group was no longer to be. Everyone was keen to talk to them. Another bonus was the latest DVD movies which made for much-anticipated movie nights.

With their arrival, my workload increased. Hobart was sending us forecasts for the Amery Shelf, where the Twin Otter was flying to drop off fuel. I'd relay our local conditions and would work with them so they could forecast conditions for the flights. On the 3rd we heard the AA had left Hobart early that evening, heading to Davis. Reality had set in. Our winter was over. Shortly we'd be preparing to pack up and leave.

Around this time, the Bureau threw me a twist. Robin Thiema asked if I'd be interested in going to Casey immediately after Davis to winter. I'd be allowed a short break back in Yeppoon with my family, but they were desperate for an OIC for Casey as two blokes had dropped out and they'd run out of time to find and train a replacement. I'd get a month or six weeks back home before shipping out and wouldn't have to face any training except for fire training.

It was a hard decision. On the one hand, I'd finally get to Casey, something which had always eluded me, and it would be a short winter of only eight months – from late February until October. On the other hand, it was a big ask of my family. After the year in Davis, I'd only be home for a short time before leaving them for the better part of another year.

They say the first time you go to Antarctica, it's for the experience. The second time is for the money. And the third? Because you can't make it anywhere else. It's in your blood.

I rang Deb to discuss the offer. It wasn't an easy conversation. Deb asked if I was serious, that I'd been away from the family for 15 months and was now looking at close to another year. My family needed me. I agreed, but said it was likely I would only have to work another 12 months before retiring. The money would help with uni fees and some kitchen renovations we'd planned. And not having to return to the Rockhampton office, with its proximity to helicopters and in-fighting, and having to deal with the public, would help with my nightmares. We talked pros and cons, and I said I'd ring her back the next day so she had time to think about it.

Deb knew I was finding it hard to get up at 1.30am to drive 45 kilometres from our house in Yeppoon to the Rocky office, and that I'd had a few near misses. I was comfortable down here, and we decided we could handle this.

"You're coming home before?" she asked.

"I've made it a stipulation," I reassured her. I'd take at least a month off so we could be together. I rang Robin back and told him to put my name down. For better or worse, I'd head to Casey.

***

With the ship on the way, I jumped at the chance to go out one last time with Jim for sea ice observations. Afterwards we went to Gardner Island to visit the penguin rookeries. Adults return to the same rookery where they were born to build their nests but the sheer numbers meant space and rocks were limited and stealing from one's neighbour was common practice.

The noise was intense; their short sharp grunts came non-stop. We watched one who'd claimed his spot looking at his pile of rocks, glance over to his neighbour's unattended pile, walk over, gingerly pick up a rock and calmly walk back to drop it on his pile. Fights often erupted, but this building and pinching cycle would continue until the female laid her two eggs. Both parents take turns incubating the eggs. Once they've hatched, they take turns feeding and protecting them from predators (especially skuas).

Back at Davis, I helped Gil move personal boxes of tools and gear to the green shed in preparation for the changeover. Early that evening our second lot of visitors arrived on another Twin Otter, C-GXXB. This time the Canadians (Captain Steve King, Flight Officer Zoe Lambert and Aircraft Mechanical Engineer Kevin Riehl) brought Met forecaster Jane Golding with them. Jane had gone by ship to Casey but it was decided to bring her from Casey to Davis so she could do forecasts for the Twin Otters and the helicopters when they arrived on the AA.

I was worried about Stay, the full-sized golden retriever Guide Dogs collection box, and got up early one morning on a mission to pinch her. I'd told Jim and Beacon a few days earlier that I was going to bring her with me to Casey. As the RTA (Return to Australia) officer, I needed Beacon to arrange for Stay to be secretly transported and Jim had agreed to build her a box. When I got to the bar, however, Stay wasn't there. Someone had beaten me to it. I asked Jim and Beacon but they couldn't confirm where she'd gone. Looking guilty, Dave P got involved and helped me search the base, including the old Davis Station, but with no luck.

***

Gil had started giving me Mack truck lessons because with my experience driving army trucks I'd been selected to help with the resupply. My first driving mission was to carry an open container to the nearby aerial farm, clearing the beach in preparation for the resupply. All ANARE gear was returned to the green store and finally, on the afternoon on the 16th, we could see the AA breaking through fast ice as she approached Davis. She came to a stop in heavy snow, wedged in the ice about four kilometres from the station.

As the cook for the day, I was relieved when we heard the new expeditioners wouldn't be coming ashore that night. I went onboard to meet the incoming Met crew and felt overwhelmed by all the people, who all wanted to talk. Jeremy went out early that night to brief the incoming expeditioners and returned with mail and fresh fruit, along with plant operator Gary Mason and communications officer Bob Orchard who'd come ashore to prepare for the next day's operations.

It was clear the next morning that winter was truly over, and it had nothing to do with the weather. Everyone came ashore and every available space at Davis was filled. The Twin Otters made several trips, taking the new winter crew into Mawson and bringing the relieved crew back to Davis so they could join us on the AA back to Australia.

For the next three days, I was on truck duty, driving on the Sea Ice Highway, carrying waste from Davis to the AA and returning with fresh supplies for the green store and fuel drums for the fuel farm. At times it was difficult to manoeuvre the big Mack truck, especially driving off the sea ice, which was breaking under the constant traffic, onto the beach area.

The most dramatic moment driving the truck came when I delivered a container of drums filled with waste. I was sitting in the cabin waiting for the container to be offloaded by a Caterpillar front-end loader with a large forklift upfront. Dave Power was driving and operating the Cat. There was a large bang and a crashing sound, and it seemed the whole Mack truck was crushing in around me. I didn't have any second thoughts. I grabbed my camera gear and got out of there.

For the next 20 minutes, I watched a determined but frustrated Dave as he tried to lift the heavy container from the truck. As the Cat tried to lift, its rear wheels would lift off the ice and the cabin would swing around. That's how bloody heavy it was. Usually the Aurora's crane would lift these off the truck, but at the time there were strong winds and blowing snow. To save time, the Cat was used.

The resupply finished on the 19th and I started duelling with Tim in the Met office. Just after lunch, the *Kapitan Khlebnikov* arrived, full of American tourists, waiting for the total eclipse of the sun which was due in a few days.

The formal changeover ceremony was held two days later and Jeremy handed over the keys to the incoming station leader. We were all presented with our Antarctica medals and were driven out to the AA, ready for the trip back to Fremantle via Zhong Shan.

Just after 2pm, the AA sounded her long horn and expeditioners on the ice set off flares, waving and dancing. As we started putting distance between us and the shore, I felt an immense sadness. My home for the past 12 months was fading into the distance. I'd become very attached to it and the people I'd shared my life with. The closeness we'd shared was ending. We were starting to prepare for our other lives.

The AA was chewing through the ice, leaving chunks in her wake. Algae had coloured the water brown and it was pushed onto the floes. I caught up with Sprunky, who'd come in with the AA to do the refuelling for Davis, and it was good to see him again.

At 8pm we got to within 18 nautical miles of Zhong Shan. The next morning helicopter pilots John and Rick started the base's resupply. I worked on the bridge doing METARS (met reports for the helicopters). On Sunday at 4.30pm, resupply complete, we left Antarctica behind for Australia.

It was routine practice to have an outgoing psych test, to find out how we coped with the long period of remoteness. I felt more comfortable discussing my nightmares at my appointment. That morning we gathered on the trawler deck and watched the total eclipse of the sun. It was brilliant. The following evening we finally left the sea ice pack and by the next afternoon the icebergs were gone. Day by day it got warmer and December 1 was the warmest I'd felt for a long time.

An Australian bush fly welcomed us back on the 3rd, the first I'd seen in over 12 months, and we were still 100 nautical miles off the Western Australian coast. That, more than anything else, showed we were getting close. At that evening's barbecue it felt like we were on the mainland as the flies swarmed our food.

The next morning we were stationary between Rottnest Island and Perth, with the city's tall buildings and Scarborough Beach in the distance. We lined up among a dozen container ships waiting for a pilot. He climbed aboard at 1pm and an hour later we tied up at the wharf. Compared with Hobart, there weren't many people on the dock to meet us. It was disappointing, but distance and cost meant many families couldn't fly out to Western Australia. My older brother Gerry was to be there but I couldn't see him before I went through customs and quarantine. He arrived at 3.30pm and I took the opportunity to show him through the ship. He'd been in the Australian Navy for six years and was quite impressed with the AA's setup.

Finally it was time to leave the others. It was difficult to sum up what I was feeling as I said my goodbyes, but it was genuinely like leaving a family behind.

Mark Maxwell said it best: "An inbuilt mechanism of the human condition in such a situation is to build camaraderie with those who share that isolated experience.

"My observations were that this camaraderie did indeed flourish, as evidenced by the great friendships established, an open willingness to help each other with their tasks and problems and the ability to laugh about and not seriously dwell on an individual's shortcomings or mistakes.

"Despite the requirement to be efficient and responsible in our day-to-day tasks and to be able to respond to emergency situations, we are all still human with the inherent weaknesses that the human condition demands."

But reality was waiting. Gerry took me to the home he shared with partner Rene for an evening barbecue. It was strange driving through the city; the heat, noise and traffic fumes were overwhelming. I caught the plane the next day, arriving at Rockhampton that night.

Deb, Michelle and David were at the airport and it felt good to touch them again and to see that they were safe. They were my biggest worry while I was away. My emotions tight, I felt my heart was in two pieces – one here with my family, the other down south. I'd only been back a short while, but I couldn't control the part that wanted to get down to Casey.

PART FOUR
CASEY STATION
GLIMPSE OF LEGOLAND

"Do not measure your loss by itself; if you do, it will seem intolerable; but if you will take all human affairs into account you will find that some comfort is to be derived by them."

Saint Basil (329 AD-379 AD)

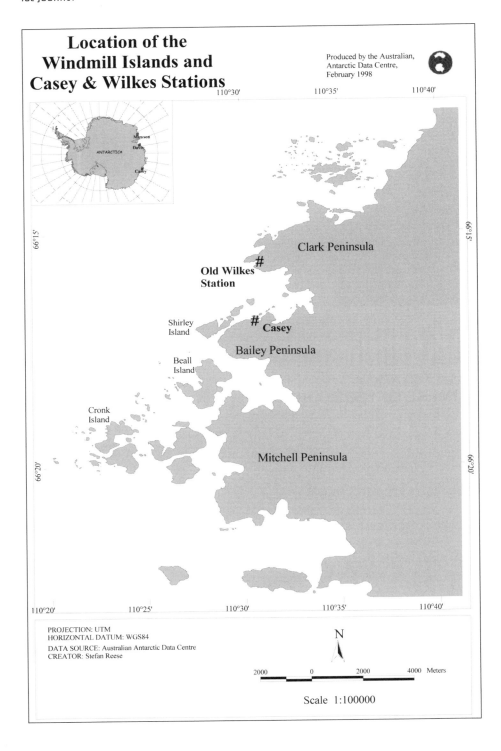

Location of the Windmill Islands and Casey & Wilkes Stations

Produced by the Australian, Antarctic Data Centre, February 1998

110°30'   110°35'   110°40'

ANTARCTICA
Mawson
Davis
Casey

66°15'   66°15'

Clark Peninsula

Old Wilkes
Station #

Shirley
Island

Casey

Bailey Peninsula

Beall
Island

Cronk
Island

Mitchell Peninsula

66°20'   66°20'

110°20'   110°25'   110°30'   110°35'   110°40'

PROJECTION: UTM
HORIZONTAL DATUM: WGS84
DATA SOURCE: Australian Antarctic Data Centre
CREATOR: Stefan Reese

N

2000   0   2000   4000 Meters

Scale 1:100000

Casey was established in February 1959 when Australia took overall responsibility for the American station Wilkes (built in 1957). Australia maintained Wilkes until 1969 when Casey station was built on nearby Bailey Peninsula. The present station, the first of the Australian Antarctic stations to be completely re-built using the brightly-coloured AANBUS building station (leading to its nickname of Legoland) was opened in 1988. Just 3880 kilometres due south of Perth, Casey is the closest of Australia's permanent Antarctic stations and sits in the low, rocky Windmill Islands and peninsulas. Near Casey Station is Law Dome, an immense icecap that was the site of a drilling project that finally reached bedrock in 1993. The ice was measured to be 1200 metres thick.

CHAPTER 21
CASEY AT LAST

Culture shock. It's the only way to describe returning to the mainland after more than a year in the spectacular, stark, forbidding Antarctic. Though I'd gone through it before when I'd returned from Macca, the longer stint away and lack of greenery at Davis made more of an impact. Flies and dust had rejoined my life. The musty, earthy smell present after rain, and the odour of freshly cut grass assaulted my senses.

We knew our family would have a limited spell together, and wanted to make the most of it. The first few weeks I stayed at home, catching up on Deb's news, the kids' big leaps, and the routine stuff like mowing lawns. Then we packed up and headed off on a family holiday for several weeks at Caloundra, Brisbane, the Gold Coast and south into New South Wales to Coffs Harbour and Port Macquarie. It was a peaceful time and I was lulled into holiday mode, enjoying body surfing and relaxing. I was starting to question my reasons for going back and had ANARE rung during that period I would have opted out. It was just too nice being home.

When the clock finally ran out, I packed reluctantly and, when I gave my family one last hug at the Rockhampton airport, I turned away. Maybe because that time with them was so short, I found that parting to be the worst.

In Hobart, I started the familiar routine of training for the different duties I'd been assigned. Mick Williams trained me to deal with the stores so I could order whatever was needed on the computer system. I'd been told I couldn't get on the ship without a dental clearance so a visit to the dentist was next. Three fillings later, I was cleared and went back to the AAD in Kingston to be kitted out. I was surprised that Uncle Don wasn't there to greet me with his cheerful smile. Phillipa Foster, who'd been at Macca with me, fitted me out and told me he'd retired. In a small way it ended an era for so many expeditioners.

Robin Thiema pulled me aside, telling me I was to report to Calvary Hospital in Hobart for some tests. It was like being in Hobart again for the first Casey preparation. I asked what was going on and he said I needed some isotope imaging done. My medical examination had picked up something but he couldn't expand on that. I had the test but still wasn't any wiser about what they were looking for.

***

Another training session, another phobia. I'd been chosen for the Breathing Apparatus Team, but unlike the basic fire training I'd done for other expeditions, this time I'd have to undertake a full course, including entering a smoke-filled container to negotiate a course full of obstacles and rescue dummies.

Since Vietnam I couldn't cope with smoke or fire. As with the scrub nurse training, I didn't want this to get in the way of my duty, so I joined the other Casey expeditioners at the TasFire Training Centre in Cambridge.

As I waited my turn the anxiety started building.

Nui Dat, Phuoc Toy Province, Vietnam

It doesn't take long before my name goes up on the noticeboard for ambush patrol. Anxiety tightens my nerves during the day before I head out with two Sergeants (one carrying a radio on his back) and 12 Sigs. I'm loaded with water canteens, ration pack, full-round magazines, ammunition belts for the M60 machine gun around my shoulder and a trusty SLR.

We reach the ambush site just before dark and lie in wait for the VC. Adrenalin keeps me alert. The jungle noises magnify as the night goes on. My army greens are wet with nervous sweat and I start imagining things. It's dark. No sense of anything outside our immediate space. My ears strain with the effort of listening for footsteps, knowing I probably wouldn't hear them if they existed. The effort of holding down the fear is tiring.

Staring at the container being filled with smoke, I knew what it would feel like stepping inside. Dark, no sense of where you are, having to feel around for everything. The sound of my own breath magnified in the breathing apparatus, danger all around. My apprehension must've showed and as I talked to Ron (chippie) and Jason (engineer), I eventually told them my concerns.

"Don't worry, Morg. You can go between us." These blokes teamed up with me and we tied ourselves together before heading in. My head was spinning and I forced myself to breathe evenly, fighting my need to gasp extra air from the regulator. Even knowing they were there at the end of the rope didn't stop the lonely feeling. I fumbled in the dark, searching for dummies, and struggled to focus.

The second time in, after lunch, was easier, as was the rest of the training the next day. I was given a message to ring Dr Peter Gormly and I found a phone, dialled the number and prayed he wasn't going to deliver bad news like before. I had to go and get another ECG stress test with isotope imaging. I questioned why because I felt fine but policy rules. It turned out that all expeditioners over 55 had to have such a test, but at the time I didn't know that.

That afternoon I went to the docks to meet the *Aurora Australis*. I'd been on the first ship out of Davis and she was now bringing in the other winter expeditioners who'd stayed on for a few more months. Watching the ship draw close and hearing the cheers from family members raised goose bumps. I greeted Chad, Nanette, Mark, Tony, Jim, Paul, Gerbil, Cathie, Cal and Sharon as they came down the gangplank. It was good to see them and be among my friends again.

On Monday morning I fronted at Calvary Hospital, apprehensive but determined they'd find nothing wrong with me. The stress test was done on a bike. I was injected with chemicals for the isotope imaging before pedalling like crazy. After 14 minutes on the hardest setting, I was sweating and puffing.

"You did well," the female attendant said. "You mustn't be too bad as others your age often only last a few minutes."

Feeling better, and medically cleared, I took a taxi on the morning of the 17th to the AA, and spent a few hours doing drills and sitting through briefings. After lunch I was free to wander Hobart, so I bought a Canon digital camera and headed with Ron to Customs House for a few beers. Di Beamish, Jim Milne, Kathryn Wheatley, Cal and Cathie came down to the dock to see me off and I gave them a final "cheers" before climbing the gangplank.

Just after 5pm the horn reverberated across the harbour and we went through the farewell routine again as the ship pulled away. Sprunky was again beside me, all set for another trip of refuelling various bases.

SITREP February 18:

Position -44.5South, 145.2East

Seas 3.4m (moderate to rough)

Speed 4.9 knots

Distance travelled last 24 hours 170 nautical miles

Air temp 13.6°C, sea temp 15.2°C

Average wind speed 45 knots from 292°

The next morning I was up on the bridge early to do meteorological work but didn't last long. My old friend seasickness had come to visit and I crawled back to my bunk for the rest of the day. Due to heavy seas, we were forced to slow to two knots during the night and I spent it sliding from one end of the bunk to the other. My stomach was churning and I don't think mine was the only one.

SITREP February 19:

Position -46.2South, 143.6East

Seas 5-6m from South West

Speed 6.3 knots

Distance travelled last 24 hours 118 nautical miles

Air temp 10.6°C, sea temp 13.2°C

Average wind speed 25 knots

The rolling motion was incessant, as was my stomach, which couldn't keep down any food or liquid, not that I was interested in either. Dr Andy Williams, the doctor going to Macquarie Island, visited my bunk to give me an injection to prevent dehydration.

SITREP February 20:

Position -48.4South, 139.3East

Seas 2-3m from North West

Speed 10.2 knots

Distance travelled last 24 hours 218 nautical miles

Air temp 9.7°C, sea temp 9.2°C

Average wind speed 24 knots from 274°

Finally my stomach stopped heaving enough for me to head to the mess for lunch. I wasn't sure whether to credit the wonderful chefs onboard or the lack of the dreaded needle but things were looking up.

SITREP February 21:

Position -51.8South, 135.3East

Seas 2-3m from South West

Speed 8.4 knots

Distance travelled last 24 hours 209 nautical miles

Air temp 2.3°C, sea temp 7.6°C

Average wind speed 24 knots from 240°

The occasional snow started falling and it was significantly colder. We gathered on the deck for the standard emergency muster and winds kept building during the day, gusting to 60 knots at night. Then it was back to the routine of sliding up and down my bunk all night. Not getting much sleep at all.

SITREP February 22:

Position -53.5South, 130.3East

Seas 2-3m from South

Speed 11.5 knots

Distance travelled last 24 hours 255 nautical miles

Air temp 3.2°C, sea temp 5.7°C

Average wind speed 20 knots from 247°

Seas were calm overnight, giving a much-needed chance to sleep. Most welcome.

SITREP February 23:

Position -57.8South, 124.5East

Seas 3-4m from West

Speed 11.4 knots

Distance travelled last 24 hours 273 nautical miles

Air temp 4.0°C, sea temp 4.8°C

Average wind speed 32 knots from 277°

I was confined mainly to my small bunk but occupied myself by emailing the family, or curling up to read. I wandered up to the bridge to do weather observations and we gathered for a quarantine lecture, after which we had to clean our shoes and boots to pass through the strict conditions. Nothing foreign could be introduced to the continent.

SITREP February 24:

Position -60.3South, 118.3East

Seas 1m from South

Speed 14.2 knots

Distance travelled last 24 hours 294 nautical miles

Air temp 0.3°C, sea temp 2.5°C

Average wind speed 20 knots

We sighted our first iceberg today, a majestic carved monument floating past us. Snow showers were continuing and a week out my stomach had settled.

SITREP February 25:

Position -64.4South, 111.1East

Seas smooth at last

Speed 15.1 knots

Distance travelled last 24 hours 286 nautical miles

Air temp 1.1°C, sea temp 1.6°C

Average wind speed 11 knots at 293°

With the crossing of the -60° line, King Neptune, well supported by his beautiful, long-suffering Queen of 200 years, came out to initiate all those for whom this was a virgin crossing. We gathered on the deck waiting for him to make his entrance after we chanted our three cheers of welcome.

The King explained what was expected of the uninitiated, and warned them: "For all of you who choose not to do as we say ... you go that way (pointing to the sea)".

He gathered several blokes, Dr Andy Williams included, into a group. "Come forth and pay your penance."

After they'd taken off their beanies and knelt before him, the King bellowed: "You have trespassed in my kingdom without so much as a 'Good day'. You, sir, will have a spoonful of the royal potion." Pointing to Dr Williams, he motioned forth his helper. Dr Williams opened his mouth but the helper ignored him, smearing a concoction of rotten fish mixture through his hair instead.

One by one, the victims had their crimes listed (vegetarian or smoker) and their cheeks slapped with Vegemite or fish mixture.

"Bring on the Royal fish," the King ordered. Rotten fish were brought out and given to the victims to pucker up and kiss. Those who had been initiated grinned and enjoyed watching the others, pleased it was a once-only initiation. That evening we had to put up with cold showers again.

Weathered icebergs were now a regular occurrence, and we entered the sea ice pack early that night. Sea conditions became smooth and we covered good ground through the grey, flat mass.

The next morning we arrived at Casey. I'd had a shocking night, full of violent nightmares, and was up at 6am. A half hour later, we pushed through and stopped at -66.1South, 110.3East.

After all those years, I had finally got there. I watched the LARC (lighter amphibious resupply cargo vessel) start operations. It was a truly fascinating piece of machinery. An aluminium craft capable of propelling itself through water as well as over land, it has large balloon tyres which provide suspension and help with flotation. It also has a crane fitted behind the operator's cabin.

For many years the LARCs were supplied and operated by the Australian Army on behalf of the AAD but are now run by P&O Polar as part of the charter of the *Aurora Australis*. Our quarantine lecture had informed us that if the LARCs were used for anything other than ANARE operations, the entire vessel had to be steam cleaned before being loaded on the AA.

Staring at the coloured buildings, my home for the next eight months, I felt satisfied. I'd finally made it, and broken the curse of Casey. Now it was time to go ashore and meet her.

CHAPTER 22
AND THE LIGHTS WENT OUT

When my turn came, I climbed aboard *Pagadroma*, the station work boat, and ventured to the Met office for changeover procedures. On the way I went to the red shed (accommodation block) to inspect my room (better than Davis) and the social area (mess smaller, but the lounge, bar and pool table better). I was due to replace Cliff Spencer, the outgoing officer-in-charge, and at 9am he started outlining my duties and taking me through the office.

After lunch, he took me on a tour on the way back from the mess. I'd been at Casey for just over three hours, and little did I know that would be all I'd remember of the station. What happened next, I only know about because someone told me the details.

Apparently, as we walked back to the Met office to continue the changeover after our late lunch, Cliff offered to show me the tank house which housed the sauna. We headed out the back towards the main communications building (which houses the Met office) and just outside the back door, found ourselves on clear ice. Cliff slipped first but managed to save himself. I wasn't as lucky. My head bounced off the ice and the report says as I got up, Cliff could see I was distressed. He put me on the steps by the tank house, talking to me, telling me to stay there and he'd go get help.

He raced to the comms building, grabbing Segun Adewumi, the Met tech who was going to Macca, and told him I was in a bad way. When they got back, I was disoriented and wandering around behind the tank house. They walked me to the medical rooms.

Dr Tanya Kelly diagnosed severe head injuries and a serious concussion. I was also hypothermic. Dr Andy Williams, who'd given me injections on the AA, and Dr Jeff Ayton, who was the Polar medical doctor based at Kingston under Dr Gormly, were brought by chopper from the AA to help. They tried to take X-rays but they weren't very clear. There was a radiographer on the

AA, and the chopper brought her in to the surgery so she could try as well. Her pictures were better but the extent of the injuries to my head and neck still couldn't be determined.

They contacted the chief neurosurgeon at the Hobart Hospital and sent scanned copies of the X-rays. The reply was decisive: "Get him out of there ASAP". The decision was made – medivac back to Australia.

Early that evening I came to. I was in a high neck brace, connected to an oxygen mask and covered in drips. It was unbearable.

I rang Deb and the kids and had a brief conversation, telling them I'd arrived and that I'd had a fall, but it was thought to be only concussion and I would come good in two or three days. Deb later told me she thought something was wrong as I was speaking very slowly and wasn't making sense. I have no recollection of the call.

Dr Jeff got on the phone after I'd finished and told Deb that in his medical opinion, "Dave should return home". He reassured her that I was coping and comfortable and promised to call with regular updates. Distance and the unknown can lead to fear. All the family had to go by was that I'd had a nasty fall, hit my head and Hobart had advised bringing me back with severe head and neck injuries.

The next day my head felt like it was about to explode. The constant pressure was relentless. I couldn't think or focus but was told I'd fallen and they were sending me back to Australia. I didn't care.

> *ANARE's First Aid Manual: "Especially if the blow to the head has been sufficient to knock the casualty out then complications are possible. But if there is loss of memory so that the injury cannot be recalled, and events leading up to the blow are hazy or unknown, then special observation is necessary as there is more chance of pressure building up inside the skull due to swelling or bleeding; this can compress the brain and kill the victim. If the level of consciousness decreases ... then the victim probably has increasing pressure inside the skull: keep the airway clear and administer oxygen; plan for urgent evacuation for life-saving emergency surgery."*

The neurosurgeon in Hobart was updated and told heavy blizzards had prevented the chopper from leaving the AA. Finally, the word came through to prepare, and I was transferred from the bed to a stretcher, packed tight to remain immobile and strapped in, a bright orange plaid blanket tucked in over me. I lay on the floor surrounded by people, and vaguely remember

Psycho (Chris Gallagher) nearby and Dr Williams putting a reassuring hand on me while discussions flew around above.

The mood was sombre and with a count, six or seven people lifted me to their waist height and started out, keeping me level as they descended the ramp outside the red shed with slow steps. Snow was falling on my face and I remember it was freezing as they approached the chopper. It'd been cleared for the medivac, with seats taken out to allow for the stretcher. Vaguely I realised people were taking photos but I didn't care; later I learned they'd been taken to be of use to the AAD in the future.

They slid me in and strapped me down while I stared at the ceiling. For once I didn't even care I was in a chopper, they'd doped me up so well. Expeditioners gathered around the door and called out various messages: "We'll miss you, mate" and "Enjoy your winter". The chopper blades started picking up speed and my head started shaking as we took off. I think Dr Kelly was with me, holding it against the vibrations.

Once on the AA, I was transferred to the hospital and when I woke up later, drips were once again attached. The ship's horn sounded and we started moving at 7pm but as I closed my eyes again, someone came in asking where my bag was.

I'd been asked to bring a spare part for the electrolyser to Casey and had put it in my bag. Shortly after the AA started moving, the Met tech remembered the part, necessary for the winter months, and the ship was halted while they searched my bag. A Zodiac came out to get it and the AA continued. It was the 27th, one day after I'd arrived.

SITREP February 27:

Air temp 2.1°, sea temp 1.4°C

Average wind speed 10 knots at 165°

I spent the next five days struggling against the pain in my head and neck but Drs Jeff and Andy kept me full of painkillers. I lay doped up in bed, an observer of the action around me.

SITREP February 28:

Position -65.1South, 110.4East

Seas 1-2m from East

Speed 13 knots

Distance travelled last 24 hours 92nm

Air temp 2.7°, sea temp 1.0°C

Average wind speed 35 knots at 103°

Thanks to the AA master and crew for a smooth and professional operation and to the medicos at Casey, on the ship and AAD, field training officers, pilots and crew for efficient medivac.

SITREP February 29:

Position -63.2South, 119.6East

Seas 3-4m from North East

Speed 8 knots

Distance travelled last 24 hours 263 nautical miles

Air temp 0.6°, sea temp 2.0°C

Average wind speed 36 knots at 097°

Ninety-eight expeditioners aboard. Rough ride once more. Forecast for more of the same after brief respite.

Thank goodness Dr Jeff had thought to call Deb, as the Bureau of Meteorology hadn't. I was employed by them and it was their responsibility to contact family of an injured employee. Deb never heard from them.

SITREP March 1:

Position -61.4South, 128.9East

Seas 2-3m from West

Speed 14.3 knots

Distance travelled last 24 hours 251nm

Air temp 3.2°C, sea temp 2.4°C

Average wind speed 20 knots at 345°

SITREP March 2:

Position -59.6South, 136.3East

Seas gathering fury North West swell 2-3m

Speed 13.9 knots

Distance travelled last 24 hours 207nm

Air temp 5.1°C, sea temp 3.1°C

Average wind speed 32 knots at 340°

SITREP March 3:

Position -58.3South, 146.6East

Moderate to rough seas with 3m South West swell

Speed 14.6 knots

Distance travelled last 24 hours 333nm

Air temp 4.4°C, sea temp 3.3°C

Average wind speed 32 knots at 295°

Doctors Andy and Jeff were starting to get me out of bed for short periods, putting me on a chair in the shower to wash me and on the loo to try and get my bowels working again. I tried eating something solid, rather than relying on drips. The first time I stood, I nearly passed out due to the increased pressure in my head. The constant headache got worse, which I hadn't thought possible.

Dr Ayton was ringing Deb every two days with updates and was able to tell her I was slowly improving. Deb and the kids were determined to meet me in Hobart.

SITREP March 4:

Position -55.4South, 156.8East

Seas 2-3m from South West

Speed 14.6 knots

Distance travelled last 24 hours 342nm

Air temp 6.8°C, sea temp 6.4°C

Average wind speed 26 knots at 285°

Dr Jeff reminded me it was my birthday. I felt every one of my 56 years but he insisted on helping me up and outside, down the hall to the mess for dinner and birthday cake – and sung in with the traditional song by all the expeditioners. It was great, but I simply couldn't appreciate it at the time. I struggled to look around the neck brace, the headache fogging my mind.

SITREP March 5:

Position -54.3South, 158.6East

Seas 1-2m from South East

Distance travelled last 24 hours 82 nautical miles

Air temp 5.1°C, sea temp 6.7°C

Average wind speed 27 knots at 160°

The AA dropped anchor in Buckles Bay, Macquarie Island, at 7am, closing the loop on my Antarctic journey. Cargo operations started a few hours later by LARC and chopper but the LARC operations were suspended due to high swell, making it too dangerous for it to pull along the AA.

SITREP March 6:

Air temp 8.4°C, sea temp 6.6°C

Average wind speed 24 knots from 310°

Sprunky started his fuel transfer from the AA to the fuel tanks ashore, and the LARC and choppers continued with the resupply. Dr Jeff wanted me to try being more mobile and he helped me to the deck to watch the activity. It was the most I'd walked in eight days and my head was spinning. But I wanted the chance to see Macca, something I didn't think I'd ever do again.

SITREP March 7:

Air temp 8.3°C, sea temp 7.0°C

Average wind speed 17 knots from 335°

Dr Jeff decided it would be good rehabilitation to visit the solid ground on Macca. Refuelling and cargo operations were finished so he talked to Rob Easther, the voyage leader, and the chopper pilot about the possibility of moving me ashore for a few hours. They agreed. Dr Jeff and Dr Andy loaded me on and we took off, all peering outside the windows. It was strange to see a base with water on both sides and I couldn't get over how tiny and how narrow it looked. So very different from a few years ago. We passed over the water edged by rugged coastline and circled over the old buildings before setting down.

Dr Jeff had been my full-time carer since the accident and would be continuing with me to Hobart, while Dr Andy would be getting off at Macca. I went into the mess and rang my family, the first lucid conversation in a few weeks. With Dr Andy's help I visited Garden Cove and the Met office before returning three hours later to the AA. I was very tired and weak and wondered how long I'd be this fragile.

SITREP March 8:

Air temp 8.3°C, sea temp 7.0°C

Average wind speed 19 knots at 315°

It was time to say goodbye to Andy, about to start his 12-month stint as the island's doctor. Words couldn't express what I was trying to say, and my muddled head didn't help. I hoped he understood how grateful I was for his care.

SITREP March 9:

Position -54.7South, 158.4East

Seas smooth, 1-2m swell from West

Speed 13.3 knots

Distance travelled last 24 hours 26 nautical miles

Air temp 6.1°C, sea temp 9.6°C

Average wind speed 2 knots at 245°

Due to an adverse weather conditions forecast, all expeditioners were brought off Macca by lunchtime. The horn sounded at 2pm and I watched the flares being lit on a distant rock as the engines started pulling us away. I felt nothing, and certainly not the excitement or sorrow I usually had when seeing those lights.

SITREP March 10:

Position -49.4South, 153.5East

Seas 1-2m from West, South West

Speed 14 knots

Distance travelled last 24 hours 293 nautical miles

Air temp 9.2°C, sea temp 11.5°C

Average wind speed 20 knots at 245°

We are travelling better than anticipated, evading the adverse weather conditions as forecast so far.

Finally I felt strong enough to take myself to the mess for a meal without help, though Dr Jeff monitored. The bustle of returning expeditioners talking, exchanging stories and anticipating seeing their families was surreal.

SITREP March 11:

Position -45.3South, 149.5East

Seas 1-2m from South West

Speed 16.7 knots

Distance travelled last 24 hours 297 nautical miles

Air temp 10.7°C, sea temp 10.9°C

Average wind speed 10 knots at 260°

We were travelling well and expected to arrive in Hobart sometime next morning. This was the last voyage heading in for the 2003-2004 Antarctic season. As we approached port, I started having mixed feelings, knowing it was likely to be my last trip on the *Aurora Australis* and my last expedition to Antarctica. Tomorrow I'd be returning to my old life, and I wasn't sure how I felt about that.

We arrived at 8am the next day and tied up in Hobart. Dr Jeff helped me out to the deck where I searched the mass of faces for Deb, Michelle and David but couldn't find them. He told me we had to go back to the hospital ward for final packing. When I later returned to the deck, I finally saw my family.

Before I could go ashore to see them, Dr Gormly came on board and sat down with Dr Jeff and me. We talked about my injury and treatment before he told me the arrangements they'd made for me at the hospital in Hobart. The first thing would be an MRI scan on my head and X-rays on my neck had been arranged for later that afternoon.

I wasn't prepared for the strong emotions I felt when I finally got to hug my family. There but for the grace...If I'd hit a bit harder, or on a different angle ...It was nice to hold them close.

Beacon and Margaret Fulton, Robin Thiema and BoM administrator Jenny Coombes were also there. Jenny was very apologetic to Deb, realising that the department had left her out in the cold and told her to send them all the receipts for the airfares and accommodation expenses and we'd be reimbursed.

The crew of the AA brought Deb, Michelle and David on board and gave them a tour, an unexpected bonus, and they got to see where I'd been recovering and imagine what it would be like to travel the Great Southern Ocean. It was a chance to see for themselves what I'd been trying to describe for the past few years a bright highlight in an otherwise dark time.

I'd never had an MRI scan before. They loaded me in and as I started entering the tube I had a meltdown. Screaming and panting, I was trapped in a full-blown anxiety attack, one of the worst I'd ever suffered, feeling like the 20-year-old being buried in his fighting pit again. They quickly pulled me out and I sat shaking, refusing to go back in. It took a visit to a psychiatrist to talk me through what happened. I went back to try again. This time they gave me some medication and a mask. Ironically, having my face covered worked and I was able to lie still while the machine took its images.

For the next eight days I was in and out of hospital for scans and X-rays while my injuries were monitored by a neurosurgeon. Deb, Michelle and David flew back to Yeppoon on the 15th while I waited for clearance to return.

The neurosurgeon, Dr Liddell, said to me after he'd seen my scans: "Good God, you're a lucky bloke. By rights you shouldn't be here. You can still see bruising of the brain in these. The doctors who helped you did a marvellous job."

Neck X-rays showed ligament and muscle damage, especially down the left side where they had torn. It looked like I'd subconsciously tried to keep my head up when I fell, causing the damage. The neck brace stayed and I visited the physio several times.

Beacon and his wife were my lifeline during this period, driving me to doctors or errands, reassuring me when I felt down. Another strong supporter was Dr Jeff, who checked on my progress every day. I know he felt angry at how the Bureau had handled the whole matter, especially at what they'd put Deb through. Even at that point, the department had left me to my own devices.

One day a cleaning lady at the hotel asked me if I was the bloke who'd been medivacked out of Antarctica. Apparently it had been on the radio news. I told her that, yup, I was the unlucky bastard.

On the 20th Dr Liddell finally decided the bruising in my head had reduced enough for me to fly again and gave me the all-clear. Robin Thiema took me to the airport and put me on the plane, but the airline wouldn't fly me unless I signed a waiver before boarding, taking full responsibility for any further injury. I signed.

I slowly recuperated at home. Worker's Compensation covered the time off, the weekly check-ups and the physiotherapy. My head injury was progressing slowly and I suffered mild problems. Dr Liddell had told me to expect a recovery period of 12-18 months, so I wasn't worried when I had to search for a word or battled to remember something.

My neck was the main problem. I ended up seeing a pain specialist in Rockhampton who gave me a cortisone injection into the C3, C4 and C5 vertebrae. Unfortunately, while it helped with the pain, I suffered a severe reaction, vomiting and breathing difficulties. Later, boils erupted all over my body.

It was a low period. Constant pain wears a person down, and I had a lot of time on my hands. I started thinking about the Bureau's treatment (or lack of) of my family. The disappointment with my employer, who'd I been loyal to for over 30 years, kept growing. Beacon and Margaret had been grumbling about it down in Hobart, but at that point all I'd wanted was to be home with my family. Once home, Deb opened up about what she'd gone through, the lack of information and having to battle to find her way to meet me. If it had been one of the bigwigs, the reaction would've been different.

While I was laid up at Casey, Kerry Steinburner, an expeditioner who'd been at Mawson when I was at Davis, came to visit and offered to take my video camera around base so I'd have some memory of Casey. It was an incredibly kind thought and some months after getting home I put the video on. I remembered the main street and the yellow Met and communications building and followed as Kerry went into the office and taped messages from the staff.

"Hello Dave. This is your office. I think you enjoyed it," from the outgoing Met observer.

"Good luck. I would've loved to have stayed but my wife wants me home," from Cliff.

There was Fiona Gray, the wintering Met observer, waving. Poor Fiona - I was the fourth OIC going in, the other three having dropped out in quick succession for various reasons. When I'd met her, she told me she hoped I wouldn't be her fourth boss to drop out. I laughed and told her she wasn't unlucky and she didn't have to worry - I wouldn't be dropping out.

Then I appeared, lying on the hospital bed, eyes vague. We watched silently as I was carried out to the chopper and I was shocked to see how helpless and vulnerable the man on the stretcher was. I put the tape away.

One of my biggest regrets about Casey was the fact that I'd let Stay down. Unbeknown to me, she'd come in with us, carrying on the tradition of being smuggled around the bases. Before I'd left Hobart, two ex-Davis friends had told me to be on the lookout for a big box with my name on it. The box said: "To be opened only by Dave Morgan". I'd already left on the AA when the station leader discovered and opened the box. So Stay stayed, and I left.

For at least the next six months, I couldn't find the motivation to do anything. I gradually built up my strength and assessed my options. After much thought, I decided I didn't want to continue working for the Bureau and retired on 30 April, 2005, after 33 years. It was the end of another era.

In talking about Casey, I need to thank a lot of people for my medivac from the station to Australia: Dr Jeff Ayton, Dr Andy Williams, Dr Tanya Kelly (Casey Doctor), Kim (a radiographer), helicopter pilot for medivac Ric Piacenza, Casey station leader Karen, Casey nurse Dan, all Casey expeditioners involved in medivac, voyage leader Rob Easther, deputy voyage leader Shane Hunniford, the *Aurora Australis* Captain Peter and crew, Met team Cliff Spencer, Bruce Alden, Segun Adewumi, Kerry Steinberner, returning expeditioners on the AA, in Hobart Robin Thiema, Jenny Coombes, Ian Hickman, Neil Adams and my Hobart minder Geoff "Beacon" Fulton.

I owe you a lot.

EPILOGUE

"Life isn't a dress rehearsal".

- Kerry Packer

Coming back to Yeppoon, I had to accept that the Ice, though a pivotal part of my life, was in my past. With my head and neck injuries, I wouldn't be accepted for a posting down south again. For a long time I struggled with that reality, rather like someone forced into retirement before he's ready. I hadn't chosen to leave.

But the choice had been made for me. As I slowly healed, I went through different phases. One was sadness at the loss of loyalty for the Bureau, who'd provided me with a job and lots of good people to work with for the largest portion of my adult life. The Bureau of Meteorology was like a family to me, but I couldn't forgive them for the trauma they'd put my own family through when I was injured.

Deb had been forced to face her demon - the fear that her husband would be injured while far away from home. That part she could've handled, but the fact that she was left to face it alone was the part I couldn't forget. I knew my disappointment was with the system, but I ended up walking away from the lot.

I know veterans are often presented as "victims". We're not. We're achievers, every one of us. We continue to live, and to function, regardless of what goes on behind closed doors.

Casey taught me life can change so very quickly. Though it took me a while to realise it, I had achieved everything I'd set out to do. Antarctica re-affirmed what my Mum had taught me years before; it doesn't matter who you are, you can achieve anything.

Antarctica gets into your soul and consumes you; the beauty, the contrasts, the challenge of man working with Mother Nature. Not everybody who goes down gets consumed, but those who do are transformed forever.

Living in Antarctica was peaceful and so different. I could've lived there quite happily for the next 20 years. It's a better world than the mainland – no violence, no traffic, no shopping centres. You have to make your own life. Though harsh and dangerous, I felt safer down there than I ever will here.

I thought I was in control of myself. I had help and understanding from my community of expeditioners and I thought I was controlling my issues. Looking back, I was in denial.

Since coming back, I've started another phase of my life, this one a lot healthier. I've finally sought help for the nightmares that have haunted me for more than 40 years. In the months since retirement, I've been seeing a psychiatrist who's helping me work through the after-effects of Vietnam and have managed to drop from seven to ten nightmares a week to about three. I've kept it quiet for too long. Even my twin brother Don didn't know I suffered from them. My psychiatrist deals with many traumatised patients - police, fire fighters, accident victims and veterans. She's a marvellous lady.

I've had many people tell me they were envious of my experiences, my opportunities to visit the romantic land. I'm envious of them. They have normal lives and they live without PTSD. I live in constant fear of seriously injuring myself while lost in the terror of my nightmare. I've run into glass doors, dented walls and suffered shocking bruises. I envied the other expeditioners being able to tuck into their tents, while I had to tie myself to my sleeping bag, like a dog on a chain, for fear of running out of the tent before I came to my senses. To this day I can't get into a bed with sheets tucked in.

I live in fear that as I age, my heart won't be able to cope with the constant terror and one day my luck will run out. I still can't walk into a party with a number of strangers. I can't handle big crowds in shopping centres.

I don't think I'll ever get over it, but as the years pass, I try. In 2008 I was asked back to my old high school in Caloundra to be part of the Anzac Day services. Incredibly honoured, I dressed and put on my medals and sat on the stage while my hands shook with anxiety. Afterwards the principal and school captain walked me back to my car. The student shook my hand and thanked me for my service. In all the years since Vietnam, I'd never been thanked by a stranger for serving my country. I struggled to hold back my tears.

Bit by bit, I'm healing. Part of this comes from the professional help Deb had been trying to get me to seek for years. Part of this comes from the love and belief of my family. The biggest part came from Casey. Casey allowed me to stop running and face my fears, made me break my need for isolation. For that I can only thank her.

APPENDIX A

POST TRAUMATIC STRESS DISORDER

Dr John E Flanagan, MB BS BSc FRANZCP

As presently understood, Post Traumatic Stress Disorder (PTSD) was first defined in DSM III, 1980, largely as a result of study of the symptoms occurring in American Veterans of the Vietnam War. Subsequently the condition was found to be common in survivors of violent rape, torture and concentration camps, severe childhood abuse and natural or manmade disasters.

The "shell shock" of the Great War was doubtless the same condition. It was extensively studied at the time, but was later thought to be unique to that conflict and generally forgotten about.

Trauma simply means injury. Psychological Trauma is understood as the most severe form of acute stress. It is an experience of being helplessly exposed to the imminent threat of violent death or severe bodily injury or witnessing such exposure in others, while experiencing profound emotions of fear, horror or disgust. The exposure may occur over a relatively brief time, or it may be prolonged or repeated.

PTSD is a severe, enduring and disabling condition that can result from such a traumatic experience.

It is as if the "fight-flight" reaction, compounded by the inability to effectively do either, is forced into "overdrive" and then becomes unable to dampen itself as it usually does, once the stress has passed. This perpetuation of the "fight-flight" response orchestrated by an adrenalin releasing sympathetic nervous system is the most easily understood component of PTSD. The sufferer continues in a state of "hypervigilance", anxiously and suspiciously scanning their environment as if they are in a constant state of danger. The sleep patterns are disrupted and there are various physical symptoms of anxiety such as tremor, startle reactions, muscle tension, palpitations, chest tightness etc. Concentration and short-term memory are also impaired.

The second component of PTSD involves various types of "re-experiencing". This results from an interference with the normal process of remembering and forgetting. The brain is normally able to "digest", over time, what happens to a person. The event is thought about at various levels and from various perspectives; it is balanced against past experiences that are held in memory and against one's beliefs and values and, according to its significance, it is eventually filed away. The memory recedes into the past and the emotions associated the memory are attenuated. Conclusions are made about how one acted and lessons are learned for future reference.

Trauma, however, can prove "indigestible" to the brain. The activation of the emotional and memory centres is so intense that the experience can't be processed and filed. It doesn't become a past but seems to be constantly present, and the brain struggles unsuccessfully for perspective and meaning. What happened can't be measured against one's previous experiences and beliefs; it was like nothing else. The memory doesn't recede into the past but remains like yesterday and most particularly, the emotional components of the memory.

The narrative component may be fragmented, out of sequence and with gaps, and there is often a searching for the missing pieces or the right sequence.

This failure to process the memory leads to the well-known "flashbacks" and nightmares. Vivid memories may occur spontaneously out of the blue and, as well, are likely to be provoked by reminders. As a result, the sufferer tends to avoid many situations and activities that could be reminiscent. This avoidance leads to withdrawal. In Dave's case, the avoidance resulted in his working in some of the most remote places on earth.

Finally, there is a numbing or loss of normal positive emotions. It is as if the trauma bulks so large that it blocks out the sufferer's capacity to experience love, happiness and enjoyment. Instead, there is a sense of alienation.

The condition may recover in the first two years. If it does not do so, it generally remains life-long. There is no cure for the condition. Treatment can help adjust to the condition and modify some of the symptoms.

Some medications can provide benefit, particularly for depression. Psychological treatment involves several components:

Education about the disorder.

Teaching methods of reducing and managing anxiety and optimising lifestyle.

Helping a person reverse the behaviours of avoidance and withdrawal and undertake activities that are rewarding.

Memory Desensitation and Cognitive Restructuring. This is a difficult and often unsuccessful treatment. On occasion it can be very helpful. The sufferer is asked to retell and re-experience the trauma in various ways and assistance is given in "reprocessing" it, thereby providing new understanding and allowing the memory to begin to move into the past. During this treatment, gaps in the memory are sometimes filled, events re-sequenced and new realisations achieved.

Dave obtained a quite different memory and understanding of his actions when under fire and a deal of relief as a result. His distressing dreams were much reduced in intensity and frequency.

Dave's therapist Glenda Gray-James, Bpsych Cert Psych MAPS Assoc MASH, MDTAQ, and Dr Flanagan form the Hillcrest Psychiatric and Psychological Services, Rockhampton.

GLOSSARY

ACV – Armoured Command Vehicle.

AA – *Aurora Australis*, Australia's Antarctic icebreaker, also known as the Orange Roughy.

ANARE – acronym for 'Australian National Antarctic Research Expeditions', which have served Australia in south Polar Regions since 1947.

Australian Antarctic Division (AAD) – an agency of the Australian Government's Department of the Environment and Heritage, the Antarctic Division (established in 1948) is responsible for the country's Antarctic research and for the administration of the Australian Antarctic Territory and Territory of Heard Island and McDonald Islands.

Antarctic Apple or Melon – a red, prefabricated fibreglass field hut made for Antarctic conditions. A melon is an elongated version of the apple.

APPI – ANARE Personal Performance Indicator assessment.

AANBUS – Australian Antarctic Building System is a modular construction system used for buildings in Antarctica. Each module is approximately 3.6 metres by 6 metres by 4 metres high.

AWS – Automatic Weather Station.

Ant Farm or Aerial Farm – VHF Antenna farm at Davis.

Anzac – Australian and New Zealand Army Corps.

Aurora – known as northern and southern polar lights, are natural light displays in the sky usually observed at night. They occur in the ionosphere.

ATK – Aeronautical Turbine Kerosene.

bivvy bag – a bivouac sack is an extremely small, lightweight waterproof shelter, and an alternative to traditional tent systems. The bag is zipped up over the users head in order to shut out the elements completely.

Baywatch – morning cleaning duties.

BANZARE – British, Australian, New Zealand Antarctic Research Expedition.

Black box or thunder box – toilet box or can.

Blue ice – Ice that occurs when snow falls on a glacier, is compressed and becomes part of the glacier that winds its way toward a body of water. It is incredibly hazardous and can often be hidden by a light layer of snow.

BA team – trained in fire-fighting techniques and the use of Breathing Apparatus.

Blah-blah meeting – the heads of each section meet every Friday with Station Leader to discuss the week events, highlights and tabling any problems.

BoM – Bureau of Meteorology.

CMF – Citizens' Military Forces.

Comms – communications.

Choppers – helicopters.

Chippie – carpenter.

CFCs – Chlorofluorocarbons.

CNN – Cable News Network television.

Crampons – attachments to outdoor footwear that feature metal parts to provide traction on snow and ice.

CSIRO – Commonwealth Scientific and Industrial Research Organisation.

C3 C4 C5 – section of the neck area cervical vertebrae.

Daks – trousers.

Ducks – old army amphibious vehicles or **LARCs;** Lighter, Amphibious Re-Supply Cargo.

diggers – nickname for Australian soldiers.

DigiCORA – an automatic sounding machine used for tracking weather balloons by satellites (GPS) for upper air information such as air pressure, temperature, humidity (PTU) and winds.

DORIS – Doppler Orbitography and Radiopositioning Integrated by Satellite; is a French satellite.

ECT – Electroconvulsive therapy.

ECG – an electrocardiogram or heart test.

Electrolyser – a machine that makes hydrogen from electricity and water.

Fire Squaw – female Fire Chief.

Fort Knox – secure storage for alcohol drinks and chocolates.

FSB – Fire Support Base (Vietnam).

GPS –Global Positioning System.

Hass house – named after Hasselborough Bay Macquarie Island.

HF radio – High Frequency radio.

HMAS – Her Majesty's Australian Ship.

Hagglunds – Swedish dual cab over-snow vehicle powered by turbo diesel engines driving four rubber tracks. It can carry four passengers in the front cab and can operate over most snow and ice terrain including sea ice and soft snow.

Haggs – See Hagglunds.

Isthmus– a narrow length of land at the northern end of Macquarie Island. The ANARE station is located on the northern end of the isthmus.

Jolly – this is an Antarctic term for going off-station for pleasure rather than work.

KK – *Kapitan Khlebnikov* a tourist ship.

Lifer – signed up for life.

LIDAR – Light Detection And Ranging instrument that began detailed study of the middle atmosphere above Davis station in early 2001.

Macca – Macquarie Island.

Met building – Bureau of Meteorology building at the various stations.

Met – Meteorology.

Madrid Protocol – protocol on Environmental Protection to the Antarctic Treaty.

METAR – weather report is used by pilots.

MRI scan – Magnetic Resonance Imaging.

Met fairies – nickname for Bureau of Meteorology workers in Antarctica.

NASA – National Aeronautics and Space Administration.

Nasho – National Serviceman.

OIC – Officer-in-charge.

PTSD – Post Traumatic Stress Disorder.

P&O – The Peninsular and Oriental Steam Navigation Company.

PCMEGA – Prince Charles Mountains Expedition, Germany and Australia.

Quad bike – Honda Trx300 four-wheel.

Rocky – Rockhampton, Queensland.

RTA – Return to Australia.

Round tripper – an expeditioner visits Antarctica only.

RSL – Returned Services League of Australia.

Reg – Regular Army volunteered to serve.

Red Shed – main accommodation building at Casey Station.

SAS – Special Air Service (Army).

SAS – Space and Atmospheric Sciences.

Science boffins – nickname for Scientists in Antarctica.

Sked – Shorten version of the word schedule.

Skuas – Subantarctic Skua bird found on Macquarie Island. South Polar Skua breeds on the Antarctic Continent. They are scavengers and predators of other seabirds and their young, eggs, fish, molluscs, crustaceans and small mammals.

SLR – Self-Loading Rifle.

Sig Sqn –Signal Squadron.

SITREP – Situation Report.

Slushy – kitchen duties as scrubbing pots, scrubbing floors, peeling potatoes etc.

Sonde package – these sounded the atmosphere and fed back information such as pressure, temperature, humidity, wind direction and speed, before bursting at between 70,000-80,000 feet, usually about 80 minutes later. Ozonesonde packages would register ozone information.

Sparky – electrician.

STD – Subscriber Trunk Dialling.

TAFE – Technical and Further Education.

TasFire – Tasmania Fire Service.

TASPAWS – Tasmanian Parks and Wildlife Service.

Tech – Technical Officer.

Tradies – Plumbers, Carpenters, Mechanics, and Electricians.

VC – Viet Cong (Vietnam).

V8 – Voyage 8 of the season.

Weather synops – Weather synopses or weather situations include time, wind direction and speed, visibility, Present weather, Past weather, cloud types and amounts of cover, temperatures, dew point, Barometric pressure etc, in coded format.

Zodiac – inflatable boat.

JOURNEY MAP INDEX

Maps © Australian Antarctic Division, Commonwealth of Australia 2010.

IMAGE INDEX

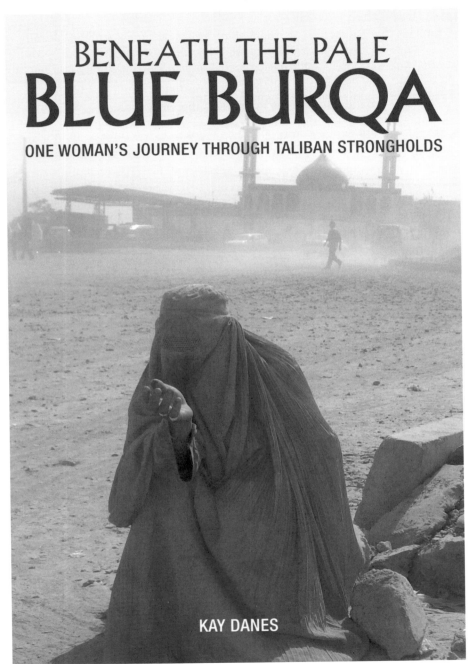

BENEATH THE PALE
BLUE BURQA
ONE WOMAN'S JOURNEY THROUGH TALIBAN STRONGHOLDS

KAY DANES

On September 11, 2001, the World as we knew it changed violently forever when ruthless Al-Qaeda terrorists launched an aerial attack on the United States of America. Just one hateful assault threatened terror from our skies worldwide, with the potential for unimaginable civilian loss spreading fear into people wanting only peace. The world was shocked, shaken and riveted to TV screens replaying horrible images for months after the atrocity.

As fear gripped the globe, Kay and Kerry Danes sat half a world away, now comfortable and secure in an Embassy after an 11-month hostage ordeal in communist Laos. Kerry Danes, an Australian Special Forces soldier, comforted his wife Kay, still struggling to come to terms with their hellish ordeal of torture, mock executions and the helplessness of leaving behind 58 political prisoners of a long forgotten war. The couple's hopes focusing only on seeing their children again. Kerry and Kay remain virtually oblivious to how the world is being held hostage to fear following 9/11.

After regaining their freedom and taking years to re-piece together family life, Kerry Danes returns to active duty with the Special Forces. Meanwhile Kay turns her dark experiences towards social justice, becoming a leading international humanitarian with a global reputation. Over the years, her diplomatic efforts have gained the respect and the ear of some of the world's most prominent individuals and political figures.

As if the Laos adventure - her husband and her jailed, children taken away – wasn't enough to put most people off travel, in November 2008 Kay embarked on a humanitarian aid mission across war-torn Afghanistan. In an old dusty Toyota mini-van, armed only with hope, Kay and her companions, a florist from Arizona, a nurse from Texas, a public servant from Australia and a US Marine Korean War veteran, drove the ancient Silk Road amidst kidnappings, suicide bombings, carnage and chaos. Their mission? To deliver life-changing opportunities and aid to people devastated by war.

This is a powerful story that will have you gripping your chair and holding your breath, as you travel with Kay through Taliban strongholds and remote wastelands of Al Qaeda terrorists. This epic journey is truly inspiring. The Afghan people she meets along the way are courageous and determined to persevere against overwhelming odds. Amidst haunting memories of her Laos ordeal, Kay is forced to overcome her personal fears, in order to contribute to the selfless efforts of all who have gone before her, to brave the perils of Afghanistan. Hers is an important contribution that will enable others a rare glimpse of places they may never visit and of people they may never meet. *Beneath the Pale Blue Burqa* proves that even in the harshest environments hopes springs eternal.

RRP: $34.99, Paper Back, 352 pages

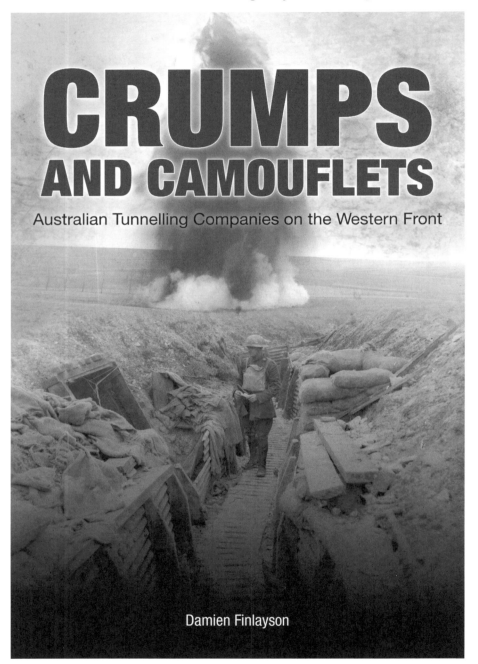

Crump

'hard hit, heavy fall, bursting shell (army slang); sound of bursting bomb or shell'

Camouflet

'subterranean cavity formed by bomb exploding beneath the surface of the earth'

"Within the vast array of Great War literature there is scant reference to the Australian tunnelling companies. I wrote this book to redress that, by telling the story of the tunnellers who, like their brother soldiers, fought a daily duel with the enemy over the wire and the enemy within – the gnawing, paralysing fear of a sudden and violent death."

Below the shattered ground that separated the British and German infantry on the Western Front in the First World War, an unseen and largely unknown war was raging, fought by miners, 'tunnellers' as they were known. They knew that, at any moment, their lives could be extinguished without warning by hundreds of tonnes of collapsed earth and debris.

These men were engaged in a desperate duel with their German opponents to destroy their opposing front lines by blowing mines, carefully placed in dark, treacherous tunnels under no man's land. At the same time, the tunnellers worked to defend their own front lines from the German miners, intent on the same deadly task. It was a war within a war in its most literal sense. The secret war culminated in the simultaneous blowing of nineteen huge mines, with a combined payload of almost 450,000 tonnes of high explosives, beneath the Messines Ridge.

Over 4,500 Australians served on the Western Front in three Australian tunnelling companies and their unique support unit, the Alphabet Company. Around 330 men did not return. The remains of most lie in carefully tended military cemeteries spread along the entire length of what was the British sector of the front, from the Belgian coast at Nieuport Bains in the north, to Bellicourt in the south. Some lie on German soil where they died in captivity. Others are lost in the dark, silent embrace of the earth and whose resting place is known unto God.

Australian tunnelling companies took part in the battles of Fromelles, Arras, Messines, Passchendaele, Cambrai, the defence of Amiens, Lys, and the famous last 100 days. *Crumps and Camouflets,* is the first complete history of Australia's role in the tunnelling war of 1914-1919, of the men and units in which they served, and of life in the tomblike tunnels of the war underground.

RRP: $34.99, Hard Back, 480 pages

ARMY·HISTORY·UNIT

PROTECTING ARMY HERITAGE
PROMOTING ARMY HISTORY

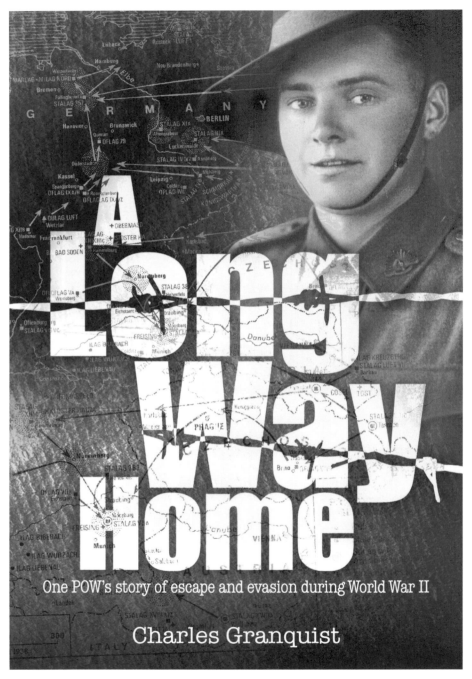

A Long Way Home

One POW's story of escape and evasion during World War II

Charles Granquist

"There is one thing that a POW learns very quickly and that is only four things matter for survival. They are food, water, shelter and clothing. The absence of any of those essentials makes life very precarious. Having them all allows you to exist, but there is one other thing that makes such an existence bearable: mateship. It shines like a beacon through the gloom. It provides the strength to battle on and survive till the sun shines again. To all my old mates, most of whom have since left this earth for that big Stalag somewhere – Thank you! I think of you often with reverence."

Charles Granquist

The son of a World War I veteran, Charles Granquist was 17 when war was declared with Germany in 1939. He lied about his age, joined the infantry and was sent to Egypt. Like so many other young men at the time, Granquist did not know what to expect. All he really cared about was doing his duty and serving his country. He never even contemplated his chances of becoming a prisoner of war.

Captured by the Germans in Greece, Granquist was determined to continue carrying the war to his captors "any way I could". In his memoir, *A Long Way Home*, he describes his shame at becoming a POW and how he believed he had failed himself, his mates and as a soldier. He orchestrated a remarkable five escape attempts, all of which ended unsuccessfully. Yet Charles refused to give up, determined to fulfil his duty as an Aussie Digger and make his own small contribution to the war effort. His story takes the reader on the rollercoaster of escape, recapture and 196 days of solitary confinement before his eventual return home with his Russian war bride.

Granquist's account of his wartime experiences adds another important chapter to the story of Australian World War II POWs, while showcasing the spirit, humour, persistence and ingenuity expected of an Aussie Digger. *A Long Way Home* is tribute to one veteran's spirit and the mateship he still holds so dear today.

RRP: $24.99, Paper Back, 208 pages

"On the 22nd April 1995, a crowd of refugees seeking shelter from a storm were fired upon by the Rwandan Patriotic Army. The horror of what followed defies description. However, that horror provided a setting for conduct, on the part of the Australians at Kibeho, which adds lustre to the proud history of Australia's service personnel in their country's cause in war and peace."

Sir William Deane, former Governor General 1996-2001

Rwanda is no stranger to violence. In 1994, an orgy of killing swept across the tiny land-locked nation and genocide, the size and magnitude unseen since the Hitler horrors of WWII, erupted. Around one million men, women and children were mercilessly shot, hacked to death or burnt alive.

To alleviate the suffering and restore order to shattered lives, a group of Australian UN peacekeepers, made up of soldiers and army medical personnel, was sent to Rwanda under a United Nations mandate. These Australians would be exposed to a lack of humanity they were not prepared for and found hard to fathom.

On 22nd April 1995, the daily horror and tragedy they had witnessed escalated out of control. At a displaced persons' camp in Kibeho, in full view of the Australian soldiers, over 4,000 unarmed men, women and children died in a hail of bullets, grenades and machete blades at the hands of the Rwandan Patriotic Army. Constrained by the UN peacekeeping Rules of Engagement, these Australians could only watch helplessly and try to assist the wounded under the gaze of the trigger-happy killers.

Pure Massacre is a record of what happened during this peacekeeping mission. Kevin "Irish" O'Halloran, a Platoon Sergeant at the time, stresses the weaknesses of the UN charter and what happens when "good men do nothing". He pulls together the perspectives of those Australian soldiers who served in Rwanda at this time. *Pure Massacre* gives a new and personal voice to the Kibeho Massacre.

It takes a special type of bravery, discipline and compassion to do what these soldiers did. Little did they know, when the second tour of Rwanda was over, that they would be the highest decorated UN peacekeeping contingent since the Korean War. For many, their service in Rwanda would come with a personal toll. No Australians died during and immediately after the massacre at Kibeho, but as *Pure Massacre* testifies, the suffering and tragedy is embedded in their memories.

RRP: $34.99, Paper Back, 320 pages

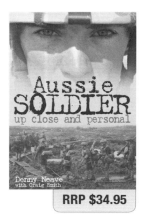
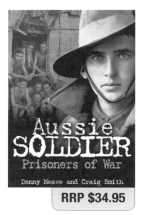
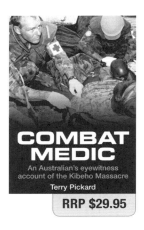
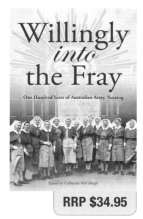

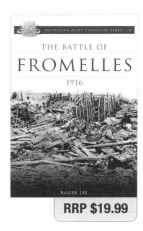

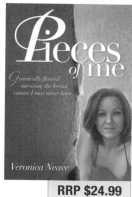

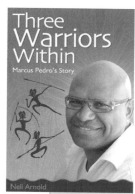